MW00390564

Adventures in Stone Artifacts

Adventures in Stone Artifacts

A Family Guide to Arrowheads and Other Artifacts

By Sandy Livoti
with Jon Kiesa

Adventure Publications, Inc.
Cambridge, Minnesota

Copyright 1997 by Sandy Livoti-Kiesa
Published by:
Adventure Publications, Inc.
P.O. Box 269
Cambridge, MN 55008
1-800-678-7006
All rights reserved

Printed in the United States of America
ISBN 1-885061-15-3

Edited by Hazel Retzlaff.
Cover and interior design by Paula Roth.
Photographs by David Kiesa.
Photos of hunting sites in Chapter 4 and the dart point in Chapter 5
    by Jon Kiesa.
Artifact illustrations by Dan Livoti.
Front cover photos:
Surface hunters. Shaun Paul (center) and older brother B.J. (right) share a
    surface hunting adventure with Graham French on a crisp October morning.
Dovetail point. A Dovetail is named after its base, which is shaped like a dove's
    tail. At almost two and one-half inches in length, this point is a fine example.
Miniature full groove axe. The small size of the granite axe head makes it an
    extraordinary artifact. It has been carefully hafted, or attached to a handle, to
    show others how it would have been held.

Dedication

*This book of adventure is
dedicated to the memory of my mother,
Marilyn Thomas Livoti*

*And is for Alissa,
with love
From Dad*

Contents

Acknowledgments

I became interested in stone artifacts and archaeology when a friend, Jon Kiesa, asked if I wanted to look for arrowheads with him. Look for what? Never heard of doing anything like that. But it sounded like fun and I was curious. Were there really arrowheads out there? Jon assured me there were.

For me, walking through a cornfield in autumn, exploring the surface of the ground for some strange, shiny stone that Indians had supposedly used was adventure enough in itself. The woods, scenery, the fresh country air, blue skies and companionship made for a great day. Then, just as we were leaving, Jon saw something. I'll always remember how I felt when I saw the small "carved" stone on the dirt. It was just as he had told me—there really are arrowheads out there. Imagine that!

After that, we searched for evidence of prehistoric activity almost every weekend and talked endlessly about artifacts. Jon brought me his books and I read about ancient relics. There was so much to learn, I started taking notes. The notes were the seeds of *Adventures in Stone Artifacts*.

When the writing began in earnest, I contacted an old friend, John B. Bryans. A book editor and publisher, John advised me on writing and getting published. For his encouragement, he has my deepest appreciation.

I also want to acknowledge Douglas J. Kullen, another specialist. The more research I did, the more I realized we would need an archaeologist's blue pencil. Despite his busy schedule, Doug graciously edited my manuscript, answered questions and supplied resource material.

Professionals in the natural gas industry, Ted Uhlemann, Cheryl Fortman, John Yater and Belinda Tyler, made helpful contributions. Ted and Cheryl provided good sources. John edited portions of the text about lithic material and furnished artifacts for pictures. Belinda assisted me in finding suitable maps.

Most of the artifacts shown in this book have not been published previously. I am indebted to Florian, Martha and Fred Centko, Nathan Hoffman, Randy Clark, Craig Werner and others for sharing them, Dr. Richard Michael Gramly for photographing the fired clay biscuits in Chapter 8 and other artifacts for Chapters 7 and 9, and Floyd Rogers for supplying flintknapping slides.

I am also grateful to Shaun, Alaina and B.J. Paul, Graham French, Carrie Rasmason, Caitlin Harrington, and their parents for cooperation with photos. To Professor Richard H. Furlow, Nancy J. Saunders, Esq., Donald A. Santefort, John E. Horton, Lori A. Myrick, Lisa Shorb, Csilla Sebestyen and colleagues and friends who encouraged me along the way—many thanks.

I appreciate the generosity of Illinois and Wisconsin landowners who have allowed Jon and me to walk their fields, and acknowledge landowners who do the same for others.

Because of the extraordinary events that delayed publishing, I would like to recognize Gerri and Gordon Slabaugh. Their guidance on sensitive issues helped me to write a more informative, comprehensive book.

Above all, I want to thank our families for their confidence and patience. I am proud to credit my son, Dan Livoti, for his illustrations and brother-in-law, David Kiesa, for photography.

And finally, thanks to my husband, Jon, for opening the door to new adventures for us all.

Foreword

A primer for young amateur archaeologists and families has been too long in coming. How often do youngsters or adults stumble upon artifacts, but never realize what they are? How many young people watch movie Westerns without thinking about the natives and early settlers who once lived in their own neighborhoods? How many school children learn a little bit about these things in their classes, but cannot find further information on the topics in their local libraries? To help others learn about our country's rich heritage, Sandy Livoti and Jon Kiesa have developed *Adventures in Stone Artifacts*.

Any introductory book must limit the amount of information with which to confront the reader. Archaeology is technically a subfield of anthropology, which over the years has borrowed from or significantly overlapped with geology, history, geography, linguistics, ethnography, botany, zoology, architecture, economics, museology, climatology and others. As a field of study which examines all cultures throughout human history and prehistory as well, its research area is potentially limitless. In this introductory book, Ms. Livoti and Mr. Kiesa properly limit the material to the absolute basics, while providing good direction for those who want to seek out more information.

This book is designed primarily as a guide for families. It can serve equally well as a guide for youngsters who have already started artifact collections and for older people who want to get started in amateur archaeology. Even seasoned artifact collectors would benefit from the tips in Chapter 4 about where to look for sites.

This book's approach to surface collecting stresses proper respect for the important laws involved. It is not a manual on how to loot or vandalize archaeological sites. Relic hunters and vandals have caused—and continue to cause—irreparable destruction of the world's archaeological resources. This book stresses the importance of responsible behavior for those who seek ancient artifacts. It is essential that youngsters learn to appreciate land ownership rights, as well as the laws protecting archaeological sites, for this respect will serve them well as they pursue their hobby into adulthood. Many grown-up avocational archaeologists would also benefit from reading—and taking to heart—the contents of Chapter 6.

Amateur archaeologists and professional archaeologists have long enjoyed a relationship which has benefits for both. From the professionals, amateurs learn the methods of field archaeology, discover the detailed scientific reconstructions of prehistoric lifeways, and obtain a renewed respect for the ancient artifacts of our ancestors. From the amateurs, professionals learn the locations of many new finds, obtain access to unique sources of archaeological data, and, often, acquire enlightening perspectives on the past. *Adventures in Stone Artifacts* will certainly help foster this kind of valuable cooperation.

There are some who will question the authors' qualifications. How, they may ask, could Ms. Livoti, a fledgling amateur archaeologist, and Mr. Kiesa, having more field experience, have had the audacity to write this kind of book? My response is twofold. First, where are the guidebooks for amateurs written by professional archaeologists? Firsthand instruction under direct professional guidance and college-level methodology texts are usually the only sources of field training for amateur archaeologists. Most of the existing methodology texts gloss over the techniques of field survey, focusing instead upon the procedures involved with site excavation and the arcane techniques involved with remote sensing, underwater archaeology and other specializations. For decades, many professionals have paid lip service to the concept of collaboration with amateurs, yet somehow none of us have managed to find the time to write a guidebook for the general public. Second, I find it highly doubtful that a professional could write a book for the public. Most archaeologists are so steeped in technical jargon and ingrained with report writing in the standard third person passive voice, that our writing is unintelligible to normal readers.

Ms. Livoti's fresh style and clear writing provide what is needed. As I helped her with this book, her sense of wonder and enthusiasm rubbed off on me, renewing my commitment to the field of archaeology. Through her thoughtful, appealing prose, I have no doubt she'll pass along the same good spirits to all of her readers.

Douglas Kullen, M.A.
Principal Investigator
Allied Archeology
Aurora, Illinois

Introduction

This book is written for youngsters, teen-agers and adults in a family-guide style. We believe individuals of almost any age can surface hunt for arrowheads and other artifacts, and we know it can be a great family activity. Discovering things together is fun! For people who enjoy rocks, nature, exercise, mystery, history, or learning about new things, arrowhead hunting has much to offer. It's an active, wholesome hobby that teaches us about other people, their cultures, and their past.

We invite you to read this guidebook independently or with family. Much of the material presented will be new to children and adults alike. When chapters are read by family members together, parents can explain information about laws, or answer questions youngsters may have on surface hunting or artifacts. You'll all learn basic terms archaeologists use and get a fundamental understanding of their field. To make it easy for everyone to identify important words, we've used bold typeface and included them in the *Glossary*.

Readers are encouraged to take an active part in cultural resource preservation by discovering, recording and reporting artifact finds. We have tried to present the facts accurately, explain techniques and procedures in an interesting way, and treat surface hunting issues objectively. The text, style and format allow:

- Children ten years and older to read the book on their own.
- Practical use of the book by children and adults together.
- The substance to be appealing, informative and valuable to adults.
- Families to share new interests and experience the thrill of learning about archaeology with each other.
- People to further develop their attitude of respect, especially toward Native American Indians.

We hope this book kindles your interest in artifacts, archaeology, site preservation and more. Getting outdoors and looking for that prehistoric tool lying on the ground is a very good way to begin. Try walking a plowed field— and take a few steps back in time. When you arrowhead hunt, you'll find the exciting world of prehistory in the stone artifacts you discover.

A Note from the Publisher

A surprising thing happened on the way to publishing this book, and it almost stopped us from publishing it. When we received the manuscript, we thought it was interesting and unique. Having two preteen children and being a family that enjoys outdoor activities and learning about new things, we found the content appealing. As I worked on the manuscript and learned about arrowheads, hammerstones, axes and other tools, I thought back to where I grew up, on a 160-acre farm in Minnesota. I thought about the rocks, remnants of glacial Lake Agassiz, buried in our fields. I remembered how my parents would plow after spring thaws, and how the rocks would end up on the surface. My sisters and I often had to help remove the stones that interfered with farming. We carried them to a rock pile just off the field, near a pasture.

Never once while picking up rocks did I think about the people who must have lived on that acreage long before my family. From my folks I learned how my grandparents built sod houses, homesteading the land early in the century. In my history classes, I learned about the pioneer settlers and European immigrants. But I don't ever recall learning about the prehistoric inhabitants or where they might have lived. Studying the manuscript, I had to wonder about the early Native Americans before me. I wondered whether they lived on the very same area of land I had. Whether they played in the same timber, climbed the same rocks, and slid on the same ice pond. Who were they? How did they live? Did they use some of the tools I was reading about? The significance of stone made into tools became apparent. Even after all that time, their stone tools might still be there! I thought about going back to walk our field. I wanted to see if any rocks had been flaked. I was curious about the rocks we had picked up and tossed. I wanted to examine our rock pile for artifacts.

The manuscript had certainly made its connection with me. Having never seen a book like it for families, we were excited about publishing another family guidebook. But during the course of publication, we ran into opposition from some people who didn't think it was a good idea at all to publish such a book.

It started with letters we had mailed to museums to request address verification for our resource section. The responses we received were voluminous and quite daunting. Our routine request had unwittingly landed us in the middle of the controversy over arrowhead hunting.

We received phone calls, letters and faxes. We heard from archaeologists who gave several versions of basically the same message. The message was that we would be committing an immoral, unethical or illegal act if we continued publication. We received multiple copies of a law that forbids artifact hunting on public lands. (We had already discussed the law and its implications in the book, but these people were concerned that we were unaware of it.) Some of the museums requested that they not be listed as resources for further study simply because the topic of the book was surface hunting. Their response was the most surprising to us, because museums typically want to advertise their locations to the public. With these responses, we knew the issue was more controversial than we thought.

We heard from a state agency, a buyer of our nature books, and were told that it had been directed by the state not to purchase this book. We heard from a Native American agency that didn't think we should publish the book. We also heard from a representative of the Department of the Interior and several professionals. Most of the professionals who called felt that historic information would be forever lost if people other than archaeologists searched for and removed artifacts. They told us when people surface hunt, artifacts end up in personal collections, all scientific knowledge about them is lost, and the historic record is permanently destroyed. They also described tragedies in which information was erased because looters had vandalized important sites. They felt that people shouldn't look for artifacts because they don't belong in private hands. Where do they belong? Some said with archaeologists, some thought in museums, and some believed that only Native Americans should have the right of ownership.

We hadn't experienced such responses prior to publishing a book before and we began to wonder if we should pursue it. We felt a little guilty for enjoying the manuscript, and even more guilty for wanting to look through the rock pile for artifacts. We didn't want to be responsible for vandalism or looting. We had no intention of encouraging people to vandalize private property or commit crimes that would result in felony convictions. And we certainly didn't want others to use the book to learn how to steal away our country's past and cause it to be lost. Would all this actually be the result of publication?

Again I thought about the rock pile. I was told that not looking for artifacts would be the responsible thing to do. That only professional archaeologists should investigate and remove things. But is the rock pile actually a site since the rocks were thrown from their original positions? Having already been brought to the surface by a plow, could I damage them more by looking? Are there any artifacts in it at all? Would I have to call a professional to do the search? Would an archaeologist want to inspect a pile of rocks just to satisfy my personal curiosity? If one came, how long would I have to wait for a visit? A week? A month? Or would it be more like a year? If I don't look or have someone else investigate, what will future landowners do? Will they want to pick through the rock pile? Will they have an appreciation for artifacts? If they do, will they share them with others? Or will they, like my parents, just want to get on with farming and move the rocks out of the way?

Besides thinking about the rocks on my land, I knew I had learned a lot from the manuscript and that I had more appreciation for artifacts and history. I wanted to know more about the Native Americans who came to North America long before my family. I thought more about their families who, generations ago, shared the same ground, handled the same rocks, and appreciated the same environment. I knew there were lessons our children could learn from studying the past, too. The lifestyles of prehistoric people are represented in the remnants of stone artifacts. When we examine stone they worked long ago, how can we not think about our own legacy? What remnants do we leave for future generations that will tell them about our way of life? A lesson such as this one will be personal for my children, because they can learn it on the land where they play. And they will be more likely to learn such a lesson from a hands-on experience. They will see the environment from a different perspective. Should we disregard all these positive effects?

We continued with publication of *Adventures in Stone Artifacts* because we believe it will have the same effect on others as it had on us. We are more conscious about preservation, not less. We want everyone, including professionals, to learn more about artifacts, not less. We can impart more information about Native Americans to our children and instill in them more respect for the Indian ways of life, not less. We moved ahead with publication not only because of these thoughts and experiences and what we think is a reasonable approach, but because of the following:

- Surface hunting can be a responsible activity for amateurs interested in archaeology. People who already hunt for artifacts, as well as those who might do so in the future, should learn responsible techniques.
- There are many more amateurs than professional archaeologists. Most finds, including significant ones, have been made by amateurs. Amateurs need a fundamental source of information directed at their level of study.
- Given cooperation and direction from professionals, amateurs can learn how

to effectively add to the body of information about the past, not deplete it.

- Exposing young people and families to amateur archaeology benefits all of us. Anyone who finds an artifact will experience a connection with folks from the past. Children exposed to surface hunting may likely grow up to be the most enthusiastic advocates for the preservation of cultural resources. (I asked a few professionals how they became involved in the field. Their answer? They hunted artifacts as kids!)

- The question of who has the right to own artifacts is a controversial social and ethical issue. Even within the professional community, there is disagreement as to how artifacts should be handled, or who should have them. As long as people respect and obey the laws, they have the freedom to make their own choices and are entitled to their own beliefs. Even the deepest personal feelings should not restrict the freedom of others to read about, handle and learn from artifacts.

- The book guides the way to ethical, legal hunting. It restricts hunting to only those items already exposed on the surface of the ground. It encourages people to report finds of artifacts to their state historic preservation agency. By receiving such information, the agency may be able to determine that in fact a significant site may exist and professionals need to be involved. The book also gives information about the laws that pertain to surface hunting, emphasizes the fact that hunting on public lands is illegal, and that certain areas are never to be hunted.

- The ultimate reason to pursue publication was that we knew we were presenting information that included views from both sides of a controversial issue. We trust intelligent people will read the book and use it wisely. We do not believe that presenting adequate information, even when some groups disagree with the content, is reckless or irresponsible.

Many professionals suggested there are better ways to learn about artifacts than looking for them, but we don't think most are practical for our readers. Working with archaeologists on supervised digs or signing up for workshops are great opportunities that we encourage. But for our family and probably many others, jobs, homework, swimming, basketball, soccer and piano lessons make another scheduled activity unlikely. We can, however, grab *Adventures in Stone Artifacts* and head for the outdoors when there are a couple of free hours to spare on a Saturday. We'll have renewed interest and appreciation for artifacts on display at our museums, too. But we won't be planning trips out of our neighborhood to look for sites so we can take all we can get.

People who hoard artifacts or surface hunt for monetary gain have little consideration for preservation and are clearly unethical in their actions. But people can and do change when given the right information and encouragement. This book gives proper instruction, encourages good attitudes, and could be just what some folks need to improve their ways. For people who have just learned about the hobby, such as ourselves, there are no past behavior patterns to modify. If we do pursue surface hunting, we'll report each and every artifact we find.

As is the case with many things, there is always the risk that someone will misuse information. But we think the odds are that *Adventures in Stone Artifacts* will have a positive impact on people and historic preservation, not a negative one. We trust this book will be read by thoughtful people who will want to use the information in the good spirit in which it was written.

Before You Hunt

Before going out to look for artifacts, adults should read this section carefully and review it with family members who will be surface hunting. To participate in this hobby, you need to be aware of laws that protect archaeological resources. A lack of knowledge about them will not protect you from a fine. It's also important to know that some professional and academic archaeologists consider amateur surface hunting outright unethical. They will not appreciate your active interest in archaeology. When you report a surface find or offer what you think is helpful information to one of these professionals, do not be surprised if you receive a very cool, if not hostile reaction.

LEGAL ASPECTS

Legally, archaeological resources are defined as any material remains of human life or activities which are at least one hundred years of age, and which are of archaeological interest. Archaeological resources include, but are not limited to: basketry, bone, bottles, ceramics, clothing, containers, cordage, debris from manufacturing materials, feathers, glassware, graves, hearths, hide, implements, ivory, metal, organic waste, ornaments, pigments, pottery, rock carvings, rock paintings, shell, shipwrecks, tools, wood, weapons and weapon projectiles, as well as flaked, ground or pecked stone. Cultural resources such as these, which are located on public and Indian lands, are protected by archaeological resource protection laws. It is illegal to hunt artifacts on these grounds or other sites where cultural resources are protected.

Policies maintained by federal and/or state administrations make it illegal to hunt on public lands. Laws governing federally owned or controlled lands make it illegal to hunt on those properties, and laws passed in individual states make hunting on state-owned or state-controlled lands illegal as well. Some states have also passed laws that prohibit hunting on private land. New Mexico, for example, has a strong anti-looting law that prohibits the looting of ruins on private property.

To arrowhead hunt legally, surface hunters must stay within the boundaries of all applicable laws. Surface hunting is generally legal on private property when you have the owner's permission. You may surface hunt only where federal, state or county regulations are not prohibitive.

To understand how cultural resources located on public and Indian lands are protected under the law, you'll want to become familiar with the regulations that apply. These regulations specify who may search for, remove and own cultural resources, set penalties for civil and criminal acts, and describe how and where archaeological investigations may be executed. There are sections that concern confidentiality of prehistoric and historic information, forfeiture of artifacts, public awareness programs, surface finds of arrowheads, and more. Before surface hunting, you should be aware of the following major laws.

Laws

Early in this century, the Antiquities Act of 1906 was passed to protect cultural resources in the United States. At that time, scientists and archaeological and anthropological organizations documented severe vandalism and looting in ruins, particularly in the Southwest. Many ruins were being plundered by looters who excavated sites and stole artifacts to sell them for profit. They essentially ripped historic information from the ground along with the artifacts, and the data necessary for understanding the culture of the people was forever lost to the scientific community. Having no access to the plundered artifacts, professionals did not have all pieces to the archaeological puzzle, and holes in the prehistoric picture became permanent. Because of losses like these, groups worked hard to pass legislation to protect cultural resources. This federal act created a system for qualified scientists to gain access to ruins for the purpose of study, and was the first to establish criminal penalties for illegally looting archaeological sites on federally owned or controlled land.

The Archaeological Resources Protection Act of 1979 (ARPA) provided further protection for public and Indian lands. It dramatically increased the penalties for illegally excavating, removing, damaging, or otherwise defacing archaeological resources on federal and Native American lands. After ARPA went into effect, people could be fined as much as $100,000, spend up to five years in prison, or both, if convicted for violations of this act. ARPA also requires that Native Americans be notified when a permit for excavation and/or removal of archaeological resources could lead to harm or destruction of religious or cultural sites on public lands.

A final rule to the Department of the Interior's Protection of Archaeological Resources Uniform Regulations amended the description of prohibited acts on public and Indian lands, and strengthened the enforcement provisions effective

February 27, 1995. This rule also required Federal Land Managers to develop programs that would increase public awareness of the need to protect cultural resources located on public and Indian lands.

The Native American Graves Protection and Repatriation Act, passed in 1990, protects Native American grave sites, and further specifies that any museum receiving federal funds must inventory and return all Native American skeletal remains and cultural artifacts to the appropriate tribe. Many museums are now in the process of returning these items.

In addition to these major federal laws, many states have regulations that protect cultural resources. State laws in coastal regions specify what may and may not be recovered from underwater, and who can be authorized to do the work. Cemeteries are also protected in some states, even if located on private land. To be sure that your activities are legal, use the following guidelines.

Stay Within the Law

- Where it is legal to hunt private property, you may do so only after you have obtained permission from the owner.
- Never hunt or collect anything on federal land. Be aware that much of the land in the Southwest and West is federally owned.
- Do not hunt or collect anything on state-owned land or in state parks until you check with state authorities to determine if it is legal.
- Do not hunt or collect anything on county-owned land, forest preserves or wildlife refuge areas until you check with county authorities to determine if it is legal.
- Never hunt or otherwise disturb any area you suspect is a burial ground, cemetery or other place with religious significance. To ascertain the existence of a burial mound or cemetery on private property, check with your state historic preservation agency for verification.
- To be absolutely certain you are surface hunting within the letter of the law, check with your Federal Land Manager, or state or county officials before you hunt.

ETHICAL ISSUES

Most experts in archaeology agree that surface hunting on private property is usually legal, but many do not believe it is ethical or responsible when it is done by amateurs. Some authorities think surface hunting could be beneficial if amateurs would only find and report, but not remove, or even touch the artifacts. Others think it's fine to touch and remove artifacts, as long as the finds are clearly documented and reported. Ownership becomes an issue for everyone when a find is significant. While some feel that artifacts should be displayed in public museums, others choose to keep their finds and assume curatorial responsibility themselves. To relay the variety and intensity of opinions on the ethical issues surrounding surface hunting, our publisher is supplying the following quotes from letters received regarding the publication of this book:

". . . we try to stress . . . that archaeological sites are an irreplaceable resource that can be seriously damaged or made unfit for scientific investigation by surface artifact collecting. . . . certain individuals will amass private collections of artifacts that have minimal value to archaeologists or the public. Archaeologists attempt to document and understand America's past, for the benefit of all citizens, before it is lost or compromised . . . . this book will . . . contribute to (this) problem."

"Often people keep these artifacts and collected oddities, but more usually the "goodies" eventually get thrown out through a thorough spring house cleaning or a family household move. What a waste!"

"Archaeologists always focus on the spatial relationships (provenance) of artifacts as they are found in a site . . . Artifacts may be pretty to look at, but without their precise provenance, they often lose much cultural and archaeological meaning."

"When the collector dies, the information he or she knows about general artifact provenance may be lost forever. With this type of collecting going on, we get more and more samples of artifacts floating disconnected in time and space, with no way to recover the meaning they might have once held as they rested in association with other artifacts in the site, in a particular landscape, at a precise point in time."

"Collecting artifacts in an unorganized manner may provide some educational opportunities, but these tend to be poor and most meager educational opportunities for children because greater insights are lost for a lack of understanding the provenance of these artifacts."

"Advise your potential readers that the full force of Federal law will be (and is) brought against illegal collectors on Federal Lands in many western states. Sentences include confiscation of all equipment, vehicles (cars, trucks, boats, helicopters), tools, et cetera, used in the crime. Felony conviction could result in probation, severe fines, house arrest, or several years in a Federal penitentiary."

"I would also suggest a chapter on the feelings of Native Americans and the pain and suffering traditional tribal members feel at seeing sacred places and ceremonial sites plundered for hobby collecting and for museum displays."

"The pothunter loots it and sells it to a middleman. The middleman sells it to a trader. The trader markets it. People buy it for ego gratification. So where is the provenance? They'll all tell you it came off of private property; most of it is looted from public lands. This has nothing to do with professional archaeology."

After the devastation of ruins by looters and vandals, it is no wonder that professionals are distressed about the preservation of cultural resources. They simply do not want to see more information destroyed. There are professionals, however, who don't equate all surface hunters with looters. There is an association for amateur archaeologists, called the American Society for Amateur Archaeology (see the *Resources*), that includes the following in its public information:

"Only a generation ago amateur and professional archaeologists, collectors, museum professionals, government agencies and the public-at-large interacted freely. In the arena of archaeological science cooperation prevailed. Discoveries of buried and forgotten art and other traces of human ingenuity were widely heralded. Now word of important finds is hushed or down-played, and the specimens themselves may be hidden from public view. Records about archaeological sites are withheld from all but a few, "approved" researchers. People are pitted against one another; arguments rage over who has the right to investigate the past. In the name of "conservation" professional archaeologists admonish amateurs who collect arrowheads and at the same time set themselves apart from the taxpayers whom they serve."

Richard Michael Gramly, Ph.D., the founder of this continent-wide, North American organization, believes that amateur archaeologists can make valuable contributions, sometimes precisely because they *are* amateurs. He maintains that people who are not professionals in archaeology are able to contribute viewpoints from entirely different perspectives, some of which could enlighten even the most learned archaeologists.

These diverse opinions about ethics can be perplexing to us all, especially when professionals tell us they chose to be archaeologists because they went arrowhead hunting as children. While some professionals will not encourage arrowhead hunting and don't recommend others to encourage it either, it's obvious that not all surface hunters grow up to be looters. Some even grow up to be very strong preservationists.

MAKING PERSONAL DECISIONS

This is only a brief treatment of the ethical issues involved in amateur archaeology. We must all obey the law, but beyond that, individuals must examine their intentions and develop their own thoughts about what is responsible behavior, and what is not. Because you know that surface hunting is a controversial issue, and you understand why amateurs and professionals are not in harmony, you need to decide what is right for you.

We hope our readers will continue to learn more about archaeology and get involved in historic preservation. An excellent way to help stop vandalism of cultural resources is to nurture your personal awareness. You can do this by joining an archaeological organization, volunteering to be a site steward for historic preservation, or signing up for a field or laboratory training program to be certified as a paraprofessional technician (see the *Resources*).

We encourage amateurs to consider the *who, what, when, where* and *why* of artifacts in the same way professionals do. When you try to provide answers to these questions, then you have accomplished the type of archaeological reporting that archaeologists value and appreciate.

To prevent information you compile from being lost, share photographs and other records of your finds with others. A well-kept record that is hoarded at home is of no use to science, and one that is destroyed in a natural disaster or discarded in the next generation is lost to posterity. In light of this, it's extremely important to pass the information on. For preserving knowledge of Native American Indians gained from your participation in this hobby, we would like to suggest guidelines for responsible behavior. The recommendations given on the following page should be acceptable to all who wish to cooperate.

We would also like to add a note about artifact preservation and cultural resource reporting. Because of the shortage of archaeologists and recent cutbacks in government spending, the professional community often cannot respond as fast as you might like. When you leave an artifact as you've found it, whether you report one or several, you may have quite a wait before getting a response from your state agency. When artifacts are found on the surface of a plowed field and the farmer needs to plow, it is better to remove them before they are moved and forever ruined by the disk.

Ethical Conduct for Arrowhead Hunters

- Make the intention of your hunting to discover, record and report.

- Always surface hunt within the law. This means having permission, staying on private property, and keeping away from burial grounds or cemeteries.

- Never dig.

- If you find anything that appears to be an artifact, sketch a map to identify its place on a site, photograph the find as you found it, and take notes about your discovery before you leave the site. Use your notes to accurately record your find in a permanent artifact journal at home.

- If you discover a site with more than two artifacts in close proximity, follow the suggestions given above, but do not disturb the finds. Report your discoveries to the landowner and contact a local professional archaeologist or send your data to the state historic preservation agency as quickly as possible.

- Ownership of finds is a matter between the landowner and you. Normally, permission to keep finds is granted with permission to hunt. Use good judgment in deciding whether you want to keep an artifact, offer it to the property owner, or lend or donate it to a museum where many others can appreciate it, too.

- Obtain a form from your state historic preservation agency or make a copy of our generic form, complete it, and mail it with your sketches and photographs to your state agency. See page 109 for the generic form and the *Resources* for agency addresses.

Figure 1-1. This projectile point was found on the side of an Illinois cornfield in springtime, just before sundown. Actual size: two and one-quarter inches.

Arrowhead Hunting and Amateur Archaeology

ARTIFACTS AND THE PAST

Have you ever wanted to travel through time, back to the past? Have you ever dreamed about living when mammoths, mastodons or giant bison walked the earth in pristine territory, where the sun was your watch, and the moon and fire were your light? Have you ever thought about what it was like to encounter an antlered deer, catch sight of a colorful pheasant, or come across a large shellfish and consider them as your sources of food? Have you ever wondered what life was like hundreds or thousands of years ago? What activities made up the daily routines? What things people did for special occasions? How they accomplished tasks without the benefit of modern tools? Or what people did for fun?

If questions like these have ever crossed your mind, then you have the curiosity and sense of discovery that make for a good arrowhead hunter and archaeologist's helper. Do you like adventure, enjoy nature, going to new places or solving riddles? Your natural inquisitiveness will help you find clues to the way people lived in earlier times. And you can discover some of these clues in stone, probably in nearby fields and streams.

1

CHAPTER 1

ARROWHEADS, BEADS, PIECES OF FIRED CLAY AND TOOLS OF STONE AND BONE FOUND BY PEOPLE LIKE YOURSELF HAVE LED TO IMPORTANT ARCHAEOLOGICAL DISCOVERIES.

Imagine walking along a country road in springtime, next to a freshly plowed cornfield. It has recently rained and something glints in the sun a few feet away. Curious, you stop and walk over to see what it is. But it's not just an old bottle cap or piece of scrap metal. It's a beautifully made arrowhead, looking as perfect as the day it was worked from stone, maybe over a thousand years ago.

Who owned this point? Was it a father hunting for food for his family? Or a warrior protecting his home and land? What position in the community did the person have? Was it an Indian chief or a young girl? And who was the last human being to see it and hold it in his or her hand, just as you are today?

That arrowhead, like every stone artifact, is a unique piece of workmanship. There were no molds or casts or assembly lines to manufacture what people needed. Instead, daily life depended on objects that individuals could chip from stone.

How could massive animals be slain without firearms? What were the best ways to skin game for food? How could pelts be cleaned and made into clothing? What natural resources could be used to adorn the body, cultivate the land or cook food? Arrowheads, ornaments and ceremonial objects, as well as tools for cutting, scraping, farming and preparing food, all enhanced the lives of the artisans and their families. Knowing about the artifacts can give you clues about the people who passed through or lived on a particular piece of land.

Many people today are interested in how folks lived thousands of years ago. Perhaps you know someone who can tell you what an ancient "celt" was used for. Or what a "thumb scraper" or common "cup stone" looks like. If you'd like to, you may discover artifacts like these and other stone tools and weapons on plowed fields, near cliffs, at creeks and in other places you can explore.

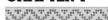

Points of Interest

How Old is Prehistoric?

How old are Indian artifacts? Most of them are so old, they're positively _prehistoric!_ Think of prehistoric as "pre-history," or before history was written. Archaeologists call stone tools, weapons and other objects "prehistoric artifacts" if they were made or used before the time people started writing down events. Objects made or used after written records were kept are known as historic artifacts. Since there is not a specific date when folks all over the country decided to write history, there is not a definite dividing line between prehistoric and historic times. While the most recent prehistoric artifacts can be about three hundred fifty years old, older artifacts date back to 13,000 B.C.—almost fifteen thousand years ago!

ARROWHEAD HUNTING

If you're searching for adventure, this book can open the door to the fascinating world of archaeology. You can hunt arrowheads and other types of artifacts and find clues to solve mysteries about the past. What exactly is **arrowhead hunting**? It's a term commonly used for **surface hunting**, which means exploring the surface of the ground in search of arrowheads _and_ stone artifacts. Though the main objective of many surface hunters is to discover an arrowhead, arrowhead hunting means looking for other artifacts as well.

Artifacts are any objects made or used by people that archaeologists study to increase our knowledge of history. Cork stopper bottles, antique barbed wire and colonial battle relics are examples of artifacts from a relatively recent time. Arrowheads made long ago are also artifacts, as are spear points, knives, grinding stones, tools such as axes and drills, pottery, pipes and more.

INDIANS CARVED AND ETCHED EFFIGIES, OR LIKENESSES, OF ANIMALS, BIRDS AND HUMAN FACES ON PIPES.

Arrowhead hunting is an experience in discovery. Just as people are fascinated and excited by sighting a rare bird they've never seen before or focusing a telescope on moon craters for the first time, you'll be thrilled to find your first artifact and speculate about its origins. Looking for and discovering artifacts is *fun*, number one. It's being outdoors in the fresh air and sunshine, and getting plenty of exercise. It's biking or hiking to hunting areas close by, or taking a family drive to the country. It's meeting new people and getting to know them. And it's informative and inexpensive, too.

As far as your schedule goes, nothing is set in prehistoric stone, so to speak. You aren't required to be there at nine o'clock sharp Saturday mornings. And you can continue to explore in the middle of an outing because no buzzers will sound to signal a break in play. You can choose whatever hours of the day you wish to hunt. You can hunt all day, make a morning, an afternoon or evening of it, or search for an hour or less. Weekends, holidays and vacations are good opportunities for arrowhead hunting because expeditions can be planned for consecutive days or scattered over several weeks.

Some adventurous activities require fees or costly equipment. Amateur archaeology does not. There are no season passes or admission tickets, and there's no need to purchase any expensive equipment to take on excursions.

Figure 1-2. Shaun Paul, age 12, Carrie Rasmason, age 12, and Graham French, age 10, arrowhead hunting with permission on a cornfield.

You can look for arrowheads and other artifacts with a friend, family member or by yourself. When you'd like to do something other than the usual, go on an arrowhead hunt. Plan an outing for a free evening and make it a whole family affair. Invite a special person to go with you, because it's lots of fun to hunt with a partner. Or ask a friend to help identify your finds. It could open up a new interest to share.

AND AMATEUR ARCHAEOLOGY...

The more you know about arrowhead hunting and the longer you do it, the better it gets. It's true! Consider the illustrated scraper and the information given in Figure 1-3. If you were to find a stone scraper, it could be a clue that spears or arrows were used in the area. Suppose you discovered a point from one of the projectile weapons. You would wonder what kind of **projectile point** it is, be curious to know what professionals have learned about it, and have questions about the people who used both the scraper and the point. Through your reading and hunting experiences, you'll learn many interesting things about archaeology, geology, geography and history. More important, your appreciation of artifacts and respect for the people who made them will increase.

The artifacts you find on the surface of the ground are called **surface finds**. Surface finds can provide valuable information to professional **archaeologists**. Any information you can provide that helps to study the past should be shared with archaeologists and other historical detectives. Conscientious **amateur archaeologists** who make contributions to the field

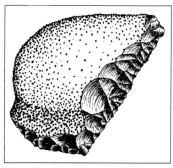

Figure 1-3. Indians made scrapers in many shapes, designs and sizes. From one to ten inches long, stone tools for cleaning animal hides and bones were made in other parts of the world as early as 500,000 B.C. In America, scraped hide was used for clothing, quivers, moccasins and tepees. Bones free of gristle were made into fishhooks, hairpins, needles and spear points.

of archaeology deserve the appreciation of any professional. A responsible surface hunter will identify finds, record them in a journal, and report discoveries to experts.

A VERSATILE HOBBY

Inside...

Arrowhead hunting is an indoor pastime, too. There are so many neat things to do and learn about, you'll find that discovery just *begins* with your search of the ground. When you're at home, go through your finds. You can clean some with a dry brush, or make a journal entry or two. After sundown, examine strange finds more thoroughly and compare them with photographs in books. Read all about artifacts and prehistory during storms, and you'll make more accurate identifications when the weather clears. If there's a light cover of snow on the ground, use your time inside to study maps. Choose some interesting areas to explore and make plans to go hunting during the next warm spell.

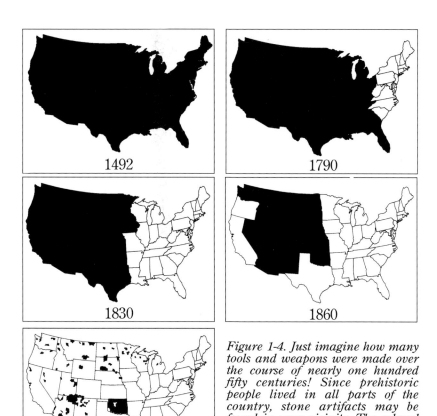

1492

1790

1830

1860

1890

Figure 1-4. Just imagine how many tools and weapons were made over the course of nearly one hundred fifty centuries! Since prehistoric people lived in all parts of the country, stone artifacts may be found in your vicinity. The colored portions of these maps indicate areas of Indian habitation at various times in history.

And out!

It's very exciting to find a nineteenth-century doll part or an Indian head penny on an arrowhead hunt. While you explore, search for other things from early times. Because different groups of people lived on the land at different times, antique buttons, marbles, horseshoes and old coins can sometimes be found on the same **sites** as prehistoric Indian artifacts. Watch for the relics of historic hunters, such as musket balls, bullets, brass shells and gun parts. And keep an eye out for logos or marks on ceramic and porcelain fragments that you can look up later and identify, too.

Figure 1-5. Jon Kiesa found this fossil of an extinct trilobite when he was ten years old. Unfortunately, it was in a limestone rock that was attached to a one-hundred-fifty-pound block of cement. Not exactly portable in a pocket, Jon and older brother David dragged the entire piece home in a Red Flyer wagon. Today, it continues to hold the record as his heaviest surface find.

You can also hunt fossils during your walk. In many places, fossils are easier to find than artifacts. These imprints in stone of marine and plant life are more ancient than relics made by people. Fossils of **trilobites**, segmented scavengers that lived in water four hundred million years ago, are even twice as old as dinosaurs!

There are remarkable things to look for on the ground and so much to discover. It's very possible to spot a sparkling **geode**, which is a hollow rock with a crystal lining, or find a pretty piece of petrified wood. You could encounter the remains of a prehistoric, spineless animal that's better known as an **invertebrate** fossil. You may even discover a turn-of-the-century sulfide marble containing a luminous figurine. Any of these are super finds to appreciate and share with family, friends and other folks you know.

▼ ▼ ▼

Arrowheads, artifacts, archaeology and *adventure!* People of all ages enjoy arrowhead hunting because it includes much more than just searching for arrowheads. When you know more about it, we think you'll enjoy it, too.

Figure 2-1. To find stone artifacts, search for the kind of rock that Indians made into sharp tools and weapons. The most common materials used were flint, chert and obsidian. Though flint is often gray, white or brown, look for mixed colors and marbled patterns, too. If you find flint nodules, it could be possible that tools were made at the site. Chert looks like flint, but it's not as fine-grained or glossy. You'll spot obsidian easily because it's black and shiny.

CHAPTER 2

Is It a Rock or an Artifact?

Have you ever counted boxcars while you waited at a train crossing? Or counted sheep to get to sleep? Can you estimate the number of books you have read? Or movies you have seen? While you surface hunt, you'll see more rocks and stones than any other thing you can count. Far more were shaped by Mother Nature than altered by people. How will you know which ones to examine? How will you decide that a stone is only a rock, when it happens to look like an ornament? How can you tell if a stone was used by folks for tasks? Or be certain that it was made into a weapon?

You will be searching for signs of **cultural** stone—stone that people either **worked** into an altered shape or used without modification. You'll be identifying artifacts by looking for markings on rock surfaces and noticing stone shapes. To know what kinds of markings to look for, it's very helpful to understand how folks changed or used rock. In order to hunt game, chop wood, prepare food or hold a ceremony, Indians made the objects they needed by either chipping or grinding stone. You'll be looking for evidence of this chipping and grinding when you arrowhead hunt. With an eye for the right signs, you can decide if you've found a rock or an artifact.

STONE ARTIFACT MATERIALS

It helps to know types of rock when you hunt for artifacts. Since there's too much stone on the ground to sort through it all, you'll need to be selective about the rocks you inspect. You can expand the time you have to hunt productively by narrowing down the materials to the kinds used to produce tools and weapons. Though many types of rock were available, Indians often chose stone that could be chipped or flaked into shape. If you hunt for stone that can be modified by **flaking**, you'll increase your chances of finding artifacts.

Stone that broke into sharp pieces was chipped into sharp tools and weapons. Sharp tips and serrated edges on projectile points allowed quick, clean kills. Butchering went more smoothly with stones that could slice. Hides could be punctured, stone and bone drilled, and fine lines etched. For arrowheads, knives, scrapers and more, the sharper the edge, the better.

The way a stone was modified depended on how the stone would break. Just as it would be difficult for you to shape a piece of pottery from clay that is too moist or too crumbly, it would also be difficult to chip a stone into a tool if you couldn't control or predict how it would break. While different kinds of stone do not break in the same way, the types that break into naturally sharp pieces have a distinct feature that sets them apart from others.

When you find a stone with a **conchoidal fracture**, you've located the right kind of stone. A conchoidal fracture is a break in stone that occurs in a circular pattern. The word "conchoidal" describes a stone surface that is slightly cupped or depressed and shell-like in appearance. A conchoidal surface is as smooth as the inside of a shell. But an edge of a stone that breaks in a conchoidal fracture, such as an edge of a shell, is sharp. Hard stone with fine crystal structures, such as flint and chert, fractures into conchoidal breaks. It may seem odd, but the harder the material, the easier it is to chip. Why? It doesn't crumble apart, as soft rock can when struck. To make a precise shape or serrate an edge, Indians had to remove small pieces, or **flakes**, in certain places without breaking the entire stone. They chipped stone that broke in conchoidal fractures into sharp weapons and tools, such as projectile points, knives, scrapers and engraving tools, called **gravers.**

Figure 2-2. To identify stone that can be flaked, look for smooth, cupped swirls and sharp edges that are characteristic of conchoidal fractures.

You can spot conchoidal fractures even if you don't know the name of the rock. To decide if a stone is the type that could have been flaked, find a broken rock to inspect—any one will do. Pick it up, examine it, and feel the broken surface. Does it have a pebbled, uneven exterior? Can you feel any grains of sand in the rock? Is it spongy in texture? Or porous? Try another one, because these types break differently and cannot be properly chipped.

The kind of stone you want to find should have a glassy appearance and smooth, slightly rippled surfaces. Try looking for hard, broken stones with sharp edges, smooth surfaces and a dull luster. Swirling, shell-like patterns on smooth surfaces are the designs you'll be seeing on worked stone.

Check out the conchoidal breaks shown in Figure 2-2 and look for stones with this feature. Distinct conchoidal fractures are usually easy to see, even on very small chips. It really doesn't matter whether you find large flakes, small chips or nodules. When you see stone that breaks into patterns with swirls, the area would be a good place to hunt.

MANY SMALL FLAKES FOUND IN ONE AREA COULD BE REMNANTS FROM TOOL AND WEAPON MAKING.

Though Indians preferred to use stone that would flake, they didn't restrict their toolmaking to just a few types of rock. Artifacts were made from banded agate, flint, jasper, quartz, quartzite, obsidian and even petrified wood. Others were created from basalt, chalcedony, chert, felsite, slate or turquoise. Still more were made of dense granite, diorite or hematite, and soft rock, such as pipestone, sandstone or soapstone. While the ability to identify stone and other mineral mixtures is very helpful, you don't have to be a geologist to arrowhead hunt effectively. Let's narrow down the materials to the rocks that were most easily flaked, commonly used, and that you are likely to find.

Flint

The most common stone material used in prehistoric times was **flint**. An important resource for tool and weapon making, flint was valued because it broke sharply in conchoidal fractures. It was also partially responsible for warmth, hot food and light, since sparks from flint started Indian campfires.

Although the fires have long since died out and grown cold, the objects made of flint remain. Flint is a very hard, fine-grained quartz material so durable that whole weapons and tools made of it can still be found today. Besides arrowheads and spear points, other artifacts you may find made of flint include knives, scrapers, gravers and spiked tools for puncturing, called **perforators**.

Veins of flint are found in rock deposits containing limestone, but flint that was moved by glaciers and tumbled about can also take the form of large, rounded pebbles, called cobbles, or **nodules**. Sometimes flowing water and underground pressure cause voids in which crystals form in flint nodules, but these can weaken the geode and cause it to break. Examine a broken surface of an artifact for bits of sparkling minerals, and you may determine that geode crystals were responsible for the damage.

Flint has a dull luster and can either be **opaque** (light doesn't pass through) or **translucent** (some light passes through). Frequently gray, white or brown, flint also appears in more lively colors and multicolored patterns. When the stone was a high-quality dark gray or especially pretty, Indians flaked it into portable pieces for future toolmaking on their travels. Often, they traded this fine material for other desirable goods as they moved from place to place. Transportation and trading provided much of the material for the flint artifacts people are finding across America today.

Chert

With the exception of geologists, archaeologists and other experts, most people confuse flint with **chert** because they look so much alike. Chert is a hard, opaque quartz material that is an impure form of flint. When flint was not available, Indians chipped and flaked chert. Both chert and flint, so useful before modern society began, have little value today and are normally considered a nuisance by those who quarry other stone. Like flint, artifacts made of chert are found in all parts of the country.

The differences between flint and chert are easier to see when a high grade of flint is placed next to a low grade of chert. Conchoidal fractures and refined flaking will be easy to see on a piece of good flint, but this may not be the case with chert. Inferior chert that refuses to break into proper conchoidal swirls cannot be worked as precisely as flint. Since lower grades of chert are harder to control during flaking, the resulting handiwork may look crude or even unfinished.

Chert usually has a dull finish and is white, light gray, brown or yellow. Indians often **heat-treated** it before chipping to improve the flaking quality of the stone. Though heat-treating darkens or reddens exterior surfaces and roughens the texture, the interior becomes almost glassy. Flaked, heat-treated stone will have yellow, orange, pink, or rose tinges and a smooth, waxy luster. Heat-treated artifacts may also have a few small, concave craters, called "pot-lids," where heat has fractured the material.

Obsidian

Obsidian, also known as "volcanic glass," is a glossy rock that comes from volcanoes. You won't mistake obsidian for flint or chert, because it's much shinier. While the color is usually black, you might see it in gray or dark brown. Conchoidal breaks in obsidian result in distinct shell patterns on surfaces. Indians liked to use obsidian for making projectile points and cutting tools because chipping resulted in longer flakes, and flaking could be done in any direction.

SCIENTISTS HAVE DETERMINED THAT SOME ARTIFACTS FOUND IN ILLINOIS, INDIANA, OHIO AND MICHIGAN WERE MADE FROM OBSIDIAN QUARRIED AT YELLOWSTONE NATIONAL PARK IN WYOMING.

Think of obsidian the way you think of glass because it handles more like glass than stone. Chips in obsidian look much like the small, concave chips that you'll see on damaged plate glass. Thin flakes of obsidian are translucent and can be as sharp as a surgeon's scalpel. Never brush away a tiny flake with bare fingers because it can cut through your skin like a glass sliver. When you touch large pieces or small flakes of obsidian, always use extreme care.

Though obsidian is most common in the Rocky Mountain regions, it can also be found in places where it's not native. Like flint, obsidian was so valued it was transported and traded, often finding its way far across the country. As a result, beautiful obsidian artifacts have surfaced all over the U.S.

HOW STONE WAS WORKED

Flaking Materials

You'll recognize worked stone more easily once you understand how it was modified. To modify stone such as flint, chert and obsidian, Indians used a stone-working technique called **flintknapping**. A process of removing flakes from rock by hitting the rock with another object, flintknapping is a trade as well as a means of chipping stone. A flintknapper needs skill, persistence, the right type of stone, and a few tools for flaking. People who lived long ago had to gather the materials before starting their work. Their most essential material was stone.

The work of prehistoric flintknappers began with flaking a stone **core**. A core is the rock that was hit. Cores produced the flakes that Indians used to make tools and weapons. Think of them in the same way you do apples—yes, apples! Just as apples diminish in size as you eat them, cores became smaller as flakes were removed. Aren't there times you start eating an apple, but can't finish it? Stone cores were also half-used. You throw out apples after eating the fruit. Cores too small to produce flaking material were left at the work site. A core is a good example of stone used by people. In the process of removing stone, the stone itself became flake scarred. Cores of any size or shape are artifacts because they're the waste material of ancient flintknapping.

To remove flakes from a core, people needed something just as hard as the stone to break it down. Another rock fit that requirement. The rock used to hit the core is called a **hammerstone**. Hammerstones were hand-held, general-purpose pounding tools that were in plentiful supply. Cobbles and pieces of rock became vital flintknapping tools when prehistoric Indians used stone to strike cores. Sometimes hammerstones were also used with another tool to refine the flakes they made.

Shaping stone required the removal of flakes in certain directions or on specific areas. Folks needed a sharper, thinner tool

17

than a hammerstone to do this. **Flaking tools** were used to chip the smaller pieces of stone that were struck from the core. Flaking tools are hard, slender objects that are not all exactly alike, but each type has a sharp point and a flat end. They were either held in a firm grip and used as the sole striking tool, pounded with a hammerstone, or pressed against the stone using the weight of the body. Instead of rock, these tools were made from antler, bone, or wood and copper.

USUALLY MADE OF ANTLER, FLAKING TOOLS WERE ALSO MADE FROM BONE OR WOOD AND COPPER.

Billets are antler flaking tools that were used with or without hammerstones. Billets were the most common flaking tool because the supply of material was ample, and the natural shape of the antler fit the needs of the job quite well. Deer and elk provided not only food for people, but antler, too. During slaughtering, Indians removed the antlers or cut off tines for flaking tools. When game was scarce, it was sometimes possible to find antlers that had been shed. This was much more difficult since mice usually ate the material before people could find it.

At certain times during flintknapping, Indians needed to have a flat, thick rock on hand. Unlike shed antler, slabs and cobbles of granite and other hard rock were fairly easy to find. The level surfaces of **anvils** and **chipping stones** provided steady bases on which they could work their stone. When one flat surface became pitted during the flaking process, the rock was often turned over and used again.

Indian flintknappers probably carried their billets and other flaking tools to and from places where they flaked stone, but heavier hammerstones, anvils and chipping stones were left at flintknapping sites. Even though people didn't produce products to the extent we do today, flintknapping sites are known as manufacturing areas. When you search for objects from the prehistoric tool kit, also look for battered or pitted rocks that were modified by the early production process.

Figure 2-3. Flintknapping specialist Floyd Rogers of Glen Ellyn, Illinois, demonstrates hard-hammer percussion. He is using a hammerstone to strike off large flakes from a good-sized piece of chert.

Flintknapping Techniques: Percussion and Pressure Flaking

People used hammerstones, flaking tools and chipping stones in different ways to get all the results they wanted. Large rock was broken down into smaller pieces by **percussion**, striking one rock against another. Indians performed **hard-hammer percussion** by holding a core or placing it on an anvil, and hitting it with a hammerstone. This method was used for removing wide or large, thin flakes and is shown in Figure 2-3.

Striking a hammerstone against a core didn't always create large flakes, especially on the first try. Sometimes it took two, three, four, or more hard hits to break it down. During this battering process, smaller flakes and chips were likely to break away from the core.

Hard-hammer percussion served a dual purpose since more than one artifact could be made from one rock. Depending on the size of the core, large flakes were chipped into projectile points and knives, scrapers and more. Smaller flakes were used to make smaller forms of the same weapons and tools. Very thin,

A FLAKE CAN BE AS BIG AS YOUR HAND, LONGER THAN YOUR FOREARM, OR SMALLER THAN YOUR FINGERNAIL.

very sharp flakes that broke off during percussion were frequently used just as they were. These sharp flakes, called **flake tools**, were often ready for use as cutting and scraping tools, and little or no further work was required. Flake tools are thin stone flakes that can be smaller than your fingernail or perhaps as big as your hand. They are not the same artifacts as the antler flaking tools used in flintknapping to make flakes, but are the *result* of hits from hammerstones and flaking tools.

Figure 2-4. Mr. Rogers used a sturdy antler billet during soft-hammer percussion to make this preform for a projectile point.

Indians used **soft-hammer percussion** to chip pieces removed from the core into objects called **preforms**. Preforms are rough forms of points or tools that are chipped into their basic shapes. To shape a stone into a preform, Indians used one of several techniques.

Normally, they held the stone in one hand against a leg, a knee, or in the lap while gripping a billet with the other hand. The billet was held in much the same way you would hold a drumstick, except more firmly. Flakes were removed by hitting the stone with the billet. Holding a stone against the body

cushioned flaking blows, allowed slightly more control over flaking, and also prevented other parts of the stone from being inadvertently spoiled.

When stone was placed on anvils, chipping could occur elsewhere as the billet knocked rock against rigid rock. But since preforms were rough forms, Indians would sometimes use anvils or chipping stones, and hammerstones during percussion as well. Placing the preform on a chipping stone, Indians held the pointed end of their billet against the stone, and hit the flat end with a hammerstone. Either method of percussion resulted in the removal of stone in long, slender flakes.

Another effective method for removing flakes in soft-hammer percussion required billets and hammerstones, but no anvils. Indians held both the preform and billet in one hand, with the sharp end of the billet toward their stone. Flakes were removed by striking the billet with the hammerstone. Once the preform was made, the object was ready for refining.

ODDLY ENOUGH, WHEN STONE IS STRUCK ON THE TOP, SHARP FLAKES FLY OFF FROM THE BOTTOM.

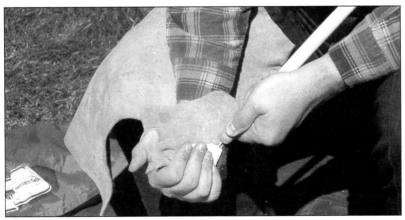

Figure 2-5. For pressure flaking, Mr. Rogers places a piece of rawhide against his palm for protection and applies pressure with a flaking tool made of wood and raw copper. These flintknapping materials are similar to those used by people thousands of years ago.

Figure 2-6. And his finished product is a beauty!

The final step in making tools and weapons was **pressure flaking**. Holding a stone firmly in one hand, Indians made minute, sharp serrations by pressing a flaking tool against thin edges of stone and slightly twisting. Stone was also pressure-flaked by using a long, pointed stick that was attached to a breast rest. To apply steady pressure, Indians placed the breast rest against the chest, the sharp end of the stick against their stone, and leaned against the flaking tool. Sometimes as many as twenty tiny flakes were chipped within one inch of stone. The precise chipping you see on edges of arrowheads, spear points, scrapers, drills and many other tools is the result of this finishing process.

PARALLEL   RANDOM   OBLIQUE

Figure 2-7. Examine flaking patterns on points and knives to appreciate a flintknapper's style and expertise. Parallel flaking has even, matching chipping on both sides of center. Random flaking is irregular, with no particular pattern. Oblique flaking is diagonal.

Amateurs should not try to knap stone without proper instruction. Since flaking tools and chipped stone edges are very sharp, there's a high likelihood of painful injury when using any of the flaking techniques. Amateurs who try the percussion and pressure flaking methods with obsidian, flint, chert, or other types of stone risk getting hurt. In addition to that, should you mistake a worked stone for Mother Nature's **non-cultural** rock and use it for chipping practice, a precious piece of prehistory would be lost. Before trying any flaking techniques, enroll in a flintknapping class at a museum or school.

Knapping tools and weapons out of stone has never been easy. Even flintknappers who lived long ago had trouble getting things to work properly at times. What do you think happened to stop the progress of the work in Figure 2-8?

Figure 2-8. A prehistoric flintknapper never completed making this point. Perhaps the artisan decided to use a more suitable piece of flint. Maybe it was a first attempt at making an arrowhead. Whatever the reason, both notches and right side were chipped, but work was abandoned before flaking the left edge and tip. What can we learn from this unfinished point? Work was completed at the base, half finished on the edges, and incomplete at the tip, so it appears this point was worked from the bottom up. Now take a close look at those rough notches. If notching was spoiled, was there really any point in finishing the weapon?

Flintknapping experts of today produce excellent replicas of stone artifacts. Their points and knives are **bifacial**, or worked on both sides, just like authentic artifacts. Inexpensive **reproductions** created by other flintknappers are **unifacial**, which means worked on only one side. These reproductions can be purchased in gift and souvenir shops, and are identifiable by the smooth, unifacial surface. Note the caliber of work on the points in Figure 2-9 and compare the reproductions with the artifacts for similarities, as well as differences.

Figure 2-9. Reproductions of arrowheads are not artifacts. Which is which? Unifacial replicas are above the pencil. Prehistoric bifacial points are beneath it. Look at flaking on surfaces, at edges and around notches to decide which points are more developed.

Pecking, Grinding and Polishing

Heavy, highly crafted objects used for ceremonies were sometimes flaked. Everyday chopping tools, such as axes and celts, were chipped now and again, too, but usually Indians pecked and ground most of their ornaments and woodcutting tools into shape. To begin, they selected a stone that was already close to the size and shape of the object they needed to make. Then, using a hammerstone in a process called **pecking**, they enhanced Mother Nature's work by battering their stone into a more desirable shape. The difference between pecking and flaking is that pieces of stone are not actually removed during pecking, but the stone is contoured by repeated blows. Indians chipped flint, but pecked granite because it wouldn't flake or crumble apart. You can identify pecking on granite or quartzite artifacts by the tiny pits or indentations on surfaces that Indians battered with another rock.

HOW WAS ROCK GROUND INTO USEFUL OBJECTS?

Stones often needed to be pecked before they were ground. Indians smoothed rough, pecked surfaces by **grinding** their stone against sandstone, limestone or abrasive bedrock. Sometimes, when the shape of the rock was already ideal for its intended purpose, Indians ground the stone without pecking it first. When a **blade** edge was needed, an end was ground until it was sharp. Extensive grinding to axe blades resulted in a dull polish, but since friction from chopping also polished sharp edges, sheens on blades will probably be from heavy use as well.

Although the supply of granite and other hard rock was plentiful in most places, pecking and grinding were tedious and time-consuming jobs. Even though it took prolonged effort to make a pecked and ground tool, some artifacts are ground so well that no pecking is left to be seen. On most tools, both pecking and grinding will be evident.

Often, flaked weapons and tools were also ground. Indians ground portions of projectile points and knives to keep edges from fracturing during the flaking process. They ground **stems** lightly to prevent them from severing sinew, gut or rawhide lashings. And they ground **bases** to prevent them from splitting spear shafts, arrows and bone handles on impact. When you see sharp edges on points or knives that have no pressure flaking, you're most likely seeing the work of light grinding.

Some types of stone have a natural glossy finish. Others have a smooth, waxy luster caused by exposure to heat from fire. But a high polish and very smooth surfaces can also result from light grinding. **Polishing**, the step that brought the beauty out of stone, was used as a finishing process. Although nobody knows precisely how polishing was done, Indians probably mixed sand with animal fat, and used leather to rub the mixture against stone. Fat would have helped brighten the banded slate and colorful stone they used for special objects. Indians took extra care buffing ceremonial stones and ornaments. Thorough polishing ensured that pecking or grinding scratches would not mar the finished products.

TIPS TO IDENTIFY WORKED STONE

Some chips you'll see on projectile points are the result of human use, and not flintknapping. On a point with a broken tip, a vertical flake that begins at the break would be an **impact fracture**. Impact fractures occurred when weapons struck bone, wood or other rigid substances so hard that the impact produced a long, lengthwise flake.

After you have examined rocks for evidence of flaking, pecking and grinding, how can you be sure that the chips and scars you see were caused by people, and *not* Mother Nature? How can you differentiate percussion and pressure flaking from chipping that occurred naturally? Or determine that a smooth stone was ground by someone long ago? You can identify more links between stone and prehistory by looking at other clues.

Figure 2-10. To identify worked stone, look for pressure flaking, percussion shaping, pecking, or grinding on broken rocks you pick up or turn over. When cultural stone does not have some kind of defined shape, deciphering what it is or what part of an artifact it came from can be anybody's guess. Except for what is believed to be a core (lower right), these fragments may have come from knives, preforms, scraping tools, or an anvil (upper right).

First, examine shapes. While you arrowhead hunt, you'll see stones that are nearly rectangular, square, triangular, oval, round, or oblong—all perfect, except for a bulge here and there, a lopsided edge, a flat tip, a slanted side, a twist at one end, a hollow spot and so forth. In these, Mother Nature has done a remarkable job of modifying stone and providing good material for Indians to improve. But most stone worked by Mother Nature and not by people has an irregular shape. Battering by glaciers, crashing down a cliff, or colliding with rock in swift water could have given a stone its present form. Heavy animals with sharp hooves can also modify stone by stepping on it. Most large chunks of Mother Nature's non-cultural rock will lack sharp definition in shape. Small pieces of flint, chert and obsidian that are not worked will usually have an extremely irregular outline. Large flakes will have a blocky appearance and instead of flake removal scars, surfaces will be riddled with cracks. After checking for surface modifications that could have been made by people, remember that most artifacts, even crude ones, will have more defined shapes than those modified by nature.

Next, think about where you found the stone. **Provenance** is the special, spatial relationship artifacts have with each other in a site. A knife and scraper near charred food remains, fragments of animal bone, or campfire rock tell us much more about a prehistoric scenario than a knife found by itself. When a stone with questionable work is in close proximity to an obvious artifact, the source of the work can be determined by comparing edge and surface flaking, and taking other archaeological clues into account.

ARCHAEOLOGISTS ALWAYS FOCUS ON PROVENANCE OF ARTIFACTS, BECAUSE THE INFORMATION GAINED IN A SITE PROVIDES GREAT CULTURAL AND ARCHAEOLOGICAL MEANING.

The moving and mixing of stone and the loss of archaeological context happens most on plowed fields, at places with significant erosion, and where water currents are strong. Moving stone from its original place in the soil destroys the provenance of an artifact. Without provenance, it becomes much harder for both amateurs and professionals to differentiate artifacts from non-cultural stone.

Provenance can make a big difference when you're looking at a stone that has conchoidal surfaces and sharp edges, but no pressure flaking. Some types of scrapers can have odd angles at sharp edges, but Mother Nature's stone that breaks in conchoidal fractures can also have edges with sharp angles. Stone edges *not* worked by people are often slightly smooth. This is a very fine distinction that's hard to determine, especially when artifacts and non-cultural stone have moved from their original places in the ground. Whenever stone has been moved and when pressure flaking is absent, give any smooth edges on sharp angles a very close second look. Keep in mind that although these areas may never have been altered by people, the stone could have been used as a flake tool and might be an artifact.

When you're looking at smooth stone, you can examine the direction of grinding scars. Think of grinding scars on stone in the same way that you think of the tiny lines in sanded wood— as minute, parallel scratches. Artifacts that have been ground by people will have consistent scars going in one direction in one area. When scratches are randomly scattered over stone surfaces, Mother Nature has done the work. Scars other than those made by people can be caused by soil movements, plow impacts or trampling from livestock. These can occur at any angle or over entire surfaces.

The trouble with grinding scars is their size. Because they are so small, they're usually hard to see. Pebbly earth that has grated against buried stone over the years adds to the problem. Most grinding scars on artifacts that have surfaced have been worn out or rubbed down by the environment and erosion. When you can't make out definite grinding scars, look at surfaces of stone for a dull sheen. Find areas that are more smooth or places with a different texture. Examine oval or round stones for a flat, defined surface that comes to an edge. Draw your finger across surfaces and along edges to feel the differences.

On plowed fields, you'll often see long, slender gashes on pieces of sandstone and limestone. Shallow, concave depressions on these types of rock could be old scars from prehistoric grinding. Indians often used small pieces of rough stone to sharpen antler, bone and other types of stone, and large, level rocks to straighten wood for spear shafts and arrows. Whether portable or stationary, a **grinding stone** that was used for sharpening and straightening would be an **abrading stone**.

You can distinguish an abrading stone from a plow-nicked stone by examining the pattern of abrasions. In abrading stones, shallow grooves are usually parallel and run along the length of the stone. Check the color of the abraded areas, since grooved

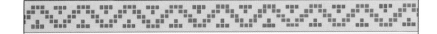

Points of Interest

Check Your Breaks for Patina

A **patina** is a hard, lustrous coating that forms on stone surfaces only over long periods of time. Many artifacts have a beautiful patina. To see what one looks like, examine a broken stone. Choose a rock having a sheen and compare the break with the outside surface. If the broken surface has the same luster as the exterior, you are seeing a patina. Because a patina forms only on surfaces, you can conclude that a rock broke long ago when the gloss is uniform over all surfaces. If a break is recent, the broken surface will not have the same luster as the rest of the stone. While you arrowhead hunt, check the breaks on broken artifacts for a patina. If damage is recent, there's a chance a plow may have been responsible and another part of the artifact could be lying nearby.

lines in abrading stones will have nearly the same color as the rest of the rock. Fresh marks from recent damage will be shades lighter than the exterior color. Inspect the edges of the furrows, too. Edges of abrasions that were ground long ago will be smoother than the sharp nicks from a plow disk.

An oval or round rock with a very smooth surface is especially hard to identify as having been ground by people, because it has nearly the same type of surface as the smooth rock you'll find in or near water. To identify it as a food grinding stone, called a **mano**, look at your surroundings once again. This time, take note of the rock types in the vicinity you are hunting. Inspect stones that don't seem to belong to the area, because Indians may have brought their manos with them from distant places. Then check those stones for a flattened side with one-way scars, and a round, convex side for cupping in the palm of the hand.

No matter what the shape may be, when an artifact is well defined and polished, you'll spot it more easily among other stone. Keep an eye out for smooth stones—both large and small—that do not resemble any of the surrounding rocks. These may have holes, grooves, etched decorations, flat sides, a sharp edge, or other curious features. If a rock like this catches your attention, chances are the stone is either an ornament, a ceremonial stone or a prehistoric weight.

The more you know what to look for in stone, the more fun you'll have. The more you see, the better you'll be. But no matter how well you know your rocks, shapes, flakes, or conchoidal breaks, your hunting experiences will be rewarding. There are possibilities for surprises every time you turn a rock over to the other side—in the patterns of fossils, the radiance of pyrite, or the beauty of quartz. And sometimes, when you least expect it, the stone you're arrowhead hunting for appears in your walking path, too.

Figure 3-1. Pieces of tools and weapons are artifacts, too. Finding a broken artifact is a significant event because you will remember the day and the way you found it. This photo contains portions of knives, arrowheads, spear points and a fine flaked drill. Behind all of these finds are stories of adventure and discovery.

Discovering Stone Artifacts

What one thing helps you and your family complete the most tasks in the least amount of time? If you guessed computers, you're close. If you think it's electricity, you're right. Electricity puts the power in our saws, the vibration in wood sanders, the heat in glue guns and the twist in our screwdrivers and drills. We have food processors, electric razors and mixers for everything from milk shakes to wall paint. We can cut, slice, smooth, chop, mash and connect things faster today than ever before.

In prehistory, thousands of years ago, people had work to do that would have been easier with our modern tools and appliances. But electricity and fancy equipment weren't invented yet, and muscle just wasn't enough. How did people do their cutting, chopping and mashing chores without twentieth-century tools? What weapons did they take to hunt game? What did people use to cut through tough material, such as animal hides, or chop harder substances, such as wood? How did they fasten one thing to another? What could they use to prepare food, or wear for ornament?

Prehistoric people had to make their tools out of the natural resources of the land. Since rock was plentiful and it was harder than the things which needed to be pierced, chopped or crushed, Indians made most of their tools from stone. You already know some of the ways to recognize cultural stone and how to look for evidence of flaking, pecking and grinding. But you'll also be curious to know how a worked stone could have been used and what kind of artifact it may be. Once you've determined that a stone is *something*, you'll want to go a step further to figure out how it was used. People chipped stone into sharp objects such as spear points, arrowheads, knives, scrapers, perforators, gravers and multipurpose tools. They ground other rock into tools that would chop and pound, such as axes and celts and mauls. Folks made manos, pestles and mortars to prepare food, and shaped other rocks into game stones, ceremonial stones and ornaments. Which type of artifact could your worked stone be? What could have been its purpose?

To decide how a stone was used, think about the kinds of jobs that needed doing long ago and consider the clues of shape and size. Shape and size, together with special features you find on stone, are good indicators that can point to a common prehistoric task. Discovering a worked stone and considering its relationship to a function will help you identify it as a specific artifact. We'll cover some of the more common artifacts in this chapter to show you how the general shape and size of stone is directly related to a type of function.

SHAPE AND SIZE OF STONE

You would know a bow and arrow if you saw them, but how can you recognize artifacts that you are not familiar with? It's easier than you might think. Think how a stone could *function* as a tool or weapon. How could it have been used? It's helpful to look at the shape and size of stone in figuring out the function. How can these clues show the purpose of an artifact? How can they help you to identify it?

Imagine an egg-shaped stone that would be easy for you to hold. What could you use it for? A stone of this shape and size would be good for pounding. Pounding what? Probably just about anything, but you could certainly strike a core or hit a billet to flake stone. The shape and size of this stone have linked it to a prehistoric function. The shape, size and function point to a type of artifact. Your tool could be a hammerstone, because hammerstones are basically egg-shaped stones that were used for pounding.

Now suppose your stone is oval and easy to hold. Imagine that one side is flat. What could you use this one for? If you rubbed the flat side against another level stone, it would be ideal for mashing wild strawberries or grinding other foods. Shape and size connect it with an artifact you already know. It could be a mano since most manos have an oval shape with a flat side for grinding.

Picture a small stone with a very defined shape and a pointed projection. This one would be great for piercing holes in buckskin for straps, or etching pictures or lines in bone and leather. What would fit the description and function of your stone? Perforators are small tools that have a spiked projection for puncturing. Gravers are smaller artifacts that have a sharp tip for engraving. Perforators or gravers would be your possible artifacts.

What other clues can help to reflect a function? How can the stone and its purpose point to an artifact? Think about the shape and size your stone has, and features like grooves, flaked surfaces, drilled holes, notches, sharp edges, smooth areas or texture. Let's try this with flaking, sharp edges and type of stone.

WHY ARE ARTIFACTS IN THE SHAPE THEY'RE IN?

Visualize yourself hunting. You've spotted a game animal and your weapon is aimed. What type of shape and edges would your stone-tipped weapon need to pierce the animal hide? The tip would have to be triangular to be sharp. It would also help if your stone had sharp edges for deep penetration. Would a triangular shape and sharp edges reflect any functions? Certainly. Piercing and penetrating. Projectile points are basically triangular, and the type of stone used for points will flake into sharp edges. To tip your arrow or spear, your artifact would be a projectile point.

Suppose your aim was true and the weapon brought the animal down. How would you do the butchering? You would need a stone with sharp edges to skin and gut the carcass. Would size matter? Or shape? That would depend on the bulk of the animal you're visualizing, and how much or what part of the hide you would have to clean. Your stone should fit the requirements of the job and still be practical for you to grip. In this case, sharp edges are the best clue to function, because the tool you would need is variable in size and shape. The function, of course, is scraping. Scrapers have different shapes and sizes. Surfaces are flaked. Edges are sharp. And scrapers were used to skin and clean hides. The tool you require is a scraper.

Let's look at the oval grinding tool again, but this time include the type of stone. Imagine grinding fibrous roots with a granular rock. Since this type of rock would be rough on your hands, couldn't you use a smooth stone instead? You could, but it wouldn't work half as well. Granular rock would be better for your coarse grinding task. Here, shape and type of stone have links with function, and function with a type of artifact. Your artifact would still be a mano, but it would not be the smooth kind that worked best on softer foods.

Look at shapes and sizes, and any special characteristics you see on stone to help you determine a function. You'll arrowhead hunt effectively this way, even if you've never seen an actual artifact on the surface of the ground before.

You can discover more by knowing some facts about common weapons and tools from prehistoric life. Since arrowheads and spear points are the best-known artifacts and knives are often similar, let's start with these.

PROJECTILE POINTS AND KNIVES

A projectile point needed a sharp tip in an inverted "V" shape to penetrate thick animal hides, and a place to **haft**, or attach it to an arrow or a spear. Take a closer look at Figure 3-2, which shows basic terms and features of points and knives. The drawing illustrates typical characteristics of flaked weapons.

COMMON TERMS AND FEATURES OF
POINTS AND KNIVES

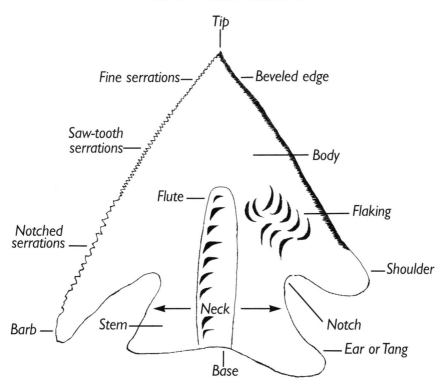

Figure 3-2. These terms identify features of projectile points and knives.

Serrations, edges resembling those on a saw, were pressure-flaked to cut like tiny teeth. **Bevels**, the result of resharpening or repair, gave edges a slight slope that helped twist points into hides on impact. **Barbs**, sharp projections jutting out on **shoulders**, were designed to stay in punctured flesh. A thrashing, wounded animal of any size was not likely to dislodge a barbed point and run away. **Ears** or **tangs**, extensions at the bottom of stems, also made for secure anchoring in hides. **Notches** were flaked for hafting to arrows, spear shafts or knife handles. Use the terms, as archaeologists do, to describe your finds of points or knives.

SHAPES, NOTCHES AND STEMS

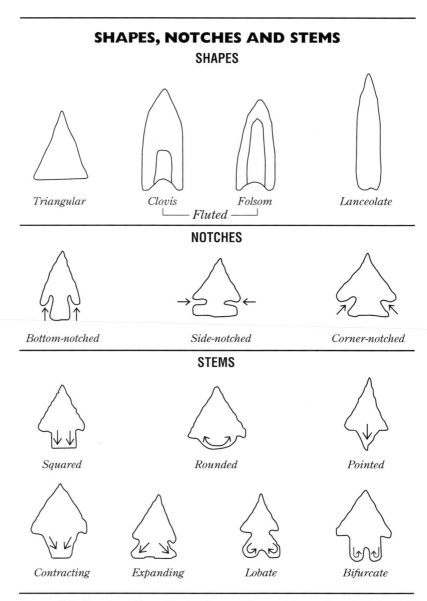

SHAPES

Triangular

Clovis

Folsom

Lanceolate

└── *Fluted* ──┘

NOTCHES

Bottom-notched

Side-notched

Corner-notched

STEMS

Squared

Rounded

Pointed

Contracting

Expanding

Lobate

Bifurcate

Figure 3-3. Compare these illustrations with your pieces of worked stone. If you find a fragment with a defined shape, notches or a stem—especially one that has tangs—the drawings can help you identify it as a point or a knife.

You will know projectile points when you see them. Clean, exposed points will *look* like arrowheads or spear points. The chart above identifies common shapes, notches and stems of various points and knives. Use the illustrations to compare and identify whole shapes, notching styles and other features, such as **lobate** ears, **bifurcate** stems, or **flutes**, on pieces of worked stone you find.

How can you tell the difference between arrowheads and spear points? It's not always easy because the shape and flaking can be similar. A good way to differentiate them is by size. Think about the size in relationship to a job, because the size of a point can be a good hint about the size of the task and the lifestyle. What tasks would require large points? Big ones. Like bringing down animals as massive as elephants. For these bigger jobs, spear points were attached to long wooden shafts and thrown with the arm. Indians used spears with large points–sometimes as long as five inches–to kill woolly mammoths, giant ground sloths and other game thousands of years ago.

BIRD POINTS AND WAR POINTS ARE TRIANGULAR ARROWHEADS THAT ARE LESS THAN ONE INCH LONG.

Spear points are usually larger than arrowheads. Arrowheads were used for smaller jobs, like bringing down deer, or shooting smaller animals such as rabbit or squirrel, long after the age of mammoths. By that time, Indians were fastening smaller points to lightweight arrows, and shooting the arrows with bows. So, measure the length to determine the point type, and you can also gain some clues about the lifestyle. Arrowheads usually will be an inch to one and one-half inches long. Points longer than two inches more likely will be spear points.

Knives were much more versatile in daily prehistoric life than spear points or arrowheads. People probably used knives more times in one day than any other tool or weapon. Indians used knives to notch the ends of spear shafts and arrows before inserting the points. They stripped bark from wood and carved slots in handles for hafting. They pried mussels apart, slashed plant food from stalks, cut fiber strands for mats and baskets, trimmed hair, and split feathers for arrows.

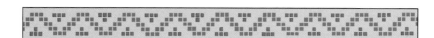

Is the Point a Knife?

Knives are commonly confused with projectile points because they look so much alike. They can have the same basic shape, flaking and edges. They both have serrations, bevels, and a stem or notches for hafting. So, what makes a point different from a **knife**?

There's a reason for the expression, "straight as an arrow." Projectile points are evenly aligned and "arrow dynamic" for flying through the air. Knives are slightly curved for cutting. Since knives were used for slashing and slicing rather than piercing, they're also sturdier than points. Indians made knives with deeper notches in wider bases to increase secure hafting and strength. They also made notches uneven to haft at an angle, and chipped unequal shoulders for enhancing blade curves. Cutting edges on knives were more important than tips. Projectile point tips are usually sharper. A lopsided, blunt projectile point is not the result of shoddy work, but a good clue that the tool is a knife.

Knives resemble points so closely in shape, size and flaking that it's easy to mistake one for the other. Also, because knives were used so extensively, what might appear to be a point could be a knife. Similarities and differences in characteristics that will help you differentiate points and knives are given in the *Points of Interest* box. Archaeologists who find broken points or knives that are missing distinguishing features use a "point/knife" classification to correctly identify them. You can follow their example by designating a debatable flaked weapon you discover as a "point or knife."

Are there any types of knives that *don't* resemble points? Definitely! And there are more than just a few. A knife will look less like a point if you consider that, because of certain features, it could not function well as a tip to a projectile weapon. For example, one diagonal tang in a base corner of your "point or knife" would indicate that the object is a knife, not a projectile point. Why? Because if the object were hafted to a spear, the tip would point in the wrong direction, not in the direction aimed. Try to imagine a very large, thick knife at the end of a projectile weapon, and a long, thin point hafted to an identical shaft. Now picture them in action. On comparison,

KNIVES CAN BE LONGER THAN SPEAR POINTS OR SMALLER THAN ARROWHEADS.

you'll probably agree that the heavier knife could reduce the distance of travel, and the bulk would prevent a clean, deep puncture. Other features, such as a curved edge opposite a straight edge, deep notches, or a broad, sturdy base, also functioned better on knives than on points. If you find a point that you suspect is a knife, examine the features even more closely. Think how you would have used it. How would it have performed, hafted to a spear shaft or arrow? Would it have worked better in a handle? Since there are characteristics you can look for that will identify certain kinds of knives, the table in Figure 3-4 provides information for recognizing both common and specialty types.

COMMON AND SPECIALTY KNIVES

FEATURES	TYPE
A triangular shape. May have rounded corners at the base.	Triangular
A rectangular shape, bifacial chipping and one beveled blade edge.	Rectangular
An elongated diamond shape with blade edges on each of the sides.	Four-blade
A half-moon or crescent shape.	Crescent
A slender leaf shape that tapers at the base.	Leaf-shape
Long, thin and tapered at the tip.	Lanceolate
Flaking on one side. Two blade edges.	Unifacial
One straight edge. Used with a slotted handle.	Side-hafted
Knife tips at both ends of the tool.	Double-pointed
One diagonal tang in the corner of the base.	Corner Tang
A stem beneath a notched base.	Double-notch

Figure 3-4. To identify a type of knife, note the shape, edge and surface chipping, the base, and other distinctive features.

When knives have characteristics that truly distinguish them from points, it's especially exciting to find one. Discovery is fun when you find crude knives, too. Rough forms of knives may not appear to have made great cutting tools, but they did the job required and served their purpose well.

SCRAPERS AND SCRAPING TOOLS

If you had lived in prehistoric times, you would have had to separate animal pelts from meat and meat from bone. You would need the hide for clothing and warmth, and the meat for food. You could use the bone for knife handles, beads, flaking tools and hooks. How would you do it? How would you remove scales from a fish? Or bark from a branch to make a spear shaft? You would need something hard, sharp and portable. And so did prehistoric people. For stripping things clean and cutting away debris, Indians flaked stone into **scrapers**.

When you arrowhead hunt for scrapers, you'll do better if you *don't* look for certain shapes. Look for sharp edges instead. Why? Most scrapers have shapes that are any which way, but scraping edges were always flaked or naturally sharp. How can you avoid mistaking a non-cultural rock with sharp edges for a scraper? It's not hard when you know a bit about the chipping you should look for on these tools.

Scrapers that have bifacial chipping have fewer areas of work on one side of the stone. The side that has the least amount of work is the underside of the tool. Chipping on both sides gives scrapers a slightly rippled edge, like the sort of edge you'd see on a conch shell. Scrapers with bifacial chipping are usually no less than the size of a half dollar.

TOOLS SUCH AS "END SCRAPERS" AND "SIDE SCRAPERS" DESCRIBE EXACTLY WHERE TO LOOK FOR THE FLAKED SCRAPING EDGE.

Chipping on only one side makes a scraper unifacial. Scrapers that have small areas of work on undersides are considered to be unifacial, too. Are flake tools with small areas of pressure flaking a type of scraper? Absolutely! So, always check both sides of thin flakes for the work. Check stones for combinations of percussion-shaped surfaces and pressure-flaked edges. Look for scraping edges along an end, on a side, or on both. When you do these things, you just may find a scraper that others have dismissed as non-cultural rock.

Scrapers were made to be used with the hands, so consider the size to connect it to a task. Indians made heavy-duty scrapers for cleaning massive animals, smaller tools for fish and small game, and **thumb scrapers** the size of your thumb for working in delicate or tight areas. For slim jobs, such as removing marrow from bones, people fluted the base of narrow tools so a long handle could be attached.

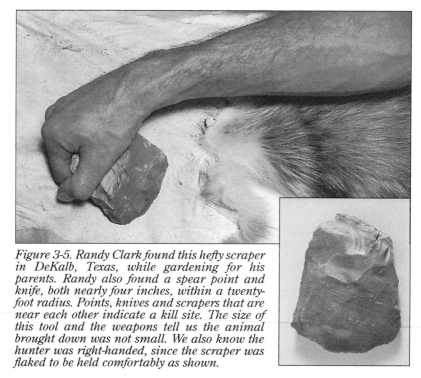

Figure 3-5. Randy Clark found this hefty scraper in DeKalb, Texas, while gardening for his parents. Randy also found a spear point and knife, both nearly four inches, within a twenty-foot radius. Points, knives and scrapers that are near each other indicate a kill site. The size of this tool and the weapons tell us the animal brought down was not small. We also know the hunter was right-handed, since the scraper was flaked to be held comfortably as shown.

Scrapers can be identified more easily when they have rock "handles." Would you cut meat with a knife that didn't have a handle, or scale fish holding a sharpened, double-sided blade? No way! And neither did prehistoric Indians when they used a sharp tool. Jagged pieces of exposed rock could slice human skin even more easily than animal hide. To avoid getting cut, they didn't chip off all exterior stone on the opposite side of the cutting edge. On broken pieces of stone with no exterior rock, Indians made scrapers safer to hold by chipping away the sharp edges on another side. If your stone has a very sharp edge on at least one side, and a rocky handle or place for a safe grip, your find may well be a scraper.

Look for a handhold on scrapers, too. Try holding them in different ways—both with your right hand and your left. Normally, a flake was removed from the stone to make a good fit for a thumb. But chipping could have occurred elsewhere to secure a grip. The scraper shown in Figure 3-5 is flaked on the reverse side for the base of a palm.

Often, more than one type of tool was needed at a time. But it was not convenient to lug a scraper and several other stone tools through forests, across prairies or up slopes. And Indians didn't wear fancy tool belts when working around their campsites. How could they have more tools available without carrying around a bunch of sharp rocks? They made handy **multipurpose tools** from scrapers.

Multipurpose tools were jacks-of-all-trades. Indians used these tools for combinations of scraping, cutting, puncturing or engraving. What do they look like? Hard to tell, because each one is different from the next. Imagine a unifacial scraper with a long, sharp edge that you could use as a knife blade. Add a perforator spike to one end for puncturing hides. Or tip it with a small, sharp graver **spur** for etching bone or antler, to be creative. You've just visualized a multipurpose tool. When looking at an actual scraper, try to find any additional flaking.

Spokeshaves are small scraping tools that were used for

COULD THE HANDIWORK OF A SPOKESHAVE CUTOUT BE FOUND ON A MULTIPURPOSE TOOL?

cleaning and smoothing sticks for spear and arrow shafts. They're easy to distinguish from other scraper types because they have one or two distinct cutouts. The shape of a spokeshave cutout is a half-moon. Look for a hollow cavity along the edge of a scraper that is more or less the size of your fingernail. Indians drew the hollow cutout over sticks to remove bark and straighten them.

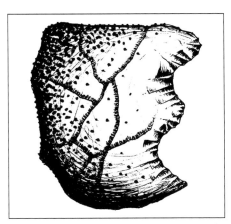

Figure 3-6. Names of artifacts can be quizzical. Spokeshaves and thumb scrapers are both scraping tools, but a spokeshave doesn't shave spokes, and a thumb scraper isn't for scraping thumbs.

CHOPPING AND POUNDING TOOLS

The most common prehistoric chopping tool is the stone **axe**. Axes are easy to figure because the purpose and name of this artifact have not changed over time. An axe is still an axe, even after thousands of years. When you think of this tool, you think of chopping wood. You also think of it as having a handle and a sharp cutting edge. Our images of axes hold true for those used long ago, too.

What about size? You might have a picture in your mind of a large, heavy tool. Most prehistoric axes are larger than other stone artifacts. Axes

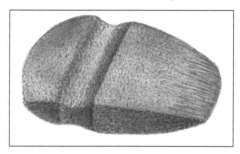

Figure 3-7. The groove in a full groove axe will extend around all four sides of the axe head.

as long as sixteen inches are fairly common and the biggest ones can weigh about thirty pounds. But you'll see axes in various sizes because miniature types were made for smaller jobs as well.

THE BLUNT END OF AN AXE COULD ALSO BE USED AS A POUNDING TOOL.

Studies on the wear of axe blades suggest that handle lengths were short, varying from only twelve to eighteen inches. With an average length of fifteen, apparently some axes were used like hatchets.

What do stone axes look like? They resemble contemporary models, but they're not as sharp or as flashy. Axe blades today are thin and made from steel. Prehistoric axes are much thicker and were made from granite, quartzite or other dense stone. Indians chose stone close to the desired shape, ground tips to a tapered edge, and made grooves for hafting to solid wood handles. Most axe types describe the characteristic of the groove, such as half groove, three-quarter groove or full groove. The pencil sketch in Figure 3-7 illustrates a full groove axe.

Figure 3-8. When an artifact has a groove and is whole, it's easy to identify it as an axe. The three-quarter groove axe is made of granite, the most common material for chopping tools, and also has some scarring from use. The surface find on the right needs a groove to prove it's an axe, but it just might be the tip of a ceremonial artifact. It has uniform beveled sides and has been broken for some time. It also appears to be polished, but never used for chopping wood. Oversized, polished tools and weapons were used in ceremonies instead. Ceremonial artifacts were too big to be functional for work, but were wonderful to see during pomp and circumstance.

Look for **celts** while you arrowhead hunt for axes. Think of them as smaller, thinner versions of axes, because the average size is only two to three inches wide and five to six inches long. You can tell a celt apart from an axe not only by shape and size, but also by the absence of a groove. Without a groove for hafting, how did people secure these tools to handles? Indians had more than one way to attach things to each other. Long chisels were mounted on wooden holders and lashed in the middle for fastening. War club stones were sewn in rawhide coverings that extended over handles. Thin monolithic axes were put in handles with hafting slots. Celts were tightly wedged in slitted handles.

Celts are sharp tools that were used like small axes in warfare, but their primary function was chopping wood. Most of them are average in workmanship, with some pecking evident.

Well-made, well-ground, rectangular celts are handsome arti-facts that are smooth to touch. You'll see them most often in granite, and occasionally in hematite, basalt or slate.

Wouldn't it have been great to find tools on the ground and simply use them as they were? Hammerstones were no-muss, no-fuss, ready-made pounding tools. As long as a rock fit nicely in the hand, any piece of hard stone would do.

You'll probably agree that hammerstones were important tools in prehistoric times. Folks used them to peck stone into shape, and also in the flintknapping process. Celts and axes are just two of many prehistoric tools that were pecked with hammerstones before surfaces were ground. When the cutting edges of chopping tools like these were damaged beyond repair, Indians did not discard the implements. After grinding down jagged blade edges, the ruined woodcutting tools, with or without a groove, were often used again as hammerstones for other pounding jobs.

Hammerstones are usually smooth cobbles of granite or quartzite. They were convenient, versatile tools good for striking, pounding, pummeling or pulverizing just about anything at all.

TO MAKE MAULS OUT OF RUINED AXES, INDIANS GROUND SHATTERED BLADE EDGES INTO ROUND TIPS.

Rocks used this way will be chipped on the ends or scarred from repeated bashing and blows.

Mauls are hafted tools that were also used for pounding. A cross between hammerstones and axes, mauls have blunt ends, which make them resemble hammerstones, and a groove for attachment to a handle, the same as axes. Because a cobble grasped with bare hands was not suitable for all tasks, some rocks were pecked and ground, and then grooved for securing to hardwood handles. The handles saved wear and tear on hands, aided leverage, added weight, and allowed people to do heavier work. Hafted mauls weighing approximately one to twenty pounds dissipated the impact of rock hitting rock, and lessened stress to the arm.

GRINDING TOOLS AND STONES FOR COOKING

Figure 3-9. What's for dinner? You're much more likely to find a mano or roller type of pestle in one piece than a whole seventy-pound mortar. Either kind of grinding stone could have been used to process food on this over-sized grinding container.

Grinding berries, nuts, seeds and roots were chores that could last for hours. Your hands would feel chafed and sore if you used a sandy, grainy stone for grinding. Smoother rock would be easier on your palms and fingers. Not only that, your food would be free of tiny rock particles that granular stones produce during grinding. But different types of jobs, such as mashing soft berries and grinding hard seeds, required different types of stone. Indians used both types of rock for their food grinding stones.

Stones for manos had to be a shape and size that could be cupped comfortably in the hand. When a person rubbed a mano against a grinding slab, the side of the stone doing the grinding wore down and became flattened. Two flat sides on a mano are clues that both sides of the tool were used for grinding.

Manos were made from smooth river rock, basalt and granite. For heavy-duty grinding, such as pulverizing seeds into flour, Indians used granular rock instead of stone that was smooth. Granular rock produced sand during grinding, which mixed with the seed flour. There was no way to avoid this, but fortunately, it wasn't harmful to stomachs.

Indians also made **pestles** to grind food. Instead of river rock or granular stone, the rock of choice was granite. Granite rocks were pecked and ground into smooth pestles of different shapes. Just as you would use a rolling pin to crush dry bread into bread crumbs, Indians used rolling pin types to grind large quantities of food. For smaller jobs, they made bell, hoof and tube shapes. Having a sort of stem as a handle, pestles were gripped at one end and food was mashed at the other.

IF YOU FIND WHAT LOOKS LIKE A VERY OLD DOOR-KNOB, IT MIGHT WELL BE A SMOOTH BELL PESTLE.

Where did all this grinding take place? Naturally, not on counters or tables. Back then food was placed on **mortars**, flat or scooped stone slabs averaging about nine by twelve inches. These platforms for grinding are the largest stone artifacts, but it's unlikely that you'll find a whole one in full view on ground surface. Why? Since they are easy to see, many have already been found. Other mortars have broken apart from exposure to natural elements.

Stone was also used in the prehistoric kitchen to cook food and line fire hearths. How can you recognize rock that folks used for these jobs? Look at color and texture, because broken pieces of **cooking stones**, **boiling stones** and **hearth stones** resemble each other. Whether broken or complete, these artifacts have one thing in common—the special characteristic of **fire-cracked** rock. Fire-cracking occurs when rock is repeatedly exposed to fire. The color and texture changes as a result of heating up and cooling down, over and over again. Blackened or reddened rock, broken or cracked from the heat of campfires, could be the result of the ancient cooking process.

Indians heated liquids and cooked their food with cooking stones and boiling stones. Stones about the size of tangerines were laid on hot coals and heated. When the stones became hot, they were placed in water for boiling, or in stews and broths for simmering. Culinary artifacts such as these can be found on campsites, where food was prepared.

GAME STONES, CEREMONIAL STONES AND ORNAMENTS

If you're guessing that **game stones** were used for entertainment, you're right. Look at shape and texture, because game stones are round and smooth. To make them, Indians chose stones that were nearly round for pecking, grinding and polishing into spheres. Game stones can be as small as marbles or as large as baseballs. Like glass marbles and rubber balls that we use for enjoyment today, stone balls can often be found where prehistoric folks lived, relaxed and played.

Disc-shaped game stones with highly polished surfaces that are not scratched or scarred may have been **ceremonial stones**. **Discoidals**, also called **chunkey stones**, could have had either a recreational or a ceremonial function. Most discoidals look like small stone wheels with two concave sides. Others have convex faces with centered indentions or a center hole. While some have evenly etched lines that archaeologists call **tally marks,** no one can say why people decorated any of these stones this way.

Though miniature stone wheels were first used in prehistoric times, early European travelers wrote descriptions about them after witnessing tribal games. Discoidals were often used in a competitive game called chunkey. In chunkey, one person rolled a disc along the ground. Two would run after it, throwing wooden poles at the spot where they expected the stone to stop. But some stones don't appear to have been played with in this rough-and-tumble fashion. Flawless stone discs are probably ceremonial instead.

YOU WOULD BE MORE LIKELY TO FIND GAME STONES ON CAMPSITES THAN HUNTING GROUNDS, BECAUSE KILL SITES WERE NOT PLACES WHERE RECREATION TOOK PLACE.

Indians made many types of finely crafted objects for rituals and used them in ceremonies rather than for work or play. To know that a stone is ceremonial, consider its size and shape. Oversized tools and weapons, such as massive axes and ten-inch knives or spear points, had a function that was suitable for ceremonies. A large, handsome object carried in a ceremony may have been a means of showing esteem and respect for others of higher rank. Bearing oversized tools and weapons might also have been a way for Indians to honor their deities.

Drilled, grooved or notched stones with well-defined shapes and smaller sizes could be ceremonial stones, too. Indians ground stones into distinct, geometric forms and worked others into birds, butterflies, boats, shapes similar to bow ties, and other designs. Although the smallest sizes were used during hunting, the largest were made for rituals. Were these types of ceremonial ornaments a sign of a hunter's expertise? Or, like dances for rain, were they an appeal for bountiful hunting? Since no one has found the evidence that indicates precisely how these ceremonial stones were used, the stories behind them have yet to be discovered.

People also wore stone for ornament. **Ornaments** for personal adornment are also well defined and polished, and sometimes decoratively etched. In order to wear a stone, Indians needed one that could be attached to a cord or strap. Though a drilled hole served this purpose well, sometimes they made a groove or chipped notches into the sides. Functional as pretty jewelry, stone ornaments were worn around the neck or tied to the arm.

▼ ▼ ▼

Remember the saying about exceptions to rules, because it also applies to shapes, sizes and features of prehistoric tools and weapons. People met their toolmaking needs with ingenuity, style and available materials. Indians flaked petrified wood points, notched scrapers for handles, and rounded arrowhead tips to scrape or stun instead of kill. They chipped **cache** blades for underground caches, chipped stone into axes, and ground barbed and fluted axes as well. They put grooves in celts, flaked flint into chipped celts, pecked double-bitted hammerstones, drilled perforated mauls, chipped unifacial points—you name it. There's a profusion of combinations. When you arrowhead hunt, be sure to keep your mind open to other possibilities in stone artifacts, too.

Figure 4-1. One of the best places to hunt for arrowheads is on a plowed field by a river. If you walk land next to a river (lower arrow), check for sandy soil, shell and smooth rocks. These features indicate that the river was bigger thousands of years ago, or that flooding has occurred. Though people may have fished, hunted or camped briefly on that field, try hunting further back and higher up, where a campsite would always stay dry (upper arrow).

Scouting for Sites

Discovering a place where early Native Americans lived or passed through is as thrilling as finding an artifact itself. Figuring out where to go is fun because you'll be using geographic clues and your imagination to find places to hunt. As you search for sites, you'll want to see your surroundings as they might have looked hundreds or thousands of years ago. Wouldn't the features of a wooded area, a bare knoll or small lake look slightly different today than in prehistoric times? Though it's wonderful to find an artifact where you'd never expect it to be, it's exciting to discover an artifact after reasoning out a location for a hunting ground or campsite.

Sometimes you'll be hunting your own land, but most other times you'll be walking a field on a ranch or farm that belongs to a good friend, a relative or new acquaintance. Do you live in the city? Ask relatives who have land in the country for permission to arrowhead hunt when you visit. If you live in the suburbs, you can ask neighbors who are having **excavations** done for permission to search for arrowheads in the evening, after the digging has stopped for the day. A location to hunt can be as close to you as home, and the availability of land with bare soil makes surface hunting convenient for just about everyone. We'll explore a variety of places that would be ideal for arrowhead hunting, but no matter where you decide to look for artifacts, you'll always need to ask permission before you walk any property. If you are young, be sure an adult accompanies you to request permission, even if the site you've spotted is just down the street.

Where are the best places to look for arrowheads and other stone artifacts? You just may live close to one, because there are *thousands* of ideal sites in the continental U.S. There are also many places that you *may not* hunt for artifacts. Government lands, public lands and certain sites, such as burial mounds or cemeteries on private land, are illegal to hunt. Anyone who chooses to disobey the laws protecting these places risks prosecution and stiff penalties. Be sure you read *Stay Within the Law* on page xxi for a complete explanation of where artifact hunting and collecting is prohibited.

Once you're familiar with the kinds of places you are allowed to hunt and you're wondering exactly where to start, put yourself in a prehistoric frame of mind. Picture yourself living in the year 2000 B.C. If you were a hunter, where would you want to live? Where would you hunt? Where would you be safe from enemies?

PLOWED FIELDS

Fresh Water

The most essential element necessary for human survival is oxygen. The next thing we all need is water. People in prehistory needed water for drinking, cooking, washing, fishing and hunting game. Indians chose campsites close to a source of fresh water not only for survival, but for convenience and protection as well.

Suppose it was your job to keep a supply of drinking water at the campsite. How would you do it? You could transport water from a stream or river to the campsite in earthenware containers of clay. **Pottery** was heavy and cumbersome when filled with liquid, and breakable. How many containers would you have been able to carry at once? How many trips would you make? You wouldn't want to walk a long way over plains or through thick woods to get to and from a water source, and neither did the Indians. For convenience, they camped near rivers, lakes and large streams. Rivers and lakes also protected campsites on one side by providing a natural barrier of water. Indians who lived on land next to large bodies of water could spot intruders coming across well before they reached the shore.

Small streams, springs, spring-fed ponds and creeks provided other sources of fresh water for Indians. Just like rivers and lakes, these places attracted game. Bear, moose, raccoon, elk, coyote, deer and other animals needed water for drinking, cooling off or catching fish. And where the game was, Indian hunters were, too.

FIRST, LOOK FOR WATER. WHEN YOU'VE FOUND IT, SURFACE HUNT HIGHER LAND NEARBY.

Hunt plowed fields near any fresh water source. Since flooding could occur during heavy rains or in springtime, camps would remain dry when they were higher than shorelines. Choose land as the Indians did, back far enough to be safe from flood waters.

Figure 4-2. Look for rises on plowed fields. Where fields are not level, check the higher areas first.

Slopes

Rises on fields and crests of bare knolls or hills near water are very good spots to surface hunt. Why would a higher area be better to hunt than level or lower places? You'll see more stones and rocks at the top of an incline than at the base. Rain washes the soil off rises and bare hilltops, and exposes stones that were covered in dirt. Frequent or heavy rains can move topsoil and flakes down the sides of slopes and deposit them at the base. Stones originally at the base and flakes that have moved there often become covered with the eroded topsoil.

On a rise in a plowed field, inspect the highest area first for whole artifacts. Slowly work your way to the bottom, looking for flakes that jut out of the ground. If you find a broken artifact at the base of a slope, it may have moved from another spot. Whenever you discover fragments of worked stone on uneven ground, check the entire area carefully for more artifacts.

Figure 4-3. When a deep washout snakes down a rise, begin searching at the top of the incline and work your way down to the bottom.

Washouts

Search other areas in fields where rain has moved topsoil, too. **Washouts**, the grooves or furrows created by heavy rain in soft earth, are great spots for finding artifacts. Go straight to any washouts when you're hunting a plowed field and walk the entire length of the furrows, top to bottom. Jon Kiesa did and found his first whole projectile point, shown in Figure 4-4.

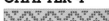

Figure 4-4. This side-notched point was buried in a cornfield, but rather than being plowed to the surface, it was exposed in a washout by rain.

Surface Changes

Site surfaces change with the weather. A field producing a smattering of flint at one time can become a surface hunter's dream just days after heavy rains wash the earth. Later, seasons pass, soil shifts or erodes, and *bingo*! New artifacts appear on surface turf. So, don't give up on the first try, especially if you've found evidence that Indians were on the land. Go again after a good rain or during a different season. It's entirely possible you'll find more. We'll take a closer look at the best weather conditions and seasons for hunting in the next chapter.

"HUNTED OUT" HUNTING AREAS

When arrowheads have been found in certain areas in past years, sometimes people think there are none left. But are those places really "hunted out?" During earlier arrowhead hunts, was anyone looking for *tools*? Beautiful scrapers, drills, hammerstones, abrading stones and others may have been overlooked or mistaken for broken pieces of rock or non-cultural stone. These sites can still have abundant artifacts and are well worth checking out.

FORMER HUNTING GROUNDS

You'll miss some ancient hunting grounds if you only search plowed fields, so you'll need to look in other places. We know that Indians hunted game along streams, springs, ponds and creeks, and at rivers and lakes. Look for points in shallow water and you may find whole or broken spear points, or arrowheads. If a hunter wounded a game animal cooling off in a lake and the animal dislodged the weapon, the point would have been lost in the water. An arrow missing an animal in water would have been lost to the hunter, too. Since water levels can change over time, deep water thousands of years ago could be shallow enough to wade in today, and points would be easy to see. Rapid currents moving lost points to shorelines can also put them in places where you could find them.

CHILDREN HAVE FOUND BONES OF EXTINCT ANIMALS AND ANCIENT WEAPONS ON FORMER HUNTING GROUNDS IN ALASKA.

When a hunter takes a position well above the level of an animal's nose, the animal is less likely to detect the human scent. Game is easier to see from a higher vantage point, and shooting down works with gravity, not against it. So, search the low areas near fresh water very thoroughly and look for scrapers. Why scrapers? Animals were not only killed, but often cleaned at hunting grounds, too. Scrapers and knives can be found at sites where hides were cleaned immediately after a kill. Banks of rivers and streams, and salt licks near springs are excellent places to explore. Search any embankments for spear points and arrowheads, too.

Are there deer in your vicinity? Or other kinds of game, such as beaver, porcupine, pheasant or fox? Present animal habitats in your area can help you find former hunting grounds. When land is inhabited by game animals, your chances will be better for finding scrapers, knives and projectile points.

ANIMAL BURROWS

Animals sometimes uncover artifacts when they dig to make burrows. Watch for animal holes in forest floors, meadows, pastures, fields and natural surfaces you walk. If you happen upon a burrow, keep clear of the entrance, be cautious, and take care not to disturb any sleeping animals inside. If you see an artifact, use a long stick to retrieve it.

Figure 4-5. Notice the accumulation of dirt and rock near the entrance to this burrow. We inspected it for artifacts from a distance of about one yard, but saw no arrowheads among the stones. Perhaps better luck next time.

DRY CREEKS AND STREAMS

Dry creeks and streams are easy places to hunt for artifacts because you can see the soil without having to peer through water. You can pick up rocks, turn them over, and keep your feet dry at the same time, too. At a creek or stream flowing with water, look for large, dry washouts that fork off from the flow. These washouts once coursed with cool water that would have quenched the thirst of both people and game.

In woods, find dry grooves in the earth winding through the trees. The earth at the bottom of the grooves will be scattered with rock and leaves, and large patches of soil will be cracked

IF A CLAY CONTAINER BROKE AT A WATER SOURCE, THERE COULD BE FRAGMENTS OF POTTERY REMAINING AT THE SITE.

and dry. Look for points, scrapers and chopping tools between stones and on slopes of the furrows.

When you walk the grooves of dry creeks or streams, always pay attention to the way that you came and remember to keep an eye on your watch. Time slips by when you're absorbed in a search, and it might take a bit longer than you think to get back to your starting point.

FLINT

If you find flint in its natural state or in small chips, it's a good indicator that artifacts may be in the area. Normally, flint was taken from its source to a campsite for working into tools and weapons. If you find an **outcropping**, it could mean you're getting warm because Indians camped near sources of flint. Rock formations that protrude above the ground, flint outcroppings are most common in Colorado and Wyoming. When you see an outcropping, check for stone with conchoidal fractures, and hunt land next to a natural source of fresh water, such as a creek, stream or spring.

You can still find flint even if you don't live near an outcropping. Remember, high-quality flint was transported to places far away. To find it, look for chips. When you find an abundance of flint chips, it means you're getting hot. Residue chips and flakes from toolmaking can be a sign that you've found a campsite.

If you are fortunate and discover an artifact in a concentrated scatter, you'll need to record the information and refrain from collecting flakes. The number of flakes will help archaeologists assess the size of the site and estimate how long prehistoric people stayed in the area. Instructions for recording artifacts and flake scatters are given in Chapter 6.

LOOKOUT SITES

Lookout sites are areas on high, level ground where sentinels were posted to watch for enemies and game. Sentinels at these vantage points could easily see human and animal movement on the land below. Since there was no way to predict when intruders or game animals would appear, posting at a lookout site usually required long hours on the job. If you had to spend the day on a bluff watching for enemies and waiting for game, how would you pass the time? You'd probably sharpen weapons and make tools, just as Indians did. Check ground surfaces on level tops of cliffs for residue flakes from flintknapping.

When you find what might be a lookout site, scout nearby for plowed fields. Land in the vicinity of bluffs—especially bluffs overlooking a river—was usually chosen for campsites. For all types of artifacts, explore the fields near any bluffs, cliffs and lookout sites.

> BESIDES CAMPSITES, WHERE ELSE COULD INDIANS HAVE FLAKED STONE INTO USEFUL OBJECTS?

BUFFALO JUMPS

Surface hunt the land at the bottom of bluffs and cliffs, and you just may discover a **buffalo jump**. The most efficient way to kill buffalo was to drive them in a herd to the end of a high cliff. Once there, the animals would crash into each other and tumble to their deaths. Since hunters did the slaughtering at the base, investigate the area for scrapers and knives—and then try to find the Indian campsite. One buffalo alone would provide plenty of meat, and more could feed several families. Look for protective places where people could live and you may discover another site nearby. To identify a campsite by its stone, consider that a grass fire wouldn't change stone color or texture as much as prolonged or repeated heating. If you find heavy flake scatters, compare flint or chert for heat-treatment, and sandstone for fire-cracking.

Natural Resources

Indians used natural materials for food, shelter and clothing, and set up camp near plentiful sources. Early Native Americans living in western parts of the country ground a vitamin-rich flour from pinyon tree seeds, burned pinyon wood for heat, cooking and aroma, and used larger timbers for dwellings. Folks camping in foothills used yucca plants to make clothes and baskets. Many more people made baskets from sweetgrass and strips of ash, and sometimes stamped them with designs they carved in potatoes. There were leaves and roots of native plants to collect for herbal medicines, hickory nuts and acorns to gather, and wild blackberries, onions and sassafras to find. Native Americans across the country used shells and feathers for breastplates, created tepee ornaments from buffalo hide, and made porcupine quill designs on toy birch bark canoes. Indians were able to find and use all types of natural resources. To locate places where they stayed, look for natural resources native to your area that prehistoric people would have put to good use.

PROTECTIVE PLACES

Indians considered nature's gifts when they chose a place to live, but they also took into account the need for shelter from the elements. To find campsites, explore places that provided protection from harsh weather.

Water and wind could harm a campsite in a very short period of time. Indians lived on level areas of higher ground to avoid campsite flooding, so search flat areas of large knolls or hills that are located near water. What types of terrain would protect against wind? Outcroppings of rock would provide just the right kind of shelter, and campsites nestled in valleys would be safe, too.

How easily could campsites be defended against enemy attack? What geographic features of the land would protect prehistoric families? River islands provided good places to live since intruders could not get across the water without first being seen. And campsites on plateaus were hard to reach on at least one side. Take the easiest route to places you see where entry is protected on one or more sides.

BLOWOUTS

If there are artifacts beneath prairie surfaces, dust storms can uncover them in places called **blowouts**. Blowouts occur in Great Plains states east of the Rockies in Colorado, Montana, New Mexico and Wyoming, and on the plains of the Dakotas, Kansas, Nebraska, Oklahoma and Texas. Scout for areas free of sagebrush and prairie grass, where sandy soil has been blown away. Blowouts hundreds of feet wide are more easily spotted from a distance, and smaller bare areas a few feet in diameter are better seen close up. Walk the prairies for blowouts and return to them after gusty windstorms. Anywhere in the country, strong winds can move sand, so be sure to spot-check eroded areas. In the following chapter, you'll discover more ways to hunt successfully by studying the effects of weather and erosion.

BUFFALO WALLOWS

Buffalo, with their thick heavy coats, sorely needed water for drinking and cooling off. They would often gather at **buffalo wallows** on prairies for water, mud or moisture. At buffalo wallows, there were moist spots to sit in to relieve discomfort when a hot sun blazed overhead. Wallows on plains were usually the only places for miles around where water could always be found. Indians knew the cool mud would feel good to the animals, and they usually camped nearby. They hunted buffalo there, and smaller game that was attracted to the area, too. Rabbits and game birds were easy to hunt in the grasses that grew near the wallows. Look for dark areas of waterlogged earth with grasses growing nearby. Search for buffalo wallows between springs or small creeks, and you're likely to discover a weapon or tool that was used during prehistoric hunting.

SHORELINES

When ancient fishing equipment was lost in the water, it literally sank like a rock. While you're at the shore, look for drilled or notched **net weights** from fishing nets, and keep an eye out for slender bone fishhooks that may have washed up to shore. Search coastlines, waterfronts and sandbars. Check lakefronts,

INDIANS MADE CRUDE SIDE-NOTCHED NET WEIGHTS BY CHIPPING ROUGH NOTCHES INTO OPPOSITE SIDES OF PEBBLES OR SMALL CORES.

river banks and beaches on river islands, too. Ceremonial objects and pottery, as well as projectile weapons, knives, axes and celts, are just some of the objects prehistoric people may have brought along with them to shore.

At campsites near ocean beaches and fresh water shorelines, keep an eye out for turtle shell from Indian rattles and shells with small, drilled holes. Most of us have seen shells with small water holes in them. How can you tell a drilled, cultural hole from a water-worn, non-cultural cavity? To prevent cracking or breakage, Indians alternately drilled both sides of brittle shell until the tool passed through the middle. Drilled holes are narrower in the center and wider on the surface faces. Look for bored holes like these in shell pendants and other ornaments.

Watch for holes in clam or mussel shells, too, but look for larger, circular cutouts instead of narrow holes. Indians removed circles of shell, drilled holes in the cutouts, and used the cutouts for buttons. Factory workers in the 1800s also made buttons from shells, but in large quantities. They discarded batches of used shells with four to six holes along shorelines. Shells with cutouts are the waste material from early button making and are interesting artifacts you can search for as well.

HEARTHS

A discolored, circular area of earth may mark the location of a prehistoric hearth or fire pit. To find the spots where fires were tended, look for black-ringed or round, reddish patches of earth that are different in texture from the surrounding ground, and examine the soil for specks of charcoal. Remember that stone used for lining hearths and cooking also will be blackened or fire-reddened. If you find chunky pieces that have a different color and texture from other rocks of the same material, try to find the reason for the alteration.

Notify a professional archaeologist if you think you've found a hearth or fire pit. Discovery of either one of these is a strong indication that you have located a prehistoric home. We can learn about the natural resources available to former occupants of the site by knowing what was cooked and eaten. An archaeologist can excavate a hearth for fish and animal bones, charred nutshells, plant seeds and other resources that nourished the inhabitants. You'll learn how to effectively give and get assistance from professionals in Chapter 6.

HOME SWEET HOME

No matter where you live or what the terrain might be, don't forget to check your own back yard. If your family is building a deck, putting in a pool, extending a driveway, or adding a garage to your home, you've lucked out! Search the construction site for stray projectile points. Holes for basketball hoops and posts for mailboxes, fences or decks can range from one to four feet deep. When post holes are planned, offer to lend a hand with the digging. Is anyone planting flower gardens, vegetable patches, shrubs or trees? Be there to help. Interesting items, some of Indian origin, have been unearthed in these ways by home-owners and their children. Even if you don't find indications of Indian or colonial activity, it's fun working together on outdoor projects and family members will appreciate your help.

OTHER SOURCES

History

Become familiar with Native American history. You'll learn more about where early American Indians lived, discover the trade routes, and understand the hardships of travel. You can visit historic sites designated by the government to appreciate Native American history, too. Remember that historic sites are protected by law and any type of artifact hunting and collecting is prohibited. But Indians hunted land which extended well beyond the present boundaries of these protected areas, and plots of land close to historic sites can be privately owned. You may be able to hunt private property close to historic sites, provided you get permission from the owner. If you want to surface hunt land immediately next to historic sites, be sure you ask the owner exactly where the property line ends, and always stay within the private property boundaries.

Areas within many miles of historic sites are good places to discover artifacts from both colonial and prehistoric times. It was always necessary to have food, fresh water and a home that would provide protection. Since Indians living at different times in history often chose the same places to live, surface finds ranging from hundreds to thousands of years old can sometimes be found in the same general area.

Figure 4-6. Some Indians buried their dead in mounds, carefully choosing the site, such as a bluff overlooking a river.

Occasionally, you might find a place to hunt that is perfectly level, except for a small, lone hill. If it has an even, conical shape, or is rectangular with a flat top, it could be a burial mound. Never hunt or disturb the area of a burial mound. Before government intervention, many mounds were excavated and looted for the beautiful artifacts buried with the deceased. Today, digging into mounds or surface hunting on them is prohibited by the government, and severe penalties are imposed on those who disobey the law.

Mounds are special sites that people should treat with the utmost respect. Because the discovery of a burial mound is significant, the landowner may have it recorded as a site in the National Register of Historic Places (**NRHP**). A mound can be nominated for a place in the NRHP by notifying a state historic preservation agency. Details for nomination are given in the *State Historic Preservation Agencies* section of the *Resources*, and you'll learn more about laws that affect surface hunting in Chapter 6.

Museums and Maps

A trip to your local museum is always an education. Find out which early Native American tribes lived in your area, what their customs were, and how events of the time affected their lives. Museums will often have old maps on display that show the locales of Indian territory, Yankee and Confederate forts, battle sites and the like. For information on various museums in your state, contact a State Historic Preservation Officer (**SHPO**) at your state agency listed in the *Resources*.

Maps are excellent resources for studying the geography of your vicinity, too. The U.S. Geological Survey (**USGS**) produces just about any kind of map you can think of. A county **topographic map**, state geologic map or sectional map may contain just the sort of information you'll need to explore your local area. USGS topographic maps are especially helpful because they show accurate locations of lakes, rivers, streams, wooded areas and contours of the land. Use the *Maps* section of the *Resources* to learn more and find out how you can get them.

People You Know

What do your relatives know about local or Native American history? Ask your grandparents, aunts, uncles and cousins, as well as parents and siblings, about stories that have been passed down through the generations. Perhaps they'll remember discoveries of stone artifacts that no one could identify at the time. Does your family have friends who are amateur archaeologists? Maybe an old family friend will tell you about an unusual rock that was found by homesteaders many years ago. Talk to them and see what you can learn.

Organizations in your community can be another good source for information on local history. Contact archaeological societies, Scout leaders, Indian guides and 4-H Club members. Speak with teachers, instructors, professors and other educators in your local school district because they would be able to help, too.

▼ ▼ ▼

Choose your own way to scout for outlying sites. You can hop on your bike and explore, or scan the territory while riding in a car. Survey the area when you travel and imagine the terrain as it would have been hundreds or thousands of years ago. Wherever you go, take a good look at the lay of the land. Remember the reasons why Native Americans lived where they did. Think about the role geography played in their lives—the importance of fresh water, high bluffs, sheltered valleys, river islands and more. Consider how the presence of these natural features affected their choices for campsites and hunting grounds. Once you've reflected on these things, you'll never look at river banks, plowed fields, prairies or cliffs in quite the same way again.

Figure 5-1. Cup stone?
Cup stones are common, but curious, artifacts. Notice the round depression in the center of this sandstone rock. There's another small "cup" like it on the other side. More than one of these cultural hollows is often seen on cup stones. What made the indentations? There is evidence of grinding or pecking, but no proof that links cup stones to their use. Some believe they were used as fire-starting rocks. To start a fire, people needed dry leaves or perhaps a fine wood dust, and sparks. Indians ground sticks into rock to make the wood dust and struck one piece of flint against another for sparks. When sparks flew into the finely ground wood, a fire could be ignited.

Or nut stone?
Others think Indians may have used the stones to crack nutshells apart or grind nutmeats. People favoring these explanations call them nut stones. But how were nuts cracked in exactly the same spot on a rock? Why would folks use uneven surfaces instead of the flat side of a stone for grinding? Can you think of a different way a stone such as this might have been used? Until someone finds undisturbed evidence next to a cup stone—or nut stone—or can prove its function in another way, the artifact will remain a mystery.

Going Hunting

Whenever you go arrowhead hunting, you'll find adventures in stone artifacts. A fabulous thing about it is that you can do it year-round. You know how to identify flaked, pecked and ground stone, and where to hunt, but once you're out in the field, how can you increase your chances of finding the small stone that happens to be an artifact? It's very helpful to know what conditions will change the position of stone on plowed fields, where the best hunting is in each season, and what kinds of weather and time of day are most desirable. You can practice some special surface hunting techniques to make discovering artifacts easier, too. To improve your arrowhead hunting adventure more than ever, let's start by taking a closer look at the most common place to hunt—plowed fields.

PLOWED FIELDS AND WEATHER

Keep your eye on the weather before you plan a trip to a plowed field, because the best time to go is after a hard rain. A stone caked with mud or a broken rock covered with soil can easily be mistaken for a clump of dirt. You'll find it much easier to see rocks and stones once the dirt is washed off, so walk fields after downpours. How soon should you go? Some successful hunters like to go on muddy adventures immediately after storms. But if there's a forecast for heavy rainfall Friday night and clear skies for the weekend, you can plan to go hunting Saturday or Sunday and do just as well.

The same water that washes rocks will alter the surfaces of plowed fields and the position of artifacts. Stubble from the previous harvest will shift very slightly from a drenching rain. Often, the change in position of a corncob or soybean plant is just enough to expose a stone edge that was completely hidden before. Heavy rain will flush flakes away from stalks, stems and leaves, and carry small rocks along the washouts and gullies it creates. Hail pummeling the ground will force stubble and stone to move once again. Since surfaces of plowed fields change with the weather, people who enjoy arrowhead hunting walk the same fields every few weeks before plowing. So, go back to that field you've already walked and retrace your steps. You'll be amazed how much you "missed" the first time around.

WEATHER AND EROSION ARE THE MOST COMMON NATURAL CAUSES THAT CHANGE THE POSITIONS OF ARTIFACTS.

You can look forward to seasonal changes in hunting surfaces, too. Weather and time give plowed fields even more appeal by modifying surfaces in cycles. Environmental changes from freezing, thawing and parching, as well as snows, floods and erosion, cause soil and stone to shift each year. Over time, buried artifacts move up. Chips appear on top as if by magic. Here and there, large flakes protrude from dry cracks. Deeper down, artifacts enter the range of the plow disk. Fields barren of cultural stone in one year might yield artifacts the next. If you haven't been able to find an artifact on a plowed field by a fresh water source, don't give up. With a little luck and a rainstorm, the day for discovery could be the very next time you hunt.

SEASONAL CHANGES

Spring

The best season to hunt plowed fields is spring. Springtime for northern arrowhead hunters has less to do with the calendar and more to do with the weather. For them, spring begins when the snow has melted and the ground has thawed. For surface hunters across the U.S., the season ends when fields are seeded.

Springtime means rain—and lots of it. Since the best time to hunt is after a heavy shower or a thunderstorm, you can experience great arrowhead hunting many times during the season. In spring, new crops of artifacts appear for discovery. How does the weather produce these crops? Ice, snow, warm spells and cold temperatures in winter followed by spring thaws push stone up where earth is loosely packed. Spring rains will clean stones you would have missed had you walked the land in the previous season. Before plowing, walk fields. Discover artifacts that may have lain on the surface during winter. Look over the new spring crop of stone. You might just save several artifacts from plow damage in the months ahead.

SURFACE HUNT IN SPRING AND YOU'LL SEE MORE STONE THAN IN ANY OTHER SEASON.

Late in the season, farmers work the soil and move more stone. Rock may be churned up from half a foot or more below the surface, so keep your ears tuned for the sound of tractors. Tractors plowing fields are your signal that prime time for spring surface hunting is approaching. After fields are plowed, wait for another spring shower before hunting, since rocks that were buried will be caked with dirt. Be sure to make time to go after it rains, because you may have only a short time to look through this new batch of stone. Farmers seed soon after they plow. Seeded fields *cannot* be walked without risk of damage to the crop. Once crops are planted, it's time to move on to different kinds of sites.

Summer

Summer brings out the best of other kinds of sites. During hot weather, search cooler places. Choose areas at fresh water sources and use the water to refresh yourself in the heat of the day. At rivers and lakes, you'll see larger beaches than you would have in spring. Water levels will be lower, so you'll have more surface area to hunt. You won't miss the evidence of spring flooding along lakefronts and on river banks. The same flood waters that brought hundreds of shells, tree branches, steel buoys and lead fishing weights to shore may also have beached an artifact or two. Keep cool in summer by wading in water and walking sandbars, and you may come across an artifact among the stones and shells on the beach.

If your family likes boating, rafting or canoeing, take a side trip to a river island and check out the view from an islander's perspective. Could the island have been a place where Indians would have lived or hunted? It might be very possible, so scout the beaches and banks, and walk any paths through timber. Peek into dead tree hollows for a weapon stash and scan the branches of massive old trees for a point that missed its mark. A find like one of these would be hundreds of years old and you'd be very lucky indeed to discover it! It's always great fun to arrowhead hunt in woods, because you just never know where an artifact might be.

A POND MAY ACTUALLY BE A KETTLE LAKE, WHICH IS A POTHOLE IN ROCK FORMED BY THE MELTING OF AN ISOLATED BLOCK OF GLACIAL ICE.

Take nature walks in summertime and choose places that have streams, creeks or springs. Search embankments where spring rains have eroded silt and you might see an artifact jutting out. In the cool of the forest, look for the grooves of dry creeks and walk the rocky furrows. Check tree-lined gullies that could have been filled with stream water long ago. To find other sources of water, watch for redwing blackbirds, mallards and terns. Listen for the honk of Canadian geese or the cry of sea gulls. Their presence will alert you that a pond, marsh or kettle lake is near. Keep a sharp eye out for scrapers, knives and points when you find natural water sources that are attracting wildlife.

Hunt for buffalo wallows on prairies and plains. Search bluffs and cliffs for buffalo jumps, lookout sites and small areas providing shelter in rock walls. Investigate your vicinity for outcroppings, knolls, hills and caves. Look for the holes of prairie dog communities and other animal burrows as you hunt, since burrowing animals move stones and artifacts. Remember to keep your distance when checking the entrances.

By midsummer, watch for fields that have not been plowed since the last harvest. These will be easy to distinguish from fields full of cotton, rice, wheat, squash or other crops. Look for low gray stubble and weeds on fallow fields, and get permission to walk them for arrowheads.

Figure 5-2. Jon Kiesa tested the fire-starting theory on a non-cultural sandstone cobble. The sandstone ground the stick as coarse sandpaper would, but after thirty minutes, the depression created from grinding was larger than the amount of wood dust produced. Particles that were ground were sticking in the hollow and smoothing down the grinding area. Is this why there is often more than one hollow on a cup stone? Did Indians have to use a gritty new surface to make more fire-starting material? Jon used two pieces of non-cultural flint to make sparks, but the wood dust wouldn't ignite. Sand from the stone had mixed with the ground wood and prevented a fire from catching. Surely these problems occurred with Indians, too. If fires were carefully tended so they would not go out, why are there so many cup stones? Is it because it took more than one stone to make enough material to start one fire?

Autumn

Autumn—with its cool, crisp air and beautiful scenery—is an excellent season for arrowhead hunting anywhere you go. You'll enjoy walking fields, woods and prairies even more when nature is at its finest. In fall, hiking is so comfortable that just when you think the weather couldn't be more perfect, the unbeatable colors of Indian summer appear for mid-season adventures. Be sure to fit some nature walks into your free time while foliage is on the trees instead of the ground. Once the leaves are down and branches are bare, you'll see the geography of the land clearly.

Streams and creeks in forests, plowed fields beyond trees, ponds and marshes in wetlands, and contours of the land will be conspicuous in late fall.

Include an arrowhead hunting adventure in your holiday plans by setting an hour or two aside to enjoy the outdoors. An outing with your relatives will be remembered long after the holiday when a family member finds a special stone. Just imagine the excitement you'll all experience at the discovery of an Indian artifact on Thanksgiving day! The **cup stone** shown at the beginning of this chapter is a good example of a well-remembered holiday find.

Autumn is the second best season for hunting plowed fields. After summer crops are harvested, you can return to fields you walked in spring. If you live in the South, where farmers reap melons, okra, peanuts, sugar cane, tomatoes, cotton and spinach, you'll need to choose your hunting hours wisely since fields will be re-seeded again after plowing. Those of you in the North can walk fields until snow begins to stick.

SPRING AND FALL ARE THE TWO BEST SEASONS FOR HUNTING PLOWED FIELDS.

To hinder erosion, many northern farmers leave stubble in place after harvest and do not plow before winter. Walk fields in fall and you'll see new stubble in different places, cracked earth from summer heat, washouts from repeated rain, and other erosion from flooding or windstorms. The surface of an autumn field will not be the same as it was in spring. Check out the fields you liked at the beginning of the year and find some new ones to look over.

Winter

Add arrowhead hunting to your winter list of favorite outdoor activities. How can you arrowhead hunt during winter? In southern states where there is little or no snow, you can walk the surface of the ground and see it just as well as in any other season. In northern states such as Maine, Minnesota, Montana or Wisconsin, the amount of hunting you do will depend on the snow, ice and cold. Mild winters with little snow or ice provide the best opportunities for hunting. Take advantage of the periods when there is no snow, because even a light dusting will obstruct your view of the ground. Hunt during mild spells, and you'll walk muddy surfaces much like they are in spring.

Snowfalls, ice storms and cold snaps that alternate with partial thaws during winter increase the rate of surface changes on plowed fields. It's good when the ground freezes and there's a light snow, because it will also increase your chances of success when a warm spell follows and the ground thaws. Thawing topsoil will shift flakes into places where you just might see them, and melting snow or ice will wash the rocks. In Connecticut, Illinois, New Jersey, Ohio, Oregon and other states where weather can fluctuate above and below freezing, you'll do best when you hunt plowed fields.

You can also hunt other types of sites in wintertime, provided the ground is partially thawed and clear of snow. Cold temperatures will freeze stones to the ground. In partially thawed soil, you may find that some are stuck. Never force one from its position or scratch soil away to get a flake up or turn a rock over. For safe removal, bring along a thermos of hot water. Pour some on the surrounding soil to melt the ice. If this does not loosen the area around a large find, leave the stone in place. You can always visit the site again in warmer weather and re-examine it then.

ARROWHEAD HUNT IN WINTER WHEN THE GROUND IS NOT COVERED WITH ICE OR SNOW.

Broken stone, bone and **sherds**, which are fragments of pottery, can look alike when surfaces are coated with icy dirt. Do not pour water or scrape off frozen soil on objects you pick up, because it may harm an artifact. Clean icy winter finds when you get home. We'll cover safe methods for cleaning artifact materials in Chapter 7.

BEST WEATHER

You can arrowhead hunt in just about any kind of weather. You'll experience the influences of nature while hunting in the sun, under cloudy skies, in a light drizzle, during rain, or even when scattered snowflakes are falling. Each kind of weather has its own special advantages for hunting surfaces of the ground.

Many arrowhead hunters like sunny days. The dull luster of flint and the shine of obsidian are easier to spot since their surfaces reflect strong sunlight. A stone that reflects light is one way to distinguish white flint or yellow chert from other stones close by that have similar colors. Pick a beautiful sunny day to hunt and you may discover more flint on plowed fields, plains, bluffs, or beaches than you ever expected to find.

Some people prefer a bit of cloud cover when they're walking in open spaces. Walking beneath clouds makes for very comfortable hunting. You'll enjoy brief periods of natural shade when fluffy cumulus clouds pass in front of the sun. Bands of thin cirrus clouds high in the sky will also provide some shade. Try hunting under low stratus clouds, and you might find that you like overcast skies the best.

When you hunt on partially cloudy days, sometimes you'll catch a refreshing sun shower. A brief sprinkle or drizzle, and even a fine mist will clean dusty stones quickly and cool you off if you're hot. Some hunters like to go out during rain since stones are easier to see while they're wet. When you hunt in dry weather and experience these kinds of precipitation, decide whether you want to continue or take a break and find some cover. After hard, sudden showers, be sure to check the rain-wash at the bottom of gullies and look over areas that you've just finished hunting.

If you're hunting a plowed field and hear thunder rumbling in the distance, do not continue to hunt. Get off the field as quickly as possible. You can find cover in a car, in woods, or at a stable, barn or farmhouse. When you're on an open plain and see lightning flash, get into your car if it's near, or lie flat on the ground, especially when cracks of thunder have immediately followed. Do not take cover under a lone tree. After showers or thunderstorms, look for rainbows and sundogs in the sky and enjoy the natural, changing beauty of the day.

FIND APPROPRIATE COVER WHEN YOU HEAR THUNDER.

You can enjoy surface hunting while snowflakes are falling, too. When soil is warmer than the air and temperatures are at freezing, flakes will melt as they touch down. A snowflake or two that sticks will not be enough to conceal your view and it's a perfect time to see stone that is wet.

BEST TIME OF DAY

You can hunt at any time between sunup and sundown, but the best time of day depends on your preference of weather. Some people who enjoy surface hunting on sunny days feel the best time to hunt is around noon. It's easier to focus on stone when you see it in uniform light. With the sun directly overhead, you won't be stepping in and out of your shadow. Wear a visor, sunbonnet, cap, or wide-brimmed hat to avoid a glare and watch for dull lusters that reflect sunlight. Some folks wear sunglasses, but you may find that stone lusters are harder to see. Experiment with a pair to see how you like it. If you discover that you do your best hunting in the sun at midday, plan to enjoy your lunch before or after prime time.

What is the best way to hunt during mornings, late afternoons or evenings, when rays are at slanted angles and glare is strong? To keep the sun out of your eyes, walk with your back to it. Suppose you're walking the rows in a plowed field and the sun is at your side. Adjust your hat and body position to alter the glare. Instead of looking back and forth between sunlit earth and the shaded ground in your shadow, you might prefer to focus on the sunny areas. If you're facing a rising or setting sun, wear your visor, and concentrate on stone color and shape just ahead.

On overcast days or when intermittent clouds hide the sun, any time is a good time to hunt. During cloud cover, you'll walk without a strong shadow, and shading of the ground will be relatively even. On partially cloudy days, be sure to take your sunglasses off when sunlight is blocked so you won't miss any flint.

TIPS AND TECHNIQUES

It's very important to be able to identify portions of weapons and tools because you will come across more parts and pieces than whole artifacts. Tangs, tips, eared bases of drills, bodies of knives, and portions of scrapers are all considered good finds. Examine the surrounding ground carefully when you discover a broken artifact since another part of it may be lying nearby. If not, keep in mind that broken pieces mean there may be more artifacts in the area. So, continue hunting! Your first whole point could be just a few yards away.

The best way to find artifacts is to walk *slowly*. The faster you walk while you arrowhead hunt, the less you will find. Search the ground in front of you up to about two yards. Look to your left and right to see the soil at your sides. Scan further ahead for objects that are reflecting light. Since your angle of vision will change as you move nearer, the gloss of a stone may not be as apparent when you reach it. Set your sight on the area and check it out immediately.

When you walk a plowed field, walk the lengths between rows instead of crossing over them. By walking rows, not only will you have a clear view of stone up ahead, but you'll be able to see one side of two rows at once. Walk across rows, and you might miss worked stone caught in stalks or stems. Watch for small stones trapped in stubble as you go.

Are you surface hunting with a partner? Switch directions and overlap the areas you've searched. Since stubble moves slightly from walking, what one misses, the other might find. If the earth is soft, check for artifacts exposed in footprints.

Figure 5-3. These tangs were seen jutting up from the ground from a distance of about two yards, while in a crouch. Would it be a whole artifact? Praise the Lord, bless the people, let's dance—it was whole! Do the tangs look familiar? They belong to the prehistoric dart point shown at bottom right in Chapter 2, Figure 2-9.

Stop often to scrutinize the ground around you. Crouch down, and you'll change your viewing angle. Inspect the immediate vicinity in a crouch to see other stones hidden under leaves, pods, rinds and other natural debris.

Pick up rocks and stones that catch your interest. Remember, you are not just looking for arrowheads. There are scrapers, multipurpose tools, game stones, drills, grinding stones, ornaments and other artifacts to discover. Wipe off excess dirt or rinse stone in a nearby creek to get a better look at shapes, surfaces and edges.

Turn rocks over gently as you walk, even if they do not appear to be cultural. Manos that were smoothed on one side and chipping stones that were nicked could be overlooked if you don't check both sides. Granite or quartzite rocks that can be gripped in a hand should be examined for scars or gashes from hammerstone use on ends.

Hold a clean flake up to sunlight and view it from different angles. Chipping that is hard to see can be much more apparent when you examine it this way. When a stone catches your interest but it's caked with hardened soil, bring it home for cleaning. Do not discard a rock or stone you're unsure of because dirt can conceal pecking, one-way grinding scars or delicate flaking. If after cleaning you realize people have not used it, you can safely pitch it at home.

TO INCREASE YOUR CHANCES OF DISCOVERING AN ETCHED STONE, TURN ROCKS OVER TO SEE THE OTHER SIDE.

Suppose you discover a stray scraper in a field that doesn't have any other flint or chert. Try to find the area where there was more activity. Any worked stone means prehistoric people were there, but the question is *where*? Indians may have had a campsite eighty feet to the right, a tool manufacturing area on the north side of the field, or a lookout site just one-quarter mile down the road, so consider your surroundings carefully. You may discover other artifacts that match the style or material of your original find.

Whether you continue to surface hunt or decide to scout the vicinity, you can enjoy your search more by being prepared. Sometimes, going hunting will be a spur-of-the-moment decision. Other times, you'll plan an outing a few days in advance. What can you bring to make your time outdoors more fun? What things are essential to have at the site when you discover an artifact? How should you dress to be most comfortable? Let's explore more ways to enhance your hunting experience.

WHAT TO BRING

Since hands and pockets can get soiled from finds you choose to keep, pack a couple of old washcloths or hand towels to wipe dirt off stones and fingers. You might also decide to wrap the finds in terry cloth to protect against chipping as you hunt.

In cool or cold weather, bring facial tissues. You may be walking fields, but your nose is likely to run. In summer, a cotton bandanna or handkerchief will come in handy. On a hot day, dip your cloth into a clean, cool stream and blot your face and neck to refresh yourself.

Points of Interest

Arrowhead Hunting Sticks

Many people who arrowhead hunt like to use a stick to turn stones. Use a flint-flipping stick, and you'll reduce the number of times you bend over. A flint-flipping stick is like a thin walking stick. You can use it to keep your hands dry at creeks, press back prickly branches in timber paths, or flip chips of flint. Find a straight, lightweight stick with enough length to touch the ground in front of you. Look for a thicker stick and it can double as a walking stick. Use a walking stick, and you'll keep your footing as you cross streams, climb slopes or walk rocky ground. Like other amenities you take along on outings, bring a good stick home with you for your next outdoor experience.

In hot weather or on clear days with direct sun, take along sun block to prevent sunburn. Bring insect repellent to ward off mosquitoes if you're hunting after a rain. Apply it as needed during spring and summer seasons.

It's easy to work up an appetite outdoors and hard to leave a good spot in the middle of a hunt, so eat a good meal before you go. If you plan to hunt for more than a few hours, fill a canteen with water or juice and pack some snacks high in carbohydrates to keep you energized. Drink liquids *before* you get thirsty and eat small quantities of food during breaks.

Do you have other things in mind you'd like to bring? A magnifying glass, a small brush to clean dirt off stone, binoculars, or instant heat packets to warm hands are good choices. They're all easily portable and at just the right moment, you'll appreciate having them on you. Consider taking along a small first aid kit for unforeseen situations, too.

To be prepared for the discovery of an artifact, don't leave home without your camera. When you see a partially covered artifact or a piece of worked stone in full view, you'll want to snap a picture of it in the original spot and at least one more of the surrounding geography. A photograph of an artifact lying on a bean field, by a prairie path, on excavated dirt at a construction site, or at any other location is a record that helps document the find. So, try shooting artifacts from different angles or hunting sites from various positions, and take snapshots of sunsets and wildlife, too. You'll share the thrill of discovery with family members and friends much more if you have a number of photographs to recall the day. Since you may want to create a collage of hunting pictures, we'll look at ideas for photo displays in Chapter 10.

TAKE A CAMERA TO RECORD FINDS AND COMPACT SUPPLIES FOR TRAVELING LIGHT.

A pocket-sized pad and a pencil or pen will be necessary for jotting notes at the site. While you're out in the field, you'll want to draft a description of the artifact, explain the geography of its site, and define the location of the artifact within the site. When you carry a pad and pencil, you can draw a **sketch map** of the area, too. A sketch map is a diagram of the geography of the land that has a mark showing the location of an artifact. To sketch a precise map, you should pack a compass. An easy way to show the location of a find is to mark the spot on a USGS topographic map (see the *Maps* section). Pack a copy of one that covers the area you plan to explore. Reliable notes, and sketching or marking a map on site make it a cinch to accurately record your find in a journal later at home. You'll learn how to take good notes and make sketch maps in the next chapter, and how to keep an accurate journal in Chapter 10.

Carry your supplies in a fanny pack, tote bag or small knapsack. When you keep a knapsack stocked with basics ahead of time, you'll be prepared to hunt comfortably at a moment's notice. If you prefer to forego provisions and rough it instead, think about slipping a pack of gum, mints or a roll of hard candy into your pocket, and take along a miniature carrying case to tote your finds.

If you and your family are scheduling a full day for arrowhead hunting, choose a site near a park. At many parks, you'll have access to public facilities. Refill your canteen with cold water, take some time to freshen up, and share your most interesting finds. Relax and enjoy your afternoon break with good company and an appetizing picnic lunch.

WHAT TO WEAR

You know how much the weather affects the movement of soil, stone and artifacts. You'll also want to know how it can affect you. While you hunt, mild to moderate changes can occur. Changing weather is part of the fun of hunting because of the surprises it brings. A moderate breeze can strengthen or soften. A sprinkle can follow a mist. The sun can chase away fog or hide under clouds just a few miles away. How can you be prepared for fluctuating weather? It's really very simple. Consider where you plan to hunt, note the weather, and dress for the conditions.

Since you'll do a fair amount of walking, the first thing to concentrate on is your feet. If you plan to hike through woods after a rain or walk wet fields, marsh areas, streams, creeks, or other places near water, wear boots to keep your feet dry. Rubber boots are best for walking muddy ground after a rain, but waterproofing your leather boots will work, too. Boots with deep treads are best for hiking or climbing. A laced boot that covers your ankles will help support you on rough ground, and a high boot will protect your lower legs. You can wear sturdy sneakers or other firm shoes for walks on dry, level ground. For hunting in cool weather or walking wet surfaces, wear liners under a regular pair of socks. Liners will help keep your feet warm and dry at the same time. In cold weather, pull a thick pair of wool socks over them before slipping into boots.

Always wear comfortable clothing. Since you'll be bending over, crouching down, walking up steep grades, or searching the sides of embankments, wear looser clothes that won't restrict your movement. Choose jeans or pants with deep pockets and shirts with pocket flaps to carry small or special finds. Wear a camp jacket with lots of pockets or a fishing vest, and you won't need to strap on a fanny pack or backpack. If you have a waterproof jacket, bring it along on overcast days in case the weather changes to a sprinkle or drizzle.

Keep in mind that whenever you are out in open places, the weather will tend to be more intense. When there's a cool breeze at home, pack earmuffs and goggles to protect ears and eyes. There could be a cold wind blowing sand on a plain. If it's chilly, dress warmly and bring your gloves. It might be ten degrees colder where you'll be hunting. Temperatures can either be hotter or cooler in the middle of a field, so put on a hat. You'll feel cooler in the heat and warmer if it's cold.

WEAR BOOTS TO HUNT PLOWED FIELDS IN SPRINGTIME BECAUSE THE GROUND WILL BE EXTREMELY MUDDY.

The best way to prepare for possible changes in weather is to dress in layers. In any kind of weather, layer your clothes to adapt to rising and falling temperatures. When it's brisk or cold, begin with a pair of long johns and wear a jacket over a flannel shirt and sweater. If the air gets warmer, you can adjust to the change by removing one layer. In warm weather, peel off the extra shirt or sweater you wore for the cool of early morning. Stow it in your knapsack, or tie it around your waist to keep your hands free.

▼ ▼ ▼

Your adventures in stone artifacts will be different every time you hunt. You'll have a fresh, new experience after a rain shower, in the midst of a dry spell, in winter as you hunt between snowfalls, or during a peaceful evening as you close the day with nature. Everybody has a special way of arrowhead hunting. We've given you some ideas about techniques you can use, what you can expect when you hunt, and what you can bring and wear when you go. To hunt most effectively, mix and match the information to find the ways that work best for you.

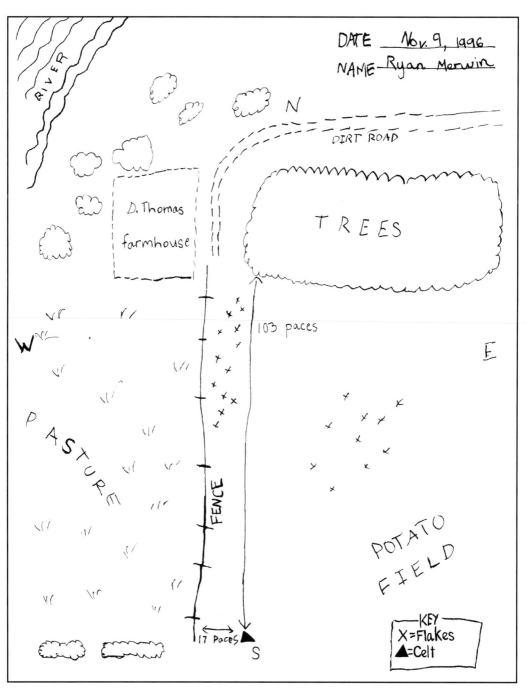

Figure 6-1. Use your artistic talent to record artifacts you discover and mark the spot on a sketch map. To convey information clearly, detail the map accurately and label the features.

Getting Permission

You've just learned about practical things you can bring with you on outings. You may have already decided that a few of the items you'll pack will be a camera, compass and bandanna. While you're out hunting, sometimes you'll find that you forgot something. It might be gloves, tissues, a visor or your sun block. It's not uncommon to forget a small item, but one thing you should never overlook when you hunt is responsibility. Responsibility is as much a part of arrowhead hunting as discovery. It will help you meet others, expand your learning, and increase your adventures, too.

It's very simple to hunt in a responsible way. The most important thing you have to do is obey the law. In the *Before You Hunt* section, we stated that there are places where you may not hunt for artifacts, we talked about laws that protect cultural resources, and discussed ethical issues that concern surface hunting. After you've finished reading this chapter, be sure you and your family get together and review *Ethical Conduct for Arrowhead Hunters* on page xxv. It details some of the significant material you'll learn about here.

Most of you have probably seen "No Trespassing" or "No Hunting" signs posted on trees, fences or at entrances to rural driveways. Some people put up warning signs because they do not want hunters trespassing on their property. If you walk on these properties without getting permission first, it won't matter to them whether you want to hunt for rabbit, prairie chickens, deer, ducks, mushrooms—or arrowheads. It's imperative that, as an amateur archaeologist, you demonstrate the utmost respect for the people you meet and those you don't see. You'll need to be considerate of the rights, property and opinions of others. We know you'll regard the following material to be as important as the subjects covered in the other chapters, because what we're about to explore concerns surface hunting, archaeology and you.

OBTAIN PERMISSION AND EXTEND COURTESIES

You already have some understanding of the significance of finding artifacts. While amateur archaeology teaches us about people and their lifestyles, we can also learn about the importance of provenance, and make discoveries that lead to professional study. Surface hunting is a highly responsible hobby, not only because of the role you play in finding surface artifacts, but because the majority of time it involves other people and their land. Property owners have the right to give permission for people to be on the land they own—their **private property**.

ASK THE LANDOWNER FOR PERMISSION

Before you surface hunt on private property, the first thing you'll need to do is ask the landowner for permission.

You must have landowner permission to hunt, because it is trespassing to walk the property without the owner's express consent. In addition, if an artifact is discovered and removed without the landowner's knowledge, it is considered looting. The looting of even a single artifact is illegal.

People who loot are more interested in hoarding their finds or selling the relics than in historic preservation. Looting causes archaeological information that would have been available to science to be lost. Because looters have been responsible for so much site damage and destruction, laws were passed to protect cultural resources on public and Indian lands. Despite the laws, looting continues—and professional archaeological study suffers. Some people who are concerned about historic preservation think of surface hunting in much the same way they think of looting. They believe that individuals who surface hunt and others who loot will deplete our country's archaeological resources and cause more information to be lost. These folks are so distressed about the loss of cultural resources that they refer to surface hunting and looting as pothunting. But **pothunters** ignore rules, and damage or destroy sites just to get the artifacts. Despite what some think, you should not confuse pothunting and looting with lawful surface hunting.

Because you are a responsible surface hunter, if you see a site that you think looks interesting and it belongs to a neighbor, a friend's family or someone you haven't met, you need to get approval before walking it. If you are young, ask a parent or older family member to accompany you, or go with a friend and ask for permission in pairs.

UNLESS YOU ALREADY KNOW THE LANDOWNER, HUNT WITH NO MORE THAN ONE PARTNER TO INCREASE YOUR CHANCES OF GETTING A "YES."

Good etiquette is a plus in every social situation, and you can extend some courtesies before speaking with the landowner. If you're biking or driving a car, park near the entrance to the property and out of the way of the driveway. If you are hiking, leave any supplies you may have brought near the property entrance, too. Stay on sidewalks and driveways to get to the door. After ringing the bell, move a few feet back so anyone inside can see you before opening it.

To ask permission, say "hello," introduce yourselves and make your request. Many rural landowners are open-minded to surface hunting and have already had others come knocking before you. In some areas, it wouldn't be the first time someone asked, "Would it be all right if we walked your field?" or, "Is that your land by the creek? May we walk it for arrowheads?"

The subject is so interesting that sometimes landowners will strike up a conversation about it. Some may tell you about arrowheads they've found, give helpful tips on the best ways to find them, or even offer to show you artifacts they've discovered while working the land. Remember to apply the same rules you use with any new people you meet. Be polite but remain outside, even if invited in.

At other times, landowners will direct you to neighbors who would be likely to grant permission. They might tell you to try a neighboring farm or the ranch just over the hill, and supply the name of the individual to speak with. If you are a newcomer to the area, ask the landowner if you can mention his or her name when you visit the neighbor. A local reference could be very helpful and your good communication will be an asset. Always thank the landowner graciously for any advice you receive.

KEEP THE PROPERTY LINES IN MIND AND DO NOT WANDER ONTO THE NEIGHBOR'S LAND.

When you get permission, find out the boundaries of the property lines. The owner may point out telephone poles, tree lines, gravel service roads, fences or drainage ditches to indicate the property limits. Ask the landowner whether you've parked in an acceptable spot, and then you can begin to hunt.

Gather your supplies and take them with you to the hunting site. If you'll be walking in a fenced area, be sure to close the gate when you come and go. When you walk near edges of plowed fields, pick up any large, non-cultural stones as you go and pitch them off to the side. Always keep the area as clean as you found it. When you have snacks, don't litter.

You may think about bringing your pet dog, but even well-behaved dogs will want to roam in the fresh air and open spaces. There will be animal burrows to investigate and there may be livestock to bark at or chase. To avoid commotion, leave your pooch at home.

POSTED SIGNS

Landowners will appreciate that you've asked for permission—especially if they've caught trespassers on their land in the past. People put up signs such as "Keep Out," "No Trespassing," "No Fishing," or "No Hunting" for a variety of personal reasons. You'll see signs such as these as you travel along a country road, at the fringes of wooded areas, or next to shorelines. Landowners will often make exceptions to those who show respect for their rights. By acknowledging posted signs and asking permission for an exception, you are honoring their right to make a decision about the property. If you see an area that you'd like to hunt and it has a sign posted, ask to find out if you can walk it.

Look for the nearest house and try your luck. If a farmhouse is in back of a plowed field, do not park at the edge of the field and walk across it to get to the house. Instead, find the road that intersects with the driveway. At times, you'll have to do a bit of investigating to find the right house. A farmhouse might seem as though it belongs with a field, but the owner of the land may actually live one mile up the road. Check it out to make your arrowhead hunting adventures more successful.

REPEATED VISITS

Property owners may invite you to stop by and chat once you've finished hunting. They'll probably be curious to see what you've found, too. These are wonderful opportunities to get to know new friends better, share information, and learn more about artifacts that have been discovered in the area. When you become even better acquainted, some may tell you it's not necessary to ask permission every time you want to arrowhead hunt. No matter how well you know each other and despite the generous offer, it's always best to check with the landowner before hunting. A recently seeded field may not look as if it's been planted and walking on it will harm the crop. A temperamental bull may be grazing just over the hill. Or a section of land may have become unsafe for sure footing. Make it a rule on repeated visits to the same hunting sites, to ask permission each time.

WHEN PERMISSION IS DENIED

Treat all landowners with respect, whether they grant or deny permission. Property owners have valid personal reasons for withholding consent. The field may have been treated with chemicals and would be unsafe for you to walk. The soil may have been plowed like a garden and is ready to be seeded. Or the field may already have been planted.

DON'T GIVE UP ON PERMISSION WHEN YOUR REQUEST IS DENIED, BECAUSE YOU MIGHT OBTAIN IT AT YOUR NEXT STOP.

Occasionally, the person you talk to isn't the owner of the land. A rancher could be leasing the property. A person might own the farmhouse, but not the field you want to hunt. Or a family member may not feel comfortable granting permission because the head of the household isn't home to approve it. The important things to remember are to be polite at all times, and not to get discouraged if your request is denied.

When you experience situations like these, keep trying. Chances are good that you'll find a place to hunt. Sometimes, a renter will give you the address or phone number of the landowner and leave it to you to follow up. An individual might suggest that you come back over the weekend, when the property owner is home. If someone suggests that you try again next season, write down the address and tuck it away for the future. Try focusing more of your attention on getting information instead of permission. Ask people if they can recommend other places in the vicinity that you would be able hunt.

HUNT WITHIN THE LAW

It's very important to know and obey laws that regulate activities. Cyclists are required to observe traffic laws and use bike paths when available. Where signs prohibit skateboarding, skaters must ride their boards elsewhere. Hunters and fishermen may hunt or fish only at designated areas during certain times of the year. Laws are passed and signs are posted when activities affect a number of people, places or things.

As a surface hunter, you'll need to be aware that cultural resource laws protect certain areas of land. At these places, you may not arrowhead hunt legally or remove any artifact you might happen to see. People who disobey archaeological resource protection laws put themselves at risk for arrest, court, fines and imprisonment. Sometimes, you'll see posted signs that will tell you cultural resource protection laws apply, and other times you won't. Where sites are undergoing professional study, information is not made available to the general community. Watch for signs as you scout for sites and never hunt in areas that warn:

```
PROTECTED

ARCHAEOLOGICAL AREA.
NO ARTIFACT COLLECTING OR DIGGING.
VIOLATORS WILL BE PROSECUTED.
```

As you drive past woods or bike along a country road, it's possible that you may be scouting for sites in an area where it would be unlawful to hunt. It is illegal to disturb or collect artifacts from any burial sites, public lands and government-owned places, such as historic sites, national and state parks, county forest preserves, wildlife refuge areas and military bases.

The U.S. Department of the Interior's Bureau of Land Management describes **public land** as all land owned by the U.S. government that is not reserved for other purposes. Your state land management office, an SHPO, Federal Land Manager or county official can provide you with specific information about places where artifact hunting would be off-limits. You can also contact public agencies, such as the Army Corps of Engineers,

Forest Service or National Park Service, when you have any concerns about hunting certain areas of your vicinity.

The easiest and most practical way to select appropriate places to explore is to limit your arrowhead hunting to private property. It's usually legal to hunt private property when you have the permission of the owner, so always get consent to hunt. *Do not* surface hunt on federal, state, county or other public land.

NEVER DIG

Pipeline or building construction and other disturbances to the ground caused by excavation can unearth artifacts and expose archaeological sites. In many cases, **site protection regulations** prohibit further commercial digging until archaeological testing has been performed and/or archaeological clearance has been received. An individual who digs with an object as small as a teaspoon can disturb a buried artifact, too.

Improper digging can damage artifacts and destroy sites. To preserve historic records as you search for artifacts, *do not dig*. Archaeological excavations are the domain of professionals. Your SHPO will record the sites you report and, if necessary, a professional archaeologist will follow up. The archaeologist will have proper authorization to excavate, and it will be done in a safe and appropriate manner. Remember, amateur archaeologists *discover*. Professional archaeologists *uncover*.

TAKE NOTES AT THE SITE

In the last chapter, we talked a little bit about note-taking and sketch maps. The notes you take at a site are a good source of archaeological information, so the more facts you record, the better. You'll be transferring the notes to an artifact journal later, and filling out a report form as well. Since the journal is a permanent diary of your surface finds and the form will be read by professionals, you'll want to take notes as accurately and completely as you can.

When you discover an artifact, it will be a moment you'll never forget. The combination of timing, luck, and finding the right clues are part of the adventure of surface hunting. Think about it. On a large plowed field, how can you predict that an artifact will be lying in one of the rows that you choose to walk? Or know where to find it before a rainstorm moves it under a leaf, and out of your view? Take some time to enjoy the lucky discovery before pulling out your pad and pencil.

AN ANCIENT INDIAN VILLAGE WAS EXCAVATED BY ARCHAEOLOGISTS IN ARIZONA AFTER ARTIFACTS WERE DISCOVERED BY WORKERS LAYING A PIPELINE.

The most important information necessary for accurate reporting is the location of the artifact. The address of the property owner is a good start, but it's very easy to be much more specific. You can describe the exact location by walking and counting. To mark the spot, place your knapsack or sweater next to your find, or use a stick to flag it. Walk to at least two nearby markers, such as a barn and a fence post, and count your paces as you go. By recording the number of paces between the markers and the artifact, you'll provide a good description of its location on a field.

Look for landmarks in the area that will describe the site of an artifact on a larger scale. Try to estimate the number of feet to a telephone pole, natural gas pipeline marker, radio tower or other fixed structures you see. Or walk to a nearby slope, pond, creek, tree line or service road, and count paces as your measure.

Take notes about the physical features of the land, describing both the site and the field conditions. Is the site on level ground near a bluff? Adjacent to any rivers or streams? Just west of a thickly wooded area? On a freshly plowed potato field? Or is it at the southern edge of a small marsh?

Any opinions you have about a find are very useful, too. How do you think the artifact got to the surface? Do you think it was exposed by rain, wind, or river water moving back and forth over sand? Could a cow's hoof have disturbed the earth, uncovering it on a pasture? Was the topsoil of a building site scraped off by a machine? Or did a plow churn the dirt instead?

IF YOU FIND SEVERAL ARTIFACTS NEAR EACH OTHER, BE SURE TO ESTIMATE THE SIZE OF THE SITE.

Make a note about why you think the artifact is at that particular place. Do you suspect it was a campsite? A lookout site? Or a buffalo wallow? Do you believe it was left behind from a hunt? Any ideas you have should be included on your report form. Your comments and rationale about a find will be helpful to experts as they piece together the prehistoric puzzle.

The reports in Figures 6-2 and 6-3 show the types of information you should be noting. When you discover an artifact, keep the categories in mind and jot some notes about the presence of other materials you may have seen in the area, such as pottery, ceramic, bone, shell, iron or even plastic. The additional information you supply will give archaeologists a better idea about the activity that has taken place on the site. Be sure to include a map, photographs and any other attachments you feel would help to describe your find. Draw a picture of it, topside and bottom, or use a copy of an artifact photographed in this book if you see one with a very close resemblance.

Surface Find Report

Name **Ryan C. Merwin** Age **10** Date of Find **Nov. 9, 1996**
Street Address **816 East Walsh Ave.**
City **Scott Mills** State **WI** Zip **12345-6789**
Property Owner Name **David R. Thomas**
Property Owner Street Address **R.D. #2**
City **Scott Mills** County **KAY** State **WI** Zip **12345**
LOCATION OF SITE **Plowed Field. Artifact south of trees, southeast of river southeast of house, east of pasture. From corner of house closest to field, go 17 paces east and 103 paces south to artifact**

DESCRIPTION OF SITE **Found chert or flint flakes on top of field. Found most in middle of field and side closest to river. Found artifact completely uncovered on top of field.**

MATERIALS OBSERVED
X Flakes **White and gray chert or flint. Some flakes look kind of clear.**
X Tools/Weapons **Maybe a celt? Gray granite tool is 5⅛" long and 2½" wide.**
X Bone **Small animal skull teeth in it! some bones close by.**
___ Fire-cracked Rock/Hearths _____

X Historic Materials **Found pieces of a red brick, by blue glass from and old bottle, some white plastic and ceramic, a rusty bolt, shiny pieces of pottery and a button.**
ITEMS COLLECTED **Stone tool and button**
ARCHAEOLOGIST CONTACTED **X** Yes ___ No If Yes, Name **Daniel F. Engle**
ATTACHMENTS
    Sketch Map **X** Yes ___ No   Illustration(s) ___ Yes **X** No
    USGS Topographic Map ___ Yes **X** No   Additional Sheet(s) ___ Yes **X** No
    Photograph(s) **X** Yes ___ No
COMMENTS **Lots of rain on Nov 8th. Would make a good place for camping. Artifacts could be buried in the pasture and in the trees. Three pieces of a jug have a shiny glaze. Button has two tiny holes. Think it's antique**

Form Completed by **Ryan Merwin**
Contact Person **Ann Merwin** Relationship **Mother**
Signature **Ryan Merwin** Phone **(555)555-5555** Date **Nov. 11, 1996**

Figure 6-2. Your notes will become a part of a permanent archaeological record when you fill out a report form. This example shows how a young person might describe the discovery of a celt. The child's sketch map in Figure 6-1 supplements the written details given here.

Surface Find Report

Name _Ann V. Merwin_ Age _____ Date of Find _Nov. 9, 1996_

Street Address _816 East Walsh Avenue_

City _Scott Mills_ State _WI_ Zip _12345-6789_

Property Owner Name _David R. Thomas_

Property Owner Street Address _RD 2_

City _Scott Mills_ County _Kay_ State _WI_ Zip _12345_

LOCATION OF SITE _Plowed potato field is on the Thomas farmstead. Southeast of the Scott River, east of a pasture and south of a tree grove. Artifact found on the southwest corner of the field, 17 paces directly east of the pasture fence and 103 paces directly south of the far southwest corner of the trees._

DESCRIPTION OF SITE _Flakes of flint and chert seen on the surface of the field. Heavier concentrations of scatter are at mid field and on the northwest side nearest the river. Dense cluster of flakes is at the east edge of scatter nearest the river. Stone tool was completely exposed on recently plowed, level ground._

MATERIALS OBSERVED

X Flakes _white, gray and brown flint or chert. Some translucent._

X Tools/Weapons _Ground tool; may be a celt. Gray granite. 5⅛" long, 2½" wide. Possible flake tools in scatter._

X Bone _Small animal skull with teeth intact; bone fragments nearby._

? Fire-cracked Rock/Hearths _Possibly. There's an even distribution of tan sandstone over surface; some are reddened; have black spots._

X Historic Materials _Fragments of red brick, aqua bottle glass, white ceramic, rusted bolt, glazed sherds, button._

ITEMS COLLECTED _Granite stone tool and button_

ARCHAEOLOGIST CONTACTED __X_Yes ___No If Yes, Name _Daniel F. Engle_

ATTACHMENTS

Sketch Map ___Yes _X_No   Illustration(s) _X_Yes ___No

USGS Topographic Map _X_Yes ___No   Additional Sheet(s) ___Yes _X_No

Photograph(s) _X_Yes ___No

COMMENTS _Heavy rain on Nov. 8. Location is a good spot for a campsite. Artifacts may be buried in the pasture; scatter may extend into the trees. Sherds have faintly dimpled surfaces like orange skins; some have metallic lusters. White mother-of-pearl button has 2 irregular holes; may be an antique._

Form Completed by _Ann V. Merwin_

Contact Person _____ Relationship _____

Signature _Ann V. Merwin_ Phone _(555) 555-5555_ Date _Nov. 11, 1996_

Figure 6-3. This example reflects a more detailed narrative since the celt was discovered by an adult. Compare the youngster's sketch map with the adult report and you'll see that the drawing illustrates both descriptions.

MAKE OR MARK A MAP

Drawing a sketch map is not only fun, it's a good way to show the exact location of an artifact. To pinpoint the position of your find on a sketch map, you'll need to illustrate the physical appearance of the land. Your drawing may include pasture, prairie, plowed fields, hills, trees, natural or man-made sources of water, or other characteristics of the geography, such as roads, buildings or power lines. Turn to the front of the chapter again to see the map of the Thomas farm. Notice how easy it would be for anyone to find the site of the celt on the potato field by looking at the details given. A good illustration that includes paces will often show the location of an artifact more clearly than a written description. It's essential to indicate directions, so use a north arrow or abbreviations on the sides of your sketch. Be sure to include the date and your name, too.

If you find more than one artifact on a field, use different symbols in the key box. Suppose you found a scraper among a scatter of flakes. You could use a series of small "X's" to indicate the scatter and draw a triangle for the tool. If you find another artifact in the area but you're not sure what it is, pick a new symbol, such as a blank square or blackened circle, and note it as "other artifact" in the key.

USGS topographic maps show the precise features of land. When you bring a copy of a USGS map for the area you plan to hunt, the geographic features will already be completed. On topographic maps, mark the location of your find, add any landmarks you see that are not included, make a key, date it, and add your name. Try either sketching or marking a map, because both methods are excellent ways to more accurately record an artifact.

ETHICS

Your discovery of one surface artifact might just be a stray. It could be an important part of a much bigger picture, too. It may be that more artifacts have surfaced in the area or are buried nearby. What is the right thing to do when you find one? How you treat each discovery is your personal choice. Some people contact local archaeologists or state agencies and do not touch the artifacts. Others keep the artifacts but don't record the finds or report them to anyone else. Most arrowhead hunters keep a careful record of their discoveries, and also collect and care for the artifacts.

TO PREVENT FUTURE LOSS OF INFORMATION, SHARE YOUR PHOTOGRAPHS, JOURNAL NOTES AND MAPS WITH OTHERS.

We encourage you to look for fragments of worked stone and whole artifacts as responsible arrowhead hunters do. Always photograph, notate and map artifacts before you leave the site. To avoid future loss of information, notify others about your discoveries. One well-kept record is of no use to science if it's hoarded at home, destroyed in a fire or flood, or discarded in the next generation.

How you report artifacts is your personal decision. You can fill out a form for a state agency or contact a local archaeologist. You might decide to register artifacts in an archaeological society database, send photographs to artifact magazines for publication, or follow up with expert avocational archaeologists. Think about combining several of these ways to share the information.

Because you hunt legally, you have the right to collect artifacts if you choose to do so, too. In certain situations, it's better to remove an artifact than to leave it in place. A projectile point on a field that is about to be plowed could be damaged by the plow disk, or moved to another spot. A stone drill on a cattle path would be in danger of cracking or chipping. A scraper lying near the top of a steep, eroded slope will shift with rain and work its way down. A knife tip in the shallow water of a river bank could be lost to the river by the next strong current. Where provenance has already been altered and when damage, loss or more movement is likely, the artifact may be safer with you. If you decide to collect your finds, be sure to record information in a journal and follow up with others. Your responsible conduct and cooperation will be appreciated by the professionals you'll come to know.

INFORM PROFESSIONALS

The position and location of your discovery is as meaningful to experts as the object itself, and it increases in significance when there are more artifacts in the area. If you find two or three artifacts close to each other, it's considered a site and you'll need to inform professionals. Sometimes, an artifact is so rare that it should not be touched or moved. Significant or rare finds require experts to investigate the site. A single, significant find on a plowed field would be any finely crafted or highly polished object, such as a pipe, weapon or ornament, that has been inadvertently plowed from a grave. Stone artifacts with adhering resins or glues are extremely rare, and should be left as you found them, too. Don't alter the position of artifacts if you see parts of them on undisturbed surfaces. The top of an evenly grooved limestone slab that's just barely visible in a grassy field could be a stationary abrading stone that archaeologists would want to excavate. Items made of perishable material, such as buckskin, feathers, hair, horn, ivory, leather, rawhide and wood, are significant but they are not usually found on the surface. While it's possible to discover artifacts of perishable material in southern caves and dry places where rock provides shelter, they are found on open, humid sites only under special conditions. Most of the time these types of materials will have been dug from dry caves or excavated from well-preserved burials. Southern sites with perishable materials and other sites with such good preservation are extremely rare and always deserve professional study.

You don't need to be anxious about leaving an artifact as is. Remember, it's survived for hundreds or thousands of years on its own. Remaining in place until it can be safely moved won't make that much difference. Inform the property owner immediately and if you are young, tell your folks. Consult with the property owner about the significance of your find, because you'll need landowner approval before reporting it. If the landowner has no objections, contact your SHPO, a university archaeology department or local archaeologist as soon as possible.

People do not always agree about the significance of a find, so professional archaeologists recommend reporting all **authentic** artifacts to state historic preservation agencies. Why report every artifact or fragment of worked stone that you see? The information about each artifact reported becomes part of the state archaeological file. Think of one discovery as a pushpin on a map. Imagine that a month later, another surface hunter reported an artifact. Suppose eighteen more were discovered over the next year and each of these was reported, too. An accumulation of discoveries in one area would be represented by a cluster of pins. Preservation agencies can determine which places should be professionally studied by considering the number, as well as the content, of reports.

ALWAYS GET PERMISSION FROM LANDOWNERS BEFORE REPORTING AN ARTIFACT YOU DISCOVER ON THEIR PROPERTY.

Landowners who allow you to hunt on their property will usually give you permission to report, too. Even so, you should not call your SHPO to report every jagged rock that *might* be an artifact. Calls are followed up with forms and if you send them in for questionable finds, it will just add extraneous paperwork to an overworked staff. Instead, use a report form for discoveries that show clear evidence of prehistoric work or use, such as flaking, pecking, grinding, polishing, drilling, fire-cracking or heat-treating.

If you discover a whole artifact but you aren't sure what it is, note the measurements and include a good photo or drawing with your report so professionals can accurately identify it. Suppose the celt in the sample reports really wasn't a celt at all. Both reports included dimensions of the find and at least one photo. One form suggested that an illustration of the artifact was attached as well. Whether you say that a surface find is a possible celt or you write that it's most likely a spokeshave, be sure to include enough information so an archaeologist can confirm your identification.

What should you do when fragments are clearly worked, but are too small for you to identify? Don't let the size or condition of your find keep you from making a report. Many of the artifacts that archaeologists discover are also broken—but they measure, study and identify each to the best of their ability. Report fragments in the same way that you do whole artifacts. You'll learn more about how to identify artifacts and pieces of worked stone in Chapter 8.

Always notify the preservation agency promptly if the discovery is rare, or when two or more artifacts are near each other. Use the notes you take while you hunt to provide the information needed for agency records. To request state forms, refer to the *State Historic Preservation Agencies* section of the *Resources* for the address or phone number of your SHPO. If you would rather use a generic form that is identical to the example in Figures 6-2 and 6-3, you may copy the blank one on page 109. After your report is received, the SHPO will forward the information to your state museum.

OWNERSHIP OF FINDS

You do not have to give up your artifacts simply because you report them. Ownership of surface finds is a matter between the landowner and the surface hunter. Typically, when you get permission to hunt you can keep what you find.

It's a learning experience for everyone when you share information about cultural resources. Whether you've found fragments of worked stone or whole arrowheads, take some time after hunting to show your finds to the property owner. When professionals are requested to study a site, get your family and the landowner together to discuss who should be responsible for looking after the artifacts. Consider loaning or donating them to a museum in the vicinity, where people would most appreciate seeing the local discoveries.

Points of Interest

Responsible Arrowhead Hunting

Obey the law

Request permission to hunt

Respect others

Respect property

Photograph, map and record all artifacts

Get landowner approval before reporting

Report artifacts and sites

Share information with others

Never dig

Reports of finds and sites far exceed the number of archaeologists available to investigate them. Perhaps as your interest in archaeology grows through surface hunting, you may join the ranks of professional or academic archaeologists. Whenever you hunt for artifacts, make a future for yourself in archaeology by behaving in a way that is above reproach. In any event, your honorable conduct as a surface hunter will be something of which you can always be proud.

Surface Find Report

Name _____ Age _____ Date of Find _____

Street Address _____

City _____ State _____ Zip _____

Property Owner Name _____

Property Owner Street Address _____

City _____ County _____ State _____ Zip _____

LOCATION OF SITE _____
_____
_____
_____
_____

DESCRIPTION OF SITE _____
_____
_____
_____
_____

MATERIALS OBSERVED

____Flakes _____
_____

____Tools/Weapons _____
_____

____Bone _____
_____

____Fire-cracked Rock/Hearths _____
_____

____Historic Materials _____
_____
_____

ITEMS COLLECTED _____

ARCHAEOLOGIST CONTACTED ____Yes ____No   If Yes, Name _____

ATTACHMENTS

    Sketch Map   ____Yes ____No   Illustration(s)   ____Yes ____No

    USGS Topographic Map ____Yes ____No   Additional Sheet(s) ____Yes ____No

    Photograph(s)   ____Yes ____No

COMMENTS _____
_____
_____
_____
_____
_____

Form Completed by _____

Contact Person _____ Relationship _____

Signature _____ Phone _____ Date _____

Figure 7-1. When stone surfaces are heavily soiled, hoof, bell and tube pestles are easy to mistake for non-cultural rock. Check out larger rocks with defined shapes and you may discover that somebody used one for grinding long ago. You can clean stone artifacts such as these with a dry brush or rinse them with water.

Cleaning Your Finds

By the time you read this chapter, you may have developed your own opinion about touching, picking up or collecting the artifacts you discover. Like others with more experience in arrowhead hunting, some of you who are new to this hobby will decide to collect. To preserve information so you can share it with others, it is critical that you know the proper way to handle and clean the finds you bring home. If you've decided to hunt but not collect, you'll benefit from this chapter since it contains other important information about artifacts.

Whether you collect or not, hunting for worked stone is a good way to get to know non-cultural rock firsthand. You can pick it up, feel the weight, touch the surfaces, and inspect edges. When you can't decide if a stone is worked, you may decide to bring it home. Until you clean the soil off and identify what you've got, it's important to handle each of your finds as carefully as an artifact.

Sometimes, all of the rock you bring home will turn out to be worked by Mother Nature. When this happens, it's an opportunity to learn in a hands-on way. You should always inspect the natural rock you collect during outings. The more you examine, the easier it will be to spot flaking, pecking or grinding when you see it.

Treat all things you bring home from an arrowhead hunt as you would other fragile objects. To avoid cracking a brittle stone,

UNTIL YOU'VE DETERMINED THAT A FIND IS AN ARTIFACT, ANYTHING YOU BRING HOME FROM A SURFACE HUNT SHOULD BE HANDLED GENTLY.

breaking off a thin edge, or nicking a smooth surface, always be gentle when handling your finds. You'll see the rough hand of the environment in fractured flint, splintered bone, rusted iron, chipped glass, cracked glazes on ceramic, broken pottery, pieces of shell, and more. That's more than enough damage already and you won't want to add any more. During cleaning, how can you reduce the chances of further breakage, scratching, chipping or splitting?

In this chapter, you'll learn about methods which will protect worked stone and other artifacts that may be among your finds. Since you may want to know more about the artifacts you discover, we'll also be looking at laboratory tests. Use the recommended procedures to keep artifacts in your care safe for future tests.

WHEN YOU GET HOME

The first couple of things you'll want to do when you get home is wash your hands and go through your finds. Empty your tote bag and lay the finds on a clean towel. Check your pockets for small pieces because anything you miss will get washed with your clothes. When you head for the sink, keep all finds away from water. Do not rinse dirty objects as you wash up and never soak any in the sink. Certain types of materials could be damaged when cleaned this way. Water won't harm stone, glass or gold—but it could damage bone, fired clay, iron, lead or shell. Since safe cleaning for one type of material is not always right for another, don't rinse your finds all at once. You might accidentally ruin something that never should have gotten wet.

TEMPORARY STORAGE

At times, you won't be able to clean or inspect your finds as soon as you get home. You may have to go to a soccer game, fix dinner, or get to an appointment. You might even decide to relax!

On these days, put your finds and the notes you may have taken at the site into a clean plastic container. Tape a note with the landowner's name and the date to the outside, and cover it with a lid. Temporary storage reduces the chance of losing information from an outing when your schedule is tight. It's also a good way to prevent surface finds from mixing with others you bring home from different locations or on other days. Labeled containers are even more convenient for busy family members who hunt together, but who keep individual journals and unmarked finds separate. When you use temporary storage, be sure to make time to inspect your finds soon since one may be an artifact you'll need to label and record. We'll be looking at some of the ways you can do this in Chapter 10.

CLEAN FINDS CONSERVATIVELY

The best way to clean any find you bring home is conservatively. We recommend that you do not remove all of the soil. An advantage of leaving some soil intact is that it can help match an artifact to the location it was found. You should not try to scrape off smudges because the material may not always be soil. On sherds, dark spots that look like bits of dirt could be residue of food. Blood cells on a scraper will be evident in the lab, but won't be visible to the naked eye. To keep materials in shape for future tests, you'll want to keep small amounts of dirt unaltered.

When finds have been washed with rainwater and are relatively clean, examine them just as they are. If they're dry and slightly dusty, take a deep breath and blow off the residue. Wipe moderately soiled finds with a clean, dry towel or remove most of the dirt with a soft, dry brush. For badly soiled finds, use a dry towel or brush, or rinse with water if you are certain that the material is stone. Rinsing will not remove bits of hardened earth or all of the dirt stuck in crevices. Cleaning finds with any of these methods will keep them free of the types of contamination that could spoil the results of lab tests.

CHAPTER 7

You should be especially careful when handling prehistoric pottery because oil from your fingers could ruin the outcome of a test. How will you know that a sherd is hundreds or thousands of years old? Look at the veneer of surfaces and texture of clay. The surfaces of prehistoric pottery have a dull finish and may be blackened on the concave interior side. The clay, which is granular in texture, will contain tiny bits of shell or particles of grit. The surfaces of relatively recent crockery may be dimpled—like orange skins—and might have a shiny glaze or metallic luster. Even when a colored glaze has worn off, you should be able to identify newer, perhaps historic earthenware by its smooth, dense clay. Until you are certain that a sherd is not a prehistoric artifact, hold the piece by the broken edges and do not touch the surfaces.

A BEAUTIFUL PATINA ON STONE IS SO DURABLE THAT IT CANNOT BE SCRATCHED BY DRY BRUSHING OR REMOVED WITH WATER.

It's easy to mistake one type of material for another, so be especially careful if there's hardened soil or dried mud adhering to any of your finds. A pipe fragment clogged with earth may seem more like a small chunk of white chert or a piece of animal bone. Dry dirt on a prehistoric sherd could make it look like a broken, porous stone. A soiled chip of translucent flint might just turn out to be shell. When your finds are so dirty that you can't quite make out the material, it's always better to dry brush than to rinse.

Take a moment to study the table of cleaning methods on page 115. The first heading lists materials that can be found on the surface of the ground. The second lists artifacts that are made from the materials. Most of the prehistoric artifacts have already been introduced and you'll learn about the others in the next two chapters. Notice that the cleaning methods you should use are not the same for all materials. As you go through your finds, refer to the table to avoid harming any that could be

MATERIALS	ARTIFACTS		METHODS
BONE	Atlatl hook Bead Effigy Fishhook Flaking tool Gorget Hairpin	Handle Hoe Needle Ornament Pendant Projectile point Scraper	Dry brush or wipe. Do not use water.
CLAY	Bowl Cup Fired clay biscuit Marble	Pendant Pipe Sherd	If wet from dew, rain, ice, or snow, air-dry at room temperature. Dry brush only. Do not use water.
GLASS	Bead Bottle Marble	Projectile point Telegraph insulator	You may immerse glass in warm water and wash with a soft cloth. Use extra caution if handling broken or chipped glass. Pat dry.
GOLD	Coin Earring	Ornament Ring	Rinse with warm water. Do not use a brush or wipe with terry cloth, since gold is a soft metal that can be scratched. Air-dry at room temperature.
IRON	Bead Gun part	Horseshoe	Dry brush only. Do not use water.
LEAD	Bullet	Musket ball	Do nothing. If corrosion is loose, use a dry brush to remove flakes.
SHELL	Bead Bowl Button Gorget Hoe	Ornament Pendant Rattle Spoon	Dry brush or wipe. Do not use water.
STONE	Abrading stone Adze Anvil Atlatl weight Axe Bannerstone Bead Birdstone Boatstone Boiling stone Celt Ceremonial stone Chipping stone Chunkey stone Cooking stone Core Cup stone Discoidal Drill Effigy Fire-cracked rock Flake tool Game stone Gorget Graver Grinding stone	Hammerstone Handaxe Hearth stone Heat-treated stone Hoe Knife Mano Maul Mortar Multipurpose tool Net weight Nut stone Ornament Pendant Perforator Pestle Pipe Polishing stone Preform Projectile point Scraper Spade Spatulate Spokeshave Spud	Dry brush, wipe or rinse with warm water. If you prefer to rinse, air-dry at room temperature.

artifacts. Remember that some of the artifacts listed are made from more than one material, so always cross-check the first three columns. If you know what kind of artifact you've found, you can also use the table to help you determine what type of material it might be. When more than one cleaning procedure is described, choose whichever method you prefer.

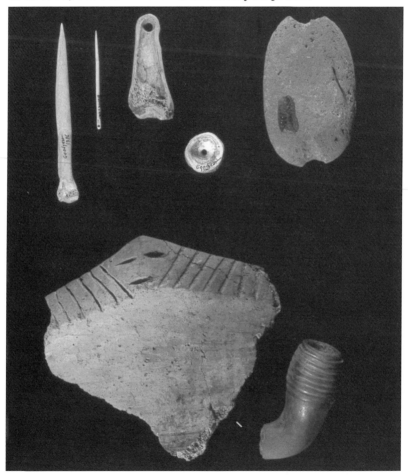

Figure 7-2. These artifacts are made of bone, stone and clay. Which should be brushed? Can any be rinsed? Top row: bone awl, needle, pendant, bead and stone net weight. Bottom row: rimsherd (human effigy) and clay smoking pipe. Needle: ca. 8500 B.C., Buhla site, Idaho. Others: A.D. 1570-90, Iroquois village, Goodyear site, Erie County, New York. Photo by R. M. Gramly.

To get your finds clean enough to examine, it's never necessary to scrub or use soap. Brush with a new paintbrush, art brush or soft-bristled toothbrush and use it only for cleaning finds. Apply light pressure, just as you do to clean your teeth. Never use a sharp, rigid object to remove soil in crevices because you might scratch or crack the material. If rinsing is safe, use your fingers to loosen the dirt. You may use a brush under running water when you know the material is stone—just don't be too particular about getting it perfectly clean. Use an old towel or extra dish drain for air-drying wet stone, and you'll keep the regular household supplies available for other family members.

LABORATORY TESTS

When archaeologists study artifacts, they use great care in taking accurate notes and measurements at sites. The finds are brought to labs for further examination and the conclusions are written in formal papers. When studies are complete, the reports are circulated or published so that new information can be shared with others. You'll see some of the artifacts that archaeologists have studied this way at museum exhibits featuring American Indians or prehistory.

Laboratory tests are especially helpful to professionals because they provide specific information about the artifacts or the history of the sites. There are several that estimate the age of materials. You've probably already heard of **radiocarbon dating**. This test measures age by the radioactive carbon in organic material. Thermoluminescent dating measures light from heated electrons. In sherds, the more light that is produced, the older the pottery. Collagen dating measures nitrogen in bone and is used to determine whether two fragments from the same deposit are the same age. A test called neutron activation analysis helps archaeologists learn the original quarries of obsidian and flint artifacts, and throws light on Indian trade routes. There are so many other tests—charcoal residue

YOU CAN SCHEDULE A LAB TEST BEFORE OR AFTER CLEANING.

Points of Interest

Practices to Avoid

Amateur archaeologists should be aware of misinformation about substances that are sometimes used to treat artifacts. You should not clean any part of any material listed in the table with acetone, alcohol, ammonia, carbonate of soda, creosote, ether, formaldehyde, gasoline, gelatin, hydrochloric acid or salt. After cleaning, do not soak your finds in vegetable oil or polish them with lanolin, petroleum jelly or grease. These agents will taint artifacts you may later decide to have analyzed. Contamination from substances such as these will reduce or destroy the chances for knowledge that can be gained through laboratory tests.

analysis, blood residue analysis, amino acid racemization, fission track dating, magnetic dating, fluorine dating, scanning electron microscopy and more—that the possibilities for further study are astounding.

Tests such as these are also available to the public. Labs at some university centers try to devote a few hours each week to the outside community and will provide technological service at no charge, or for a fee. You can learn a lot more about an artifact when you have it analyzed. Do you suspect that one of your finds was charred in an ancient fire? Could particles of food cooked long ago still be adhering to a sherd? Would you like to know the age of your scraper? Or the quarry that produced the stone of a flint knife? If you have an artifact that you would like to have tested, call a school of engineering, medicine, biological sciences or earth science and ask the departmental secretary for more information. For occasional testing, it's not uncommon to receive free service or pay the nominal cost for lab materials if the results are ultimately published, and proper acknowledgment is given to the laboratory. When you request tests frequently, expect to pay an hourly lab charge. A lot of work can be performed in just one hour, and access to extremely expensive equipment and a highly skilled operator makes the fee a very good bargain.

You may be more curious than ever about a sharp flake or a flat-sided stone that you've just cleaned. To identify an artifact or make a decision about a lab test, you'll want to give your finds a thorough inspection. So, tidy up the work area, pick a comfortable spot with good lighting, and get out your magnifying glass. To make a positive identification, try comparing your finds with the artifacts photographed in the next chapter.

Figure 8-1. To identify a round, smooth rock as a game stone, consider where you found it. The stone at the upper arrow is broken in half and looks like part of a polished marble. Since it was discovered on a river bank, this find may have been smoothed by water currents. The black stone, a discoidal (lower arrow), was discovered on a cornfield far from a source of fresh water. The location of the site, the lack of other rock like it in the area, and its smooth finish lead us to believe it was ground and buffed by people. The glass marble, another surface hunting find (center arrow), has another ninety years or so to go before it can be classified as an artifact.

Identifying Artifacts

Identifying artifacts can be a snap or just plain perplexing, but most of the time it falls somewhere in between. Identification often depends on the condition of the stone. Saw-toothed serrations on both edges of a thin, bifacial flake would identify a find as a point or knife. A flake with slight chipping, a rock with hollows, or a small flat stone could be questionable. Has a sharp rock been worked or did Mother Nature flake the edges? Did a surface become flat from human use? Would a hole be evidence of drilling? Or a groove proof of grinding? It takes time to know the difference between cultural and non-cultural stone. You'll find that identification becomes much easier with experience.

Identification of an artifact is usually a process instead of an event. It's fun because sometimes there are great surprises in store! Your ability to identify artifacts comes from what you know about worked stone and how you go about investigating your finds. You can sharpen your skills by referring to identification guidebooks, visiting museums, and going to artifact shows. As you compare finds with photos and examine other artifacts, you'll gradually become more proficient at identification. When you use resources and ask questions in the process, you'll learn even more about artifacts, materials and prehistory.

It would be wonderful to have an archaeologist as an arrowhead hunting partner, because you could ask questions while you're out in the field. You essentially have this advantage when you report an artifact and a professional studies it at the site.

CHAPTER 8

When an archaeologist comes to visit, you can learn *exactly* what you've found! If professionals feel that your report is sufficient and a trip to the site isn't indicated, ask the landowner if you may take the artifact home to study it. If you usually bring your discoveries home, you'll always want to identify them to the best of your ability. Whether you decide to leave worked stone at the site or care for it yourself, this chapter will help you identify some of the artifacts you find at the moment you first see them.

EXAMINE YOUR FINDS

To identify worked stone as you hunt, examine the finds you bring home. You'll probably have fragments, chunks and whole stones, and maybe a few other discoveries. The first thing you'll need to do is get organized. Since stones that are similar are easier to compare when they're next to each other, separate your finds into little piles. Start sorting by the type of material, such as sandstone, granite and obsidian. To separate flint and chert, you may want to refer to Chapter 2. Next, put any small, smooth stones together. Set larger rocks off to the side, jagged pieces wherever, shells here, fossils there—you can arrange your finds any way you please.

Once your finds are separated, you'll be looking for features of worked stone and shapes that are similar to artifacts. During our examination of stone in Chapter 2, we discussed flaking, pecking and grinding, and introduced chipping stones, flake tools, abrading stones, manos and other artifacts. In Chapter 3, you learned about shapes, sizes and features of projectile points, scrapers, hammerstones, pestles, chunkey stones and more. Review these chapters to become familiar with the general appearance of worked stone. Does one of your finds have a shape and size that is similar to one of these? To accurately identify it, you'll need to do a closer inspection of its features.

The best part about identifying an artifact during a thorough inspection is that you can use your sense of touch in the process.

Handling stone makes identification easier since you can hold it up close, see it from several angles, or run your fingers along a surface. So, pick up the stone you're most curious about and let the examination at home begin.

Flaking

One of the most important things to decide when examining stone is whether or not there is flaking. For worked stone that is flaked, you'll want to identify the type of chipping that was used. To describe worked stone to someone else or fill out a report for a chipped artifact, it's helpful to include information about the style and position of flaking. During a home inspection, you can make a better decision about percussion or pressure flaking by looking at the length of the strokes and noting the location of chipping. Does your find have long strokes or short chips? Is flaking on one surface, both sides or just in certain areas? Is there a pattern of uniform flaking or does chipping seem to be random? Observations like these will help you express the details about an artifact. They may also lead to clues about when it was made, since certain flaking techniques and styles came into use at different times in history. Try to determine if the artifact was percussion-flaked or pressure-flaked by inspecting it even more closely.

You'll find percussion flaking on rocks that break in conchoidal fractures. A worked fragment is percussion-flaked if you see patterns of thin, even strokes. You can also look for large strokes in patterns, long chips that go any which way, and wide flakes for handholds or grips. Look for petite chipping on top and bottom surfaces, and short strokes along edges. Turn a sharp stone on its side to inspect the line of the edge. Indians "rippled" the edges of scrapers by removing flakes from different parts of both sides. If you see ripples that are uniformly spaced, the edges were flaked by percussion. Whenever stones are shaped by soft-hammer blows, be sure to check any straight edges for pressure flaking.

If there's a regular pattern of chipping that has modified the shape of your find, you've found an artifact. On projectile points, well-made knives or large scrapers, look for percussion flaking on both sides. Chipped artifacts may also have large, broad strokes in no specific pattern. Compare a find that has **random flaking** with the **handaxe** in Figure 8-11 of the color insert. You just might decide that your stone is a percussion-flaked **side scraper**. A lot of chipping on a pebble of flint that's in the rough shape of a cone is probably an ancient flintknapping core. If your core is notched on the sides or drilled with one hole, you've found one that was made into a net weight. Pebbles other than flint may also have weighted prehistoric fishing nets, so check your stones that are about the size and shape of a cookie for crude notches on opposite sides.

Identify pressure flaking by tiny, uniform chips along edges. Sometimes, chipping will extend across the length of an entire side. Other times, only small portions of edges will be flaked. On unifacial tools, most of the edge work will be on one side. So that you won't miss small areas of flaking, inspect both sides of stone.

Use your senses of touch and sight to decide whether or not a stone is pressure-flaked. Use a well-made point or knife to start with since pressure flaking on many of these is hard to mistake. If you have a whole artifact or a fragment of stone with saw-tooth, fine or notched serrations, draw your finger over the surfaces near its edges. Feel the even, minute bumps from the chipping. When you can't decide if another stone is pressure-flaked, compare the edge work with your identified artifact by touch. It should feel like the chipped surfaces at identified serrations.

You can find pressure flaking on projectile points, knives, gravers, multipurpose tools and small to medium scrapers. Edges of spokeshaves, **thumbnail scrapers**, some **steep-edge scrapers** and other small tools may be totally pressure-flaked or not modified this way at all. Look for tiny chips on percussion-flaked stone and on flake tools that have not been otherwise altered.

Amateurs who have just begun learning about archaeology will not always recognize small areas of pressure flaking on some artifacts. Look at the drawings of the scraper in Chapter 1, Figure 1-3, and the spokeshave in Chapter 3, Figure 3-6. The pressure flaking along the scraping edges of both tools is unmistakable. Compare the chipping with the artifacts in Figures 8-4 through 8-7, and you'll spot the pressure-flaked areas much better. Try using a magnifying glass to examine questionable chipping for pressure flaking. Distinct, even chips look great under the lens. Once you see them magnified, you'll recognize the flaking more easily next time.

Probably the best way to spot pressure flaking or percussion chipping is to hold stones up to a good light. Remember that while you were in the field, sunlight reflected stone differently as you moved nearer. Walking changed your angle of vision as you hunted, but at home you'll need to change the position of the stones. To alter the reflection of light on surfaces, turn stones around and hold them at slightly different angles. It's important to turn and tilt them since one position under artificial lighting may not show flaking quite as well as another.

TO SEE FLAKING MORE CLEARLY, HOLD STONES UP TO LIGHT.

On thin flakes of flint, chert or obsidian, check for translucence under the light. In these materials, you'll see new shades of color come alive and maybe some sparkling crystals, too. If you've found pieces that you can almost see through, it could mean you've discovered a good place to hunt. Remember, Indians liked to trade high grades of stone. The piece you discovered might be a clue that they traveled through your area.

Compare your small finds with those shown in Figures 8-4 through 8-8 and think about age as you notice shapes, sizes and chipping. The oldest flaked tools that are small usually will be unifacial. You'll learn about the tools in use at different times when we look into prehistory in the next chapter.

Pecking, Grinding and More

On diorite, granite, hematite, quartzite and other hard stone, look for other work. The illustration of the full groove axe in Chapter 3, Figure 3-7, is a good example of pecking and grinding because it clearly shows where you'll see the work on a chopping tool. Compare the characteristics with the pecked axe and the grinding edge of the rectangular celt in Figure 8-11, and look through your finds to see if any show the same features. Pecked stone will have tiny pits. Ground stone will have scuff marks going in one direction. In plowed fields, pieces are much more common than large, whole artifacts. If you've hunted a field, check your stone fragments for a groove. This feature could identify it as part of an axe.

For whole axes, compare the kind of groove. Half groove types are usually found in Illinois, Iowa and Missouri, America's "axe heartland." A three-quarter groove is the most common, but a full groove is the most widespread. Full groove axes have been found in every state and into Canada and Mexico. If you've discovered a full groove axe, you've seen the oldest kind of grooved axe known in Native American prehistory.

Perhaps you've found a stone tool that looks like it may have been ideal for chiseling or chopping wood. If the tool has an end tapering into a blade edge but the body doesn't have a groove, your find could be an **adze**. Most adzes resemble celts more than anything else, so take a look at Figure 8-11 once again. Notice that both celts are smaller and thinner than the axe, and neither of the two are grooved. Not only are these same features also seen in adzes, but sizes compare with the majority of celts, too. Adzes can be under two inches or more than eight inches long, and many are in the average range of celts at five to six. Since people reworked these tools from one type to the other, how can you tell them apart? To distinguish an adze from a celt, look for a flat surface or face. If your artifact has one that runs lengthwise, it's an adze rather than a celt.

Figure 8-2. Modification of stone is plain to see on these artifacts. Included with the projectile points are triangular war points, knives and a reworked drill (bottom row, right). The obsidian point (bottom row, center) was probably a result of trade since it was found in Illinois.

Figure 8-3. There's no such thing as a typical prehistoric knife. An angular shape, chipping over all surfaces, a sturdy base, and irregularities in notching, edges and shoulders are some of the features that identify knives. Once they're hafted, the asymmetry seems to diminish.

Figure 8-4. Scrapers, scrapers and more scrapers. You can't help but love 'em! You'll likely find more of these than any other type of artifact. To discover scrapers that others have missed, examine odd shapes for flaking.

Figure 8-5. Notice the rock "handles" on most of these thumb scrapers. The round thumbnail scraper with sloped sides can also be correctly identified as a miniature steep-edge scraper (bottom row, right). All of these handy little tools are unifacial because one side is not worked. You'll see how the reverse sides are labeled in Chapter 10.

Figure 8-6. Tips on gravers are sharper than scraping tools that draw to a point and spokeshaves have small cutouts. The artifacts pictured here are unifacial tools.

Figure 8-7. You've got yourself a puzzling artifact when you can't figure out exactly what it is. A combination of flaked blade edges, sharp projections and cutouts can make for a mighty strange tool. Since rework, breaks and unfinished work complicate matters even more, refer to finds like these as multipurpose tools.

Figure 8-8. Ouch! Watch out for naturally sharp cutting edges on flake tools. These objects were great time savers. Further work was not necessary when a flake could slice or scrape as is.

Figure 8-9. Crude artifacts or nature's handiwork? Some of these "keepers" resemble artifacts pictured elsewhere in this section. If nature did the shaping, were the stones used as tools? It's a tough call when pressure flaking is absent or indistinct.

Figure 8-10. Compare rocks that have similar shapes to decide if you've found a rough form of a tool. Both of these chunks of flint were found on the same field, but only one has been shaped by percussion. The preform (right) was not refined into a chipped adze or gouge because there are small crystals in the material. Since these particles weaken stone, the tool would have been likely to break during use. Actual sizes.

Figure 8-11. The two pecked and ground celts survived woodcutting without breaking, but damage on the full groove axe is from use. Those chips at the blade edge couldn't have come from a plow, because the patina is the same on all surfaces. Why is the flaked tool that resembles a scraper photographed with these chopping tools? It's a woodcutting handaxe with a thumb groove (reverse side) for a different type of grip and worn edges from chopping, not scraping.

Figure 8-12. Inspect the centers of flat cobbles for signs of battering from a stone tool. If you think a smooth stone has been pecked, draw your finger over its surfaces to feel differences in texture. If there's more pitting on the other side, you might have a chipping stone. The hammerstones (bottom row) are nicked on the ends and there's damage in the center of both sides. People probably used these pounding tools as chipping stones, too.

Figure 8-13. We found these pebbles in three counties over a period of five months. The flattened, scuffed areas are most likely from smoothing or shaping pottery. Keep an eye out for small polishing stones as you walk for arrowheads and you might also discover a prehistoric sherd.

The bigger the artifact, the easier it is to see. In the past, large numbers of sizable artifacts, such as axes, hoes and mortars, were found by farmers, ranchers, railroad workers and surface hunters. Though they're still being recovered from highway projects and construction sites, for every complete axe, there are at least a hundred points and knives that are whole. In some parts of the country the ratio is even greater, especially on the West Coast. No matter where you live, you should not be too disappointed if you haven't found a large, whole artifact. The fun of surface hunting is not just in discovery. It's in the anticipation of what you might find and the learning process you experience as questions lead to answers.

You may have had better luck discovering a small, whole artifact that has grinding scars from use. Do you have any stones about one inch wide and under two inches long? Are there any flattened surfaces? You might have found a **polishing stone**. It's easy to think of polishing stones as miniature grinding stones because they have one-way grinding scars on one or more flat surfaces. Archaeologists believe they were used by folks who made pottery. Pebbles were probably rubbed against clay surfaces to smooth or shape it into vessels, and were ground down in the process. You'll see grinding scratches or a polish on these stones, but you'll have a hard time finding a photo of the artifacts in books. Until the use of polishing stones is established, they'll remain items of speculation.

During the time this book was being written, we discovered three polishing stones on several plowed fields. Study the finds in Figure 8-13 and notice that size seems more important than shape. If pebbles like these were used to shape pottery, it would make sense to look for sherds. Wherever you see prehistoric sherds, hunt for small stones. When you find a polishing stone but you don't see any sherds, the pottery may have long since decayed. With a polishing stone as evidence, you can still speculate that the people made pottery at the site.

REMEMBER TO EXAMINE YOUR FINDS FOR HOLES, HOLLOWS, LINES AND NARROW GROOVES.

Have you found an interesting piece of agate, limestone, sandstone or slate? Maybe you discovered a smooth stone with a defined shape, a rough stone with shallow furrows, or a rock with two level sides. Examine your finds for other features, such as pitted cavities, narrow grooves, bored holes and thin, etched lines. Do you have any flint or chert with dark pink, orange-yellow or rose-red swirls? Or a piece of sandstone with blackened or reddened areas? Check your materials for heat-treating and fire-cracking. Consider the color, texture and any cracks or small craters that prolonged heat could have caused. Compare finds that have similar shapes and sizes. Are there two pieces of flaked stone that resemble each other? Contrast the chipping. If one has precise percussion or pressure flaking, the other may be a preform of the same type of tool.

ARTIFACTS AND FEATURES

Having examined your finds in detail, you've made critical observations about shapes, sizes, special features and materials. While you'll be anxious to come to a conclusion about your most curious find, remember that identification isn't always made quickly. To be more proficient at identifying worked stone on the field or during your examination at home, you'll need to become familiar with a few more artifacts. We'll identify several that usually show distinctive features, but they may belong to more than one classification. A drilled ornament, a polished ceremonial stone and an artifact known as an **atlatl weight** are sometimes easier to spot than to classify. Though they're not nearly as common as scrapers or points, you'll often see them pictured in books and displayed at museums. If you've been fortunate enough to find a stone that's clearly and beautifully worked, you'll certainly want to know what kind of artifact it could be.

While you've hunted for the triangle shapes of projectile points, you may also have found stones and shells with holes. A stone, bone or shell with a hole near one end may be a prehistoric **pendant**. Usually between one and five inches long, most pendants have a drilled hole for threading a cord. The most common style is a bored hole in the center of one end, but it's possible to find one that has more. For secure fastening, Indians sometimes drilled pendants twice and slipped a strap through horizontal or vertical holes. They notched or grooved others, but since tied cords could stretch and slip, these types were prone to damage or loss.

A drilled hole is the main feature that could identify a pendant, but you should also consider the shape of your find. Indians often made flat, thin pendants which laid lightly and comfortably against the chest. Frequently in triangular, rectangular and teardrop shapes, they also made bell, keyhole, anchor and shovel designs. Occasionally, people wore small effigies, but these are even harder to discover than plain types. If you've found a flat pendant, you may be able to identify the outward surface by the presence of etched decorations. Though some could have entire surfaces that are incised with narrow lines, tally marks on edges are more common.

PENDANTS WERE MADE FROM SOFT, HARD AND SEMIPRECIOUS STONE, BONE, TEETH, SHELL, PRECIOUS METALS AND POTTERY SHERDS.

A drilled hole may also be an identifying feature of an atlatl weight. Pecked, ground, polished and pretty, small atlatl weights were fastened to throwing sticks, which were often used to fling spears. To understand why folks attached stone weights to sticks, you'll first need to know how they used the wooden tools.

If you used a slingshot to fling a stone, it would land much farther away than just using your arm. When people threw spears with throwing sticks, the effect was even greater. To boost the throwing distance, force and speed of spears, people placed them on **atlatls**. Atlatls, about sixteen to twenty-four inches long, are flat sticks that have a hook at one end. Indians

137

would rest a spear along the length, wedge the butt end of the spear against the hook, and use the stick to fling the weapon. A recent experiment by experts concluded that a spear thrown with an atlatl can have more than ten times the force of impact and triple the velocity of a spear thrown by hand. A professor of anthropology at the State University of New York at Brockport estimated that it may have as much of an impact as a bullet fired from a .357-caliber Magnum! Field studies on the use of atlatls support the fact that prehistoric people killed animals as large as elephants, and also suggest they were probably able to do it more easily than previously thought.

Indians attached stone to atlatls because the additional weight helped increase their leverage of the sticks. Drilled, grooved or notched, atlatl weights were much more highly prized than net weights. Less likely to be lost during hunting than crude weights

YOU MAY HAVE FOUND AN ATLATL WEIGHT WHILE YOU HUNTED FOR SPEAR POINTS AND SCRAPERS.

which went into water, atlatl weights were made in distinctive shapes and styles. If you've searched for smooth stone in well-defined shapes, you may have found one that would classify as a weight. The shapes are so distinct and the texture is so sleek, you wouldn't mistake a weight for non-cultural rock if you saw one while hunting.

Atlatl weights were usually made into **effigies** of birds or lizards, or ground into designs resembling boats or ornaments. Since the individual shapes are similar in different parts of the country, the artifacts must have had a common, but special significance. While a likeness of a snake might have symbolized the capture and swallowing of prey, birds could have represented spears in swift flight. An effigy of a bird, reptile or animal secured to an atlatl may have been a type of hunting charm.

You would have recognized an effigy of a bird if you discovered one, but you could have trouble determining the function. Though it's not uncommon to be puzzled by effigies, a sitting bird at rest would be a **birdstone**. Most birdstones won't have wings or legs, but they'll usually have a raised head, a beak, lower body and raised tail. By modifying these features, Indians made birdstones in different styles. Whether chunky, long and slender, or crude, you will not mistake the design. Occasionally, you'll see one with mouth lines and chances are you won't miss the eyes. Eyes were evidently important, because the detailing is very apparent. Since size and craftsmanship vary, a birdstone could be an atlatl weight or ceremonial stone.

BIRDSTONES, BOATSTONES, BANNERSTONES AND GORGETS COULD BE ATLATL WEIGHTS OR CEREMONIAL ORNAMENTS.

While you may not have found an effigy, you might have discovered a weight in an ornamental design. If you have a stone that reminds you of a boat, it could be a **boatstone.** Boatstones are named after watercraft because they look like smooth boats, only turned upside-down. Whether smaller atlatl weights or larger ceremonial stones, these artifacts could have pointed, curved or squared ends and bottoms that are either flat, scooped or hollowed.

Bannerstones were used with atlatls, too, and may also have been tokens of rank. Smooth and sleek, bannerstones might be in the shape of a butterfly, an hourglass, a crescent, bow tie, or a pick. Although there are rectangular, triangular, round, tubular and ridged varieties, the shapes are so unique, they'd be pretty hard to miss.

If you've found a flat, thin and polished stone with two evenly spaced holes, your find would be a **gorget**. Gorgets are drilled rectangular panels with squared, rounded or pointed ends. People occasionally decorated the edges with tally marks or etched lines into one surface. Some are made from bone or shell, but most were pecked and ground from slate. Have you found one in the eastern part of the U.S.? There's a good chance the material is soapstone.

Gorgets were attached to atlatls, used in rituals or worn as ornaments. Indians reworked broken gorgets into pendants, so examine an artifact with a drilled hole carefully to identify the original function correctly.

Suppose you've been surface hunting often, but still haven't found an atlatl weight. Don't give up on this type of artifact because it's always possible to discover one in the future. Remember to look for identifying features that Indians made for fastening. On elongated birdstones, check for drilled holes beneath the body at each end of a rectangular base. Round, short pop-eyed birdstones might have bored holes in the center. Lizard-shaped stones were almost never drilled, but they could have narrow grooves on three sides of a level base. Boatstones some-times have a central groove or are drilled near the ends. Bannerstones might be bored with a central hole or notched on opposite edges.

The function of some artifacts in the atlatl weights category is unclear. Not only that, the use of the weights has not been proved. Some atlatl weights are well over four inches in length. Were these attached to throwing sticks or were they used solely for rituals? Some weights were never drilled or grooved at all. Why not? On what part of atlatls were weights fastened? No one knows. Until someone finds a weight secured to a prehistoric object, questions about size, features and the relationship to function remain to be answered.

Spuds and **spatulates** are much larger ceremonial arti-facts that look somewhat alike. About eight to ten inches long and carefully shaped, both have narrow shafts and bases that flare. Because of their size, whole spuds and spatulates are very difficult to find.

While some well-made spuds were used as chopping tools or occasionally as weapons, highly crafted ceremonial types show no sign of wear. Spuds are usually made of light-colored flint or chert, perhaps because light shades enhanced the appearance.

Slender tools that often have a sharp, flared blade, spuds are also called flared celts.

Heavily ground and polished spatulates may have been used as spades to turn over the first earth at special sites. These artifacts, named for their spatula shape, have a short, expanded blade that's almost always flat and broad. Imagine the broad end of a spatulate with a drilled center hole. Small, short spatulates may have been worn as shovel-shaped pendants.

SPUDS WITH A FLARED BLADE ARE ALSO KNOWN AS FLARED CELTS.

PHOTOS AND ILLUSTRATIONS

A simple way to identify a surface find is to compare it with an artifact of the same type. This is easy when your find is whole or only slightly damaged. Compare your finds with photos or illustrations in books, artifact magazines, antiquity newspapers and archaeological society publications. Some of the journals, bulletins and even newsletters put out by societies have fabulous photographs of artifacts. We'll look at other ways that archaeological societies can help increase your identification skills later in this chapter.

Several sections in the *Resources* provide information that will be helpful for identification. *Additional Reading* is a source of books for reference. The titles can be found in children and adult sections of libraries, or at bookstores. Identification guides have page after page of good photographs that show distinct flaking, pecking or grinding. These books are excellent for studying features and learning where other artifacts have been found. Pictorials about archaeology, prehistoric cultures or American Indian traditions have quality drawings, as well as photos, you can study.

When using books to identify your finds, keep in mind that people do not agree about the subject of amateur archaeology. You may encounter some discouraging words about the hobby of surface hunting as you learn about knives and scrapers. The archaeological information, however, is often objective and precise, so consider purchasing a book or two and starting a library of your own. You'll enjoy the convenience of having reference material right at hand whenever you study your finds.

Read the captions that accompany photos because the written descriptions will often contain clues that can help. Does the text describe characteristics similar to your find, such as a unifacial surface? You won't know if artifacts have unifacial or bifacial surfaces by looking at photos that show only one side, so you'll need to read the descriptions. Is the artifact made of the same type of material? A black-and-white photo of a knife will not tell you that it's pink, heat-treated chert or mottled brown flint. Does the narrative give a specific name, such as Dalton, Thebes, Waubesa, or Cahokia? The name of the culture will help you estimate how old your find could be. Does it say where the artifact was found, such as a plowed field in a neighboring state? Traveling hunters might have lived in your vicinity, too. Was it discovered more recently, or decades ago? A new find may mean more could have surfaced in the area. Gathering information about other finds is helpful in identifying and discovering more about your own.

TO SEE MORE ARTIFACTS IN COLOR, CHECK OUT VIDEOS ON ARCHAEOLOGY, AMERICAN INDIANS OR MOUNDS.

Concentrate on shape and size when you compare projectile points and knives with photographs. Match the notches, stems, tangs and shoulders, and check for beveling, flutes and impact fractures. Try to identify the type of serrations you see, and look for a uniform pattern of chipping, such as **parallel flaking** or **oblique flaking**.

Compare fragments that have tips, barbs, notches, or ears to whole points in pictures, too. Artifacts with identifiable features such as these are good study pieces you should closely inspect. Careful examination of broken, flaked artifacts will increase your ability to identify worked stone when you hunt.

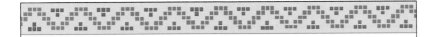

Points of Interest

Recycled Artifacts

Indians recycled long before it became popular in this day and age. Projectile points that chipped or broke were resharpened and used again. When bodies of reworked points became too narrow to function as weapon tips, they were flaked down even more into drills. Drills and perforators were made from damaged knives, and knives were made from points with ruined stems. Broken arrowheads were knapped into scrapers and if that's not enough to make your head spin, there's something else that will. Indians who found artifacts from previous times reworked those tools and weapons, too. So, if a strange and beautiful find you can't identify looks like a cross between two artifacts, remember that it could be the work of a flintknapper who recycled worked stone long ago.

Many people who search for arrowheads do not check for scrapers since they don't always have the obvious shape and detail of other tools. Though you'll find more scrapers than other types of artifacts, there are fewer photos of these than points, knives or axes. Use the photographs in the color insert to make comparisons with your finds.

MUSEUMS, CULTURAL EVENTS AND ARTIFACT SHOWS

Because good pictures are sometimes hard to find, you'll need to use other resources. To identify one of our strange rocks that didn't match photographs, we made a trip to a museum of natural history. We were thrilled to finally see an artifact that looked just like it. Our peculiar rock with hollows is the **nut stone** you saw in Chapter 5. When you can't find a suitable picture, visit a museum and examine the artifact displays. Large museums will have lots of prehistoric artifacts, and many local museums show discoveries from the vicinity. Most museums are good resources because you'll see artifacts in three dimensions and full color.

TO LEARN ABOUT REGIONAL ARTIFACTS AND PREHISTORY, ATTEND A PRESENTATION GIVEN BY AN ARCHAEOLOGIST AT A LOCAL MUSEUM, SCHOOL OR LIBRARY.

Museums with artifact exhibits may also have a reference room where you'll find more books about Indians. Check it out to see the photos available there. Get a schedule of events, since special programs that museums offer are both informative and fun. Go to a slide show about prehistoric people, a demonstration on flintknapping, or a workshop on Indian crafts. Whether you listen to a lecture on trade routes or attend a Native American pottery class, you will learn more about artifacts by looking at the lifeways of the past.

To see artifacts that were found in your area, find out if a private museum is near. Owners of private museums are usually collectors who invite the public to visit in small groups. A scheduled tour is interesting because you'll learn the stories behind many of the artifacts on display. Since the finds will be local, there's a better chance of identifying one of your own. If you see a new type of artifact, take note of the shape, size and material. Try to find one like it the next time you go hunting.

If an American Indian museum is not far, don't miss it. Take your family along to see complete displays of the evolution of Indian culture. Stop by the gift shop for artifact reproductions and crafts made by Native Americans. Sign up for a program and investigate the construction of a wigwam, or find out about Indian lore, legends or music. In *Places to Go and Things to See*, you'll find a listing by state of museums, parks, historic sites and other public places you can visit and enjoy.

There are other good resources available, whether you live near a museum or not. When powwows, traveling exhibits or Native American festivities are scheduled for your area, mark your calendar and plan to attend. You'll have fun learning about Indian art, dance, food and traditions when you participate in these colorful, cultural events. To get information in advance of activities, use the *Subscriptions* section. The publications listed will keep you informed of upcoming events, artifact shows, recent finds, new books and much more.

Be sure to go to an artifact show because you'll see many types of finds on exhibition. Amateur archaeological societies usually sponsor the shows so members can display collections, exchange information, and make sales. You'll have the chance to appreciate historic artifacts, such as calvary swords, relic guns and boot spurs. It's not uncommon for antique marbles, buttons, coins, meteorites, or fossils to be shown, too. Look through interesting back issues of society journals, artifact magazines and books. Publications are sold at a bargain price and you may want to purchase one or two. Do you have a very strange find? Bring it to a show and ask an exhibitor to help you identify it. Talk to members to learn the goals of the society and consider joining one yourself. To get started connecting with other people who have an active interest in archaeology, check *Archaeological Societies and Other Memberships*. You may find just the right one for you.

> **MEMBERSHIP IN AN ARCHAEOLOGICAL SOCIETY WILL CONNECT YOU WITH PEOPLE AT ALL LEVELS OF EXPERIENCE.**

EXCHANGE INFORMATION

A good way to learn about artifacts is to exchange information with others. Surface hunters you know will probably have finds that are similar to yours. Get together with them, compare features, and see if any match. Some amateur archaeologists will also be experienced flintknappers. Show flaked stone to skilled people who knap flint, chert and obsidian. Take a find that has you stumped to an archaeologist or a professor of anthropology. Unless your discovery is the first of a new class of artifacts, experts should be able to identify it or provide you with information.

Do you know of any teachers in local school districts who have gone on an archaeological dig? Organizations that conduct historic preservation projects sometimes invite elementary and high school instructors to participate in excavations. Teachers may also volunteer to help historic preservation specialists measure, photograph or sketch artifacts and sites. Good candidates for acceptance to archaeological teams, educators can take back what they learn to classrooms, students and local residents. Contact the faculty or history departments at schools and set up an appointment to show teachers your finds.

QUESTIONABLE FINDS

What should you do with the finds you just aren't sure about? If a find has borderline features that could make it an artifact, it's a good idea to hang onto it for a while. Remember that identification is a process. It isn't always made on the first try. Within several weeks, you might see a photo of an artifact that closely resembles your rock. In a few short months, you may determine that your find is a preform. Or, during the next season, you could discover another stone that looks like a pretty good match. Compare the two then and you may decide that one, both or neither are worked. Over time, your sources of information will grow as you network with other people. In the process of exchanging information, someone will identify it one way or the other. When you keep questionable finds, you can always examine them again as you gain more experience.

If you feel as though you've discovered a lot of nothing, remember that an unidentified find might be an artifact. Handle questionable finds as carefully as you do worked stone, save your notes or maps, and place them in temporary storage. Until you decide just exactly what you've found, you might like to call mystery finds "keepers." To get to know the types of stone finds you should think about saving, re-examine the features of a few of ours in Figure 8-9.

PUZZLING ARTIFACTS

When there's enough work on a find to identify it as an arti-fact, but you don't know *which* artifact it is, you're not alone. Small tools are hard to figure, identification isn't easy for reworked tools and weapons, and it gets more complicated when tools turned out differently than originally intended. An archae-ologist might call a flake tool with a sharp, worked tip a "graver/flake tool," or describe a stone with a single flaked edge as a "unifacial side scraper." Do as professionals do, and call a puzzling artifact by a name that would best describe the main feature and function. If you've found an artifact with two or more characteristics that could have been used for different purposes, it's correct to identify it as a multipurpose tool. Try to spot the features of bifacial scrapers and unifacial artifacts on the multi-purpose tools shown in Figure 8-7, and look for the same types of characteristics on your flaked finds.

Since some artifacts are so similar and because others mix features, it's easy to get them confused. To connect the features with the right artifacts, use the *Artifacts and Features* section. The information there will help you identify worked stone during your inspection at home. As you become familiar with individual characteristics, you'll also make better decisions about artifacts while you hunt.

PROBLEM ARTIFACTS

A problem artifact is the most difficult of all to identify. Your find will be a problem if you see that it's clearly worked, but the features don't match it to a known function. Only by answering the *who, what, when, where* and *why* of an artifact can archaeologists make specific, accurate identifications. Sometimes, these questions have not been fully answered because studies have just begun. Other times, information is just not widely available. When archaeological information is limited, refer to your find as a problem artifact.

Problem artifacts raise unusual questions. Why would prehistoric people who lived in Mississippi break projectile points and then smooth the bodies and edges? Why did others grind small stones into shapes that defy identification, and take the time to polish them so highly? Problem artifacts are also hard to classify. A grouping into an archaeological category can't be made until a purpose is determined. Unless a function is proved by professional analysis, problem artifacts will remain in a class by themselves.

How will you know that you've discovered a problem artifact? You won't, at first—but you'll start to get a clue when you try to find a matching picture. If your discovery doesn't resemble other types of artifacts you've seen, try to locate photos of problematic finds. You should be able to find at least one or two in identification guidebooks. Check recent discoveries shown in artifact magazines, antiquity newspapers and archaeological society publications, and you may have slightly more luck.

Fired clay biscuits are interesting examples of a type of problem artifact. Surfacing in Kentucky, Missouri and Illinois, twenty-six nearly identical clay discs have been found by amateurs. Over a period of three months, Barbara and Lawrence Tully found a total of seventeen in western Kentucky, on an eroded bank of the Tennessee River. While the number of their finds is the most significant, Oscar Riley found one on a plowed field in Butler County, Missouri, that matched the group. The artifacts were strange because the size and shape were uniform and each had a ring that appeared to come from a mold. But based on what is known up to this point, prehistoric Indians did not use molds.

Mr. and Mrs. Tully suspected the biscuits were used in cooking, since a crusty black material adhered to some of the clay surfaces. To have the objects analyzed and get information published, they loaned their finds to the American Society for Amateur Archaeology (ASAA), placing them in the care of Dr. Michael Gramly. Intrigued, Dr. Gramly had the black material tested at a dental school lab, where x-ray capabilities of a scanning electronic microscope were available. Scanning electron microscopy, a routine procedure used for studies of ancient artifacts, showed the deposit to be vegetal food residue. The analysis confirmed suspicions that the function of the clay discs was domestic.

In 1995, Dr. Gramly published the results in an ASAA journal issue which featured artifacts from Illinois. His article included background information about scanning electron microscopy and a photograph of the seventeen discs, taken by Mr. Tully.

On March 17, 1996, a "keeper" was discovered on a sandbank of the Illinois River in Morris, Illinois. The find was a nicely rounded object with flattened sides and a raised ring that looked like it came from a mold. It couldn't be a variation of a discoidal because the material was much lighter than stone. It seemed silly to think it was an artifact at all since prehistoric people didn't use molds. The surface hunters were stymied and the property owners didn't know quite what to make of it. What do you do with a find that resembles a white charcoal briquette? Get the landowner's permission to save it as a "keeper" and try to find out what it could be.

Two months later, during work on this chapter, a startling coincidence occurred. As we studied photos in a 1995 issue of *The Amateur Archaeologist*, Jon recognized his strange round "keeper." We were delighted to know it was an artifact and intrigued that others so similar were discovered far away. Within the week we sent a letter with its description to the ASAA. Dr. Gramly responded, agreeing that the distance between the finds was remarkable. To learn more, we decided it would be best to ship the Illinois disc to New York for comparison and further study.

In our conversations with Dr. Gramly, we learned that in an effort to determine the age, some of the biscuits had been recently tested with thermoluminescence. How exciting! What were the results? Inconclusive, because there was gypsum in the clay. There are, however, other methods that determine how old an artifact can be. The next test, called tandem linear accelerator mass spectroscopy radiocarbon dating, is expected to successfully provide data for estimating the age. Since the formal report will not be available until after this book is published, you can learn the outcome from the ASAA, listed in the *Resources*.

The best news concerned the discovery of a small vessel that had been found long before any of the biscuits. Mr. Tully noticed a stone cup in his father-in-law's collection which had the inverted shape of the discs, and realized that it wasn't a cup at all—but a steatite mold! Steatite, which is rich in talc, is a high grade of soapstone. Soapstone is a soft rock that Indians used to make vessels for cooking and storing food, and pipes. The Kentucky and Missouri discs fit in the mold, but would Jon's? Use the photo in Figure 8-14 to make the same comparison that we did.

For complex archaeological studies to begin, it often takes a significant find to draw interest and attention. Because the seventeen discs were published, more information is becoming available. Already, an additional seven have been found. Karen Masterson discovered four on a soybean field in Alexander County, Illinois—just five weeks prior to the annual ASAA meeting in the same county. After showing them to Dr. Gramly, she and her daughter, Hope Rader, searched the field again and on August 7, 1996, Hope found three more along the edge.

Dr. Gramly believes a culture known as Poverty Point made the biscuits and molds, since the people were adept at making uniform weapons, tools and ornaments. Because they also settled in the Mississippi Valley region, you'd have better luck looking for the artifacts in places where the Poverty Point folks were known to have lived. If you reside in that region, search for hunting sites near the Tennessee, Illinois, or Mississippi Rivers. Are you near any tributaries, or close to the mouth of the Ohio? Check out those areas, too. Surface hunters in Arkansas, Illinois, Kentucky, Louisiana, Mississippi, Missouri and Tennessee probably have the greatest chance of discovery.

> YOUR DISCOVERY OF A FIRED CLAY BISCUIT WOULD BE IMPORTANT TO ONGOING ARCHAEOLOGICAL STUDIES.

Why was the disc Jon found so far away from the others? Did some of the Poverty Point people live miles to the north? Could people have been manufacturing clay biscuits for trade? Or was another culture, such as the Hopewell, making discs from molds in Illinois? Since the answers to these questions are unknown at this time, keep an eye out for clay discs and molds anywhere you hunt, even if you live outside of the Mississippi Valley region. A find in any other state would be of even greater interest.

To include fired clay biscuits in an existing archeological category or add a new class of artifacts, more information is needed. Since photos are limited, study Figure 8-14 carefully. If you discover a lightweight, round object with flattened sides and a ring around the outside edge, record it well. Photograph it exactly as you found it. Make or mark a map. Take great notes,

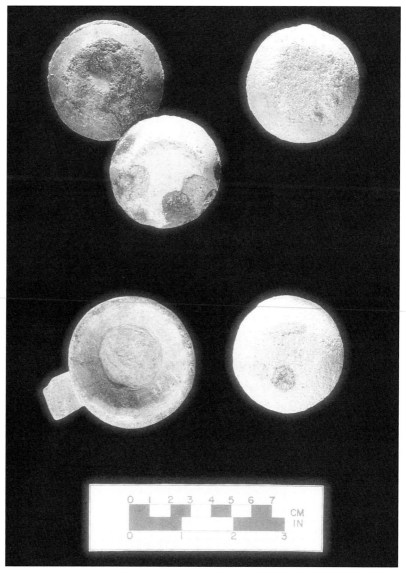

Figure 8-14. These problem artifacts are being studied by experts at the American Society for Amateur Archaeology. Barbara and Lawrence Tully found two fired clay biscuits (upper left) and fifteen others on a river bank in western Kentucky. Another (upper right) was discovered on a plowed field in Butler County, Missouri. Jon Kiesa found one more (lower right) in Grundy County, Illinois, on a sandbank of the Illinois River. To shape clay into nearly identical discs, people would have had to use some type of mold. The steatite mold (lower left) appears to fit the shape and size of the clay finds. If you discover a biscuit or mold while surface hunting, report it to professionals and contact the ASAA. Missouri disc from the Oscar Riley collection. Mold from the Curtis/Tully collection. Photo by R.M. Gramly.

do your report, and for this particular artifact, send a note to Dr. Gramly. The information you provide would be an asset to the ongoing study.

▼ ▼ ▼

You have the opportunity to learn about prehistory each time you arrowhead hunt. Whether you find a fragment of an artifact or a "keeper," keep in mind that your discovery can be significant. Consider the fate of the small disc that was found by the Illinois River. If it had been left on the sand, water would have carried it downstream. How many miles could a fast current carry a lightweight piece of clay? How much information would be altered by moving water? Would anyone find the disc and recognize it as an artifact, or would it just be seen and ignored? This artifact was not washed away by Mother Nature or forever lost to looters. It was identified by an arrowhead hunter who compared it with a photo. So, save those "keepers," compare your finds, and keep informed. Identification will always be a little easier when you plug into a network of others who are active in the study of archaeology.

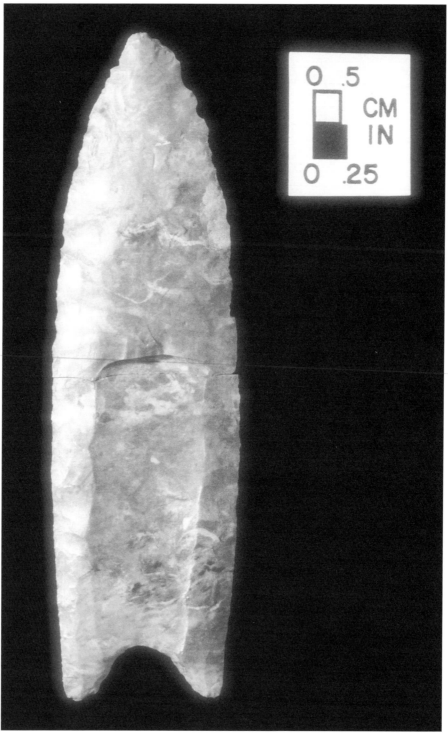

Figure 9-1. This classic, fluted Clovis point from the Lamb site in Genesee County, New York, is a magnificent specimen that would have tipped a Paleo-Indian spear. Photo by R.M. Gramly.

Prehistory Across America

Some of the artifacts pictured in this book are thousands of years apart in age. Whether stone was modified in 13,000 B.C. or at the time of Columbus—over fourteen thousand years later— flaked weapons for hunting game and tools for cleaning hide accomplished the same purposes. Because some of the same types of tools were in use throughout prehistory, you might think the lifestyle of the first Americans stayed the same, too. But during that long span of time there were gradual, distinct changes in the way Indians lived. These changes were often reflected in the kinds of tools and weapons they used, and how the objects were made.

To have a more accurate picture of prehistoric daily life and identify the tools of different times, it's helpful to know why changes took place and how the Indian culture was affected. You can also get a better idea of the approximate age of an artifact when you link it to a shorter period of history. In this chapter, we'll take you back to four prehistoric periods, and examine some of the tools and weapons in use during those times.

PREHISTORIC PERIODS

By piecing information together from artifacts and sites, archaeologists and anthropologists have divided the entire span of North American prehistory into smaller **prehistoric periods**. The Paleo-Indian, Archaic, Woodland and Mississippian periods correspond to specific prehistoric cultures. The period names are archaeological classifications that apply to both the people and the times. Folks who lived in Paleo-Indian and Archaic periods were game hunters, but Archaic people also gathered wild plants to eat. Woodland folks hunted and gathered, too, and are best known for the mounds they built. In Mississippian times, people also built mounds and most were farming the land.

In each of the periods, Indians made new tools to meet changing needs, improved existing versions, and became even more skilled in working stone. When you know some of the features of each prehistoric period, you'll narrow down the types of activities that could have occurred at the site of your find. You can also increase your chances of correctly identifying an artifact.

Archaeologists classify prehistoric periods according to *how* people lived rather than by specific dates or locations. Since the beginning and the end of one period can extend into another, they are best expressed as ranges of time. For example, while hunting and gathering was still the predominant lifestyle in one part of the country, farming was emerging in another. To be more specific, Paleo-Indians hunted game in the Rocky Mountain region while Archaic people gathered edible plants in Iowa. Woodland Indians built mounds in Illinois at the same time Mississippian farmers grew corn in Kentucky. Folks from one period lived at the same time as others did, but in a different way. Since prehistoric periods existed simultaneously and can overlap across the country, we have to begin and end them with approximate dates. Let's start our study with the Paleo-Indian period, the oldest in Native American prehistory.

PALEO-INDIAN PERIOD

Between 26,000 B.C. and 11,000 B. C., during the final stages of the last ice age, a bridge of land was exposed between Siberia and what is now Alaska. As glaciers surged and retreated to the south, game animals began to move out of the north to search for food in greener pastures. Through ice-free corridors along the Pacific Coast, they slowly migrated into Canada and the Central Plains—with Asian hunters following. In the Western Hemisphere, there is no evidence of an evolutionary process of ape-like creatures to modern man. The first folks who arrived in North America at about 13,000 B.C. were *Homo sapiens*, like ourselves. These immigrants had the same mental and physical capabilities we have, and are known as Paleo-Indian hunters.

THE HUNTERS

What was the geography like when the animals and first hunters arrived? The land had been devastated from enormous masses of earth and rock that were pushed to new places by glacial ice. Some of these masses dammed rivers and created lakes. Ponds, kettle lakes, marshes and swamps formed in potholes left by large blocks of ice. Paleo hunters were the first humans to see the deposits of sand and gravel—glacial drift—which raised valley floors and made elevated plateaus and high hills.

The **Paleo-Indian period** is the five-thousand-year span between 13,000 B.C. and 8000 B.C. To determine the age of an artifact with a **B.C.** date, just add two thousand years. For example, an artifact dated 5000 B.C. would be seven thousand years old. With a little math, it's easy to figure that Paleo artifacts can be anywhere from ten to fifteen thousand years old. This puts them near the end of the Stone Age.

The Paleo people were nomadic hunters who lived in small groups. They stayed in fertile places where game was plentiful, and moved on when the animals left to search for more food. Daily life for Paleo-Indians was not complicated, but it was also never easy. Survival during that time depended on the availability of game, their expertise in hunting it, and their success in protecting themselves.

There were at least a dozen types of large animals to hunt. Paleo-Indians got their meat, furs and antler from bear, caribou, deer, elk and moose. For approximately four thousand years, there were also three-ton woolly mammoths, giant beavers that

weighed three hundred pounds, camels, saber-toothed cats, giant bison, mastodons, lions, curved-snouted tapirs, dire wolves, massive short-faced bears and giant ground sloths. These animals became extinct at around 9000 B.C.—near the end of this period. Some believe Paleo hunters hastened the extinction, but since the animals may have died as a result of a change in climate, the actual reason is a matter of debate.

Figure 9-2. To protect themselves from lions, short-faced bears, wolves and other predators, Paleo-Indians hafted large, bifacial points to spear shafts and kept their weapons close at hand.

Paleo-Indian tools and weapons are slightly different from those made in other prehistoric periods because people brought their designs with them from distant parts of the world. The major raw materials were flint and chert. Like the points and knives from this period, many of the tools are large and sturdy, and were made from high-grade materials. Almost all Paleo artifacts were chipped into shape.

Indians used the same basic designs for scrapers in all prehistoric periods. Scrapers are thicker and rougher in appearance than well-made knives. Most Paleo scrapers will be different from others because they were often made from better materials. Since the largest game animals existed only in Paleo times, some of these scrapers are also larger. Large scrapers usually will be bifacial. A special feature that may identify smaller scrapers is a pointed graver spur. Indians flaked sharp tips on scraping tools to incise bone, antler or ivory. Many Paleo **end scrapers** have a small spur on one corner edge and others may even have two.

Paleo-Indians flaked many of their small tools on only one side and occasionally took a chip or two out along edges. If you discover a flaked tool, such as a scraper, graver, spokeshave or knife, made of flint or chert, check for a unifacial surface. An underside that has not been worked is also an earmark of Paleo times. You'll see it most often on small- to medium-sized thumb scrapers. Knives with flaking on only one side originated in this period and were also made later. You can distinguish the earliest knives by their larger size.

The convenience of tools was essential because hunters were frequently on the move. The best way to carry assorted small tools was to flake one stone into a portable combination. You may already have guessed that the most common Paleo tool is a multipurpose tool. This kind of tool was not only handy to transport from place to place, but the unique designs conserved valuable material. Look for two or more features that could have been used for different purposes. A multipurpose tool with a scraper edge might have a large perforator spike for piercing, a graver spur for etching, a spokeshave cutout for cleaning sticks, or a sharp blade edge of a knife.

THE MAJORITY OF PALEO TOOLS AND WEAPONS WERE MADE FROM FLINT AND CHERT, AND ALMOST ALL ARTIFACTS WERE FLAKED.

Paleo-Indians also made **drills**, but only in small numbers. Stone drills made in any prehistoric period will have shafts with either three or four flaked sides. Whether the shaft is triangular or squared, some bases resemble the kinds you see on projectile points and knives. Drills that are long and finely crafted may have been used as hairpins or clothing toggles. Since drills are thin, it's very hard to find a whole one on plowed fields where dirt has been churned again and again. Examine slim pieces of flint and chert for fine flaking and you may discover that it's the shaft of a drill.

To kill game, Indians flaked stone into large points and hafted them to spears. For slitting the carcasses, they used knives. Paleo points and knives resemble those from other periods because they have percussion flaking over the bodies of both sides. How will you know that a point or knife is over ten thousand years old? Since the designs of weapons and tools were brought to this country from far away, you'll see slight differences in features that were never precisely duplicated in the prehistoric periods that followed.

The discovery of a point or knife with a flute will identify a Paleo-Indian site. A fluted point has a distinct vertical flake on one or both sides that begins at the base of the body. The pencil drawing in Figure 9-2 shows how a flute thins a point at the place of attachment, "locking" the stone in the spear shaft. The design was beneficial because it also helped keep sinew, gut or other lashings from thickening spear shafts at hafting areas.

THE FIRST FOLSOM SITE WAS FOUND BY AN AFRICAN AMERICAN COWBOY ABOUT SEVENTY YEARS AGO IN NEW MEXICO.

The two major types of fluted points are **Clovis** and **Folsom**. As you saw in the photo that begins this chapter, slender Clovis points have a concave base, and ears instead of notches or stems. Large points—as long as nine or ten inches—were used to slay the biggest game, and eared bases helped keep weapons in place after striking. The first recorded find of a point of this type was named for the site near Clovis, Mexico. Because of the movement of hunters tracking animals, Clovis points can be found in most parts of the country. Take into account, however, that newer buried artifacts are closer to the surface. The oldest relics can be as much as several feet or more further down. Since it takes a lot of erosion to expose a fluted point, your discovery of a Clovis would be very special.

Folsom points bear a strong resemblance to Clovis, but they usually will be smaller and may have slightly longer flutes. To identify a Folsom point, look for a flute on one or both sides. Some extend to the middle of the body, as shown in Figure 9-3. Longer flutes can end further up, closer to the lowest part of the tip.

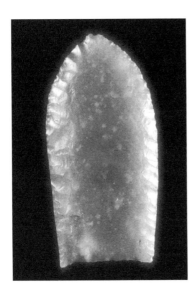

Figure 9-3. Indians liked to use better raw materials for their projectile points. This Folsom point, found in Colorado, is made from agate. About one and three-quarters inches long, it's smaller than most Clovis points. Photo by R.M. Gramly.

Lanceolates were also made in the Paleo period, but these lance-like types won't have flutes. Lanceolates are long and thin, and taper to a fine tip. Sometimes, Paleo-Indians flaked rectangular bases, stems or shoulders on their lanceolate points and knives.

Check the flaking style, too, because occasionally you'll see one with a parallel or oblique pattern. Consider the size as well, since points will be smaller than knives.

Don't be dismayed if you can't find a whole Clovis, Folsom or lanceolate artifact. Slender weapons and tools are always more susceptible to damage. Since fluted points are narrow, fluted knives are rare, and lanceolates are delicate, it's hard to find any that have not been broken or chipped.

ARCHAIC PERIOD

New types of artifacts dated between about 8000 B.C. and 1000 B.C. show that a change in lifestyle had occurred. People continued to hunt game in the **Archaic period**, but they also searched for plant food in forests, on prairies, and along lakes, marshes and rivers. For the first time in prehistory, people began to live in small villages. Several houses closely grouped in a sheltered valley or a few families banded together provided protection for all. By this time, dogs were domesticated, but they were not just Archaic pets. They also

THE HUNTERS AND GATHERERS

tracked and killed game, guarded the camps, and helped keep villages clean.

Archaeologists believe the extinction of the largest game may have started the process for a new way of life. Although Indians still hunted large animals, such as bear and deer, these hunter-gatherers stayed in one place longer, where other natural resources were plentiful. People captured birds, and caught fish, frogs and turtles with weighted nets. They collected mussels, berries, nuts, seeds and roots, and scooped minnows out of water in woven baskets. With cup stones to start their fires—or nut stones to process nuts—people enjoyed a wider variety of food, and prepared it with innovative new seasonings.

ARCHAEOLOGISTS HAVE SUBDIVIDED THE LONG SPAN OF THE ARCHAIC INTO EARLY, MIDDLE AND LATE TIMES.

Sometime early in the Archaic, pecked and ground tools came into widespread use. Granite, quartzite, hematite, glacial slate and other hard stone were available, but these materials couldn't be flaked. Indians made new kinds of tools by battering and grinding them into shape. This method of working stone had never before been used on a large scale in North America.

Stone-working technology took yet another leap forward in the variety of points and knives produced. Paleo-Indians made specialized weapons to meet their needs and Archaic people used hundreds of additional types. Since flintknapping in this period went on for seven thousand years, there's a greater chance that a point or knife you find will be from this time regardless of its size. Large spear points were resharpened, and damaged knife blades were repaired by beveling the edges. Repeated rework reduced lengths and widths, and eventually resulted in sharply sloped, beveled points that can be about the size of arrowheads. Wide, sturdy bases, thick bodies and steep, beveled edges are good clues that your find was originally much longer, and is older than you might have first thought.

In addition to the number of tools and weapons made in the Archaic, this period also has the largest number of artifact classes. To understand why different types of stone tools were important then, let's take a new look at a few you know.

You may have identified a net weight as you examined your finds at home. During this period and at later times, hunters and gatherers used stone in nets to catch fish and snare birds. To make nets heavier, they attached small net weights. Folks didn't fuss too much with these objects. They simply bored a hole through the middle of a pebble or small core, or flaked rough notches on two opposite sides. Once the nets were weighted, they were thrown to catch fish, fowl and frogs.

Most of the pecked and ground tools you are familiar with are hard evidence of the new lifeways. Archaic Indians battered stone into shapes that were necessary to prepare food. The berries, seeds and other vegetal provisions they collected were processed with pestles, manos and mortars. These artifacts came into existence along with the change in diet.

Paleo hunters traveled with their spears, but they didn't have much use for heavy, cumbersome axes. They weren't staying in one place long enough to build permanent homes and didn't need the extra baggage of celts or adzes. Because the use of axes became common after the extinction of big game, pecking and grinding techniques may have been developed to meet Archaic woodworking needs.

During these times, chopping tools were needed to clear spaces in forests for living areas, cut trees for shelter, and split wood for campfires. Wood carving and chiseling jobs required other types of sharp stone tools. To work wood, Indians used grooved axes, small pocket axes and assorted other types, celts, adzes, chisels and gouges. With these, they made house posts, dugout canoes, paddles, atlatls, handles, tool holders, mortars, bowls, birch bark baskets and probably much more. From the large number of stone axes and woodworking tools that remain, wood must have been a very important resource during Archaic and later times. Unfortunately, little is known about the wooden artifacts people crafted because the material decayed long ago.

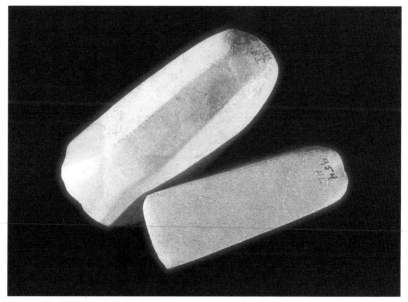

Figure 9-4. These beveled adzes were made by the Lamoka culture late in the Archaic period. One is just over four inches, the other is nearly five and both are from the state of New York. Notice the slight difference in the width of the flat surfaces. Iron Horse collection. Photo by R.M. Gramly.

Indians began making adzes early in the Archaic, at about 6500 B.C. Though the tools were well developed from the start, you may be able to distinguish Archaic adzes from those made later by taking into account several features. On one end of large adzes, look for hafting areas such as notches, grooves or knobs. Depending on the culture and the tool style, you'll see features like these on bigger adzes from Archaic times. Smaller Woodland adzes were rarely made with low grades of hard stone and usually show more polish. In the Mississippian period, stone adzes were made in small numbers. Full-size adzes from that time are long, well made and scarce.

Archaic and Woodland adzes are most common in the Northeast, Northwest and along rivers in forests where people made their watercraft. Design may vary from place to place, but the pair in Figure 9-4 shows what sort of shapes to look for. Notice that the smaller adze sharply resembles the rectangular celt shown in Chapter 8, Figure 8-11.

PRESSURE FLAKING BECAME WIDESPREAD DURING THE ARCHAIC.

Spear points from this period were notched and stemmed, and sometimes barbed to secure them in hides. Indians serrated or pressure-flaked the edges of points and knives, beveling them when necessary. Look for the work of light grinding also, at stems, bases and sides. Do you remember that when points were damaged, Indians chipped them into drills? In this period, drills with notches, square or round bases and more types were also made from scratch. Use the chart for points and knives in Chapter 3, Figure 3-3, to identify the features of drills you find.

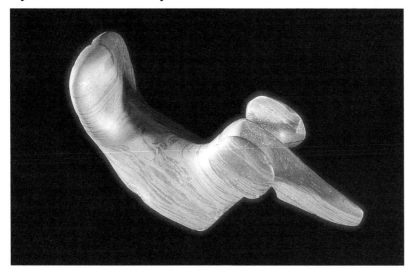

Figure 9-5. You can't miss the pop-eyes and raised tail on this exquisite birdstone. With a length of nearly six inches, it may not have been used as an atlatl weight. It was found in Jackson, Michigan, and is made from banded slate. Iron Horse collection. Photo by R.M. Gramly.

Effigies made in the mid-Archaic period were not as developed as those made in later times. By the end of this period, stone-working had improved and distinct forms of birdstones were being made. The pop-eyed birdstone in Figure 9-5 is so smooth and finely crafted, it almost looks as though it was carved from wood. It has the classic raised head, beak, lower body, and raised tail, which happens to be flared.

People didn't peck, grind and polish atlatl weights before the Archaic period, but they did make them well into Woodland times. For birdstones, boatstones and bannerstones, both Archaic and Woodland Indians preferred to use glacial slate, or if available, rose quartzite.

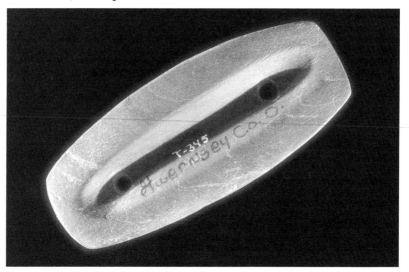

Figure 9-6. This boatstone is also made from banded slate, but it was found in Guernsey County, Ohio. The length is almost four inches. Iron Horse collection. Photo by R.M. Gramly.

You may think of dull colors when you think of slate, but grey, black, brown or blue artifacts of glacial slate are quite attractive. The banded slate artifacts in Figures 9-5 through 9-7 are various shades of blue, gray and brown. People liked to use banded slate since the colored patterns enhanced the lustrous beauty of the finished products.

Wouldn't it be wonderful to discover a polished artifact like a boatstone or a bannerstone? Notice that the two pictured were found in Ohio or Indiana. You'll have a better chance of discovering relics like these if you live in the North Central states.

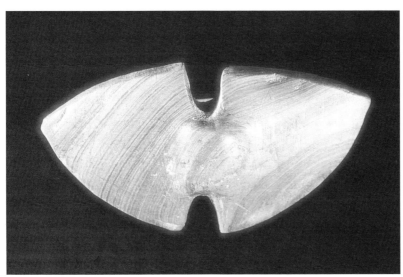

Figure 9-7. Indians liked to use banded slate for ornaments, as well as for functional tools. Double-notched and just over four inches wide, this elliptical winged bannerstone could be one or the other. Attributed to Ohio/Indiana. Iron Horse collection. Photo by R.M. Gramly.

WOODLAND PERIOD

The development of other artifacts and earthworks in the **Woodland period** reflects further changes in the Indian culture. Woodland people are known for their pottery, pipes and a settled lifestyle that included ceremonial burials and some agriculture. Still hunting and gathering, people made full use of natural resources and stayed in one place, tending beans, squash, tobacco or other small crops. From about 1000 B.C. to **A.D.** 800, larger groups lived in permanent villages. Some of these grew to be the size of small towns.

THE MOUND BUILDERS

Pottery is an important Woodland hallmark. With pottery, food could be cooked in new ways with very little waste. People boiled meat scraps, small fish and vegetables, and enjoyed stews, soups and broths. They kept food in clay pots for protection against pests and spoilage, and stored extra supplies for lean times in winter. Indians also used pottery to transport water,

167

keeping it on hand at dwellings. Pottery is significant because it influenced the supply of available food and water, and improved the way people lived.

Woodland people were not only potters. Because they constructed earthworks, archaeologists refer to the Indians of this time as Mound Builders. The first Mound Builders were the **Adena**, a people who lived in small villages throughout the Ohio Valley between 500 B.C. and A.D. 200. These folks built sturdy, circular homes with wooden posts, lashings of plant material and matting or thatch for roofs. They hunted deer, elk and raccoon, and ate snails, mussels, chestnuts, walnuts and raspberries. The Adena honored their deceased by building mounds and placing an abundance of artifacts in the graves. They built low mounds over burial pits and conical mounds that were not always erected at grave sites. Earthen effigies of birds, tortoises and humans, and some conical mounds may have been locations for rituals.

THE ADENA MADE SUPERIOR CELTS AND ADZES, AND USED ATLATLS.

The Adena layered larger numbers of their dead in gigantic funeral mounds. To erect these enormous structures, leadership, social organization and many workers were needed. One of their most impressive earthworks is the Great Serpent Mound in Ohio. Shaped like a snake, this mound is twenty feet wide, five feet high, and covers more than one-quarter mile. Why another conical burial mound is only four hundred feet away is a question archaeologists have yet to answer.

The **Hopewell** also lived in the Ohio Valley, but from about 100 B.C. to A.D. 350. Settling in Adena territory, they dominated the Midwest for almost five hundred years. Hopewell Indians were Mound Builders who are known for their fine craftsmanship. They made decorated pottery and ornamental clay pipes, and carved exquisite figures from bone and wood. The best metalworkers of their time, they made tools and many ornaments from copper and mica, and sometimes silver or gold. Copper nuggets were made into knives and axes, or alternately heated over a hot fire and hammered into thin sheets. Using flint tools, coppersmiths cut the sheets into rings, ear spools, headdresses and breastplates. Mica was easily worked and worn as shiny jewelry or made into ornamental silhouettes.

The Hopewell decorated themselves with ornaments of bone and shell, too. Both women and men wore earrings and necklaces made with animal teeth or freshwater pearls. With rings, furs, feathered capes, well-tanned animal skins and woven cloth, the Hopewell lifestyle must have seemed luxurious to others at the time.

THE HOPEWELL TRADED FINISHED WARES, SUCH AS CARVED PIPES AND CEREMONIAL KNIVES.

The Ohio, Mississippi and Missouri Rivers once served as water highways for Indian trade. Talented tradesmen, the Hopewell loaded oak canoes with their raw materials and finished wares, and traveled the rivers to destinations in widely scattered places. Following tributaries into Arkansas, North Carolina and the Appalachians, they exchanged desirable items, such as pipestone, Ohio flint or freshwater pearls, for mica, which they highly prized. They also went westward, up the Missouri, to get grizzly bear teeth and obsidian, and journeyed to the Great Lakes region for copper nuggets.

Indians who brought obsidian from the Yellowstone region may have met the Hopewell along the shores of the Mississippi. Others traveled north, up the length of the Mississippi, to trade conch shells, sharkskin and alligator teeth from the Gulf of Mexico. This route also brought in raw materials for necklaces, such as alligator or shark teeth and barracuda jaws from Florida. By establishing systematic ties and developing a trade network across approximately two-thirds of the U.S., the Hopewell changed the way commerce was conducted in Archaic times.

Trade provided luxuries for the living, but the Hopewell often obtained valued materials to place in tombs with their dead. In burial clothes decorated with freshwater pearls, the

Hopewell were laid to rest in graves laden with treasure. One grave in Hamilton County, Ohio, contained 35,000 pearl beads, 20,000 shell beads, 12,000 pearls, iron beads, nuggets of copper, iron and silver, and sheets of hammered copper and gold. Another yielded hundreds of pipes, copper effigies of birds, turtles and humans, a copper-covered wooden effigy, and a mask made from human skull fragments. A grave in Ross County produced a twenty-eight-pound copper axe, two copper breast-plates, a skull with a copper nose, and thousands of pearls,

The Hopewell sometimes built burial mounds in geometric earthworks. An enormous complex at Newark, Ohio, contains a number of burial mounds, an effigy of an eagle, and a corridor that reaches the banks of the Licking River over two miles away. This structure, containing avenues, circles and plazas, covers more than four square miles. Today, most of it lies within the borders of a golf course and a fairground.

ARROWHEADS CAME INTO EXISTENCE WHEN WOODLAND PEOPLE BEGAN USING BOWS AND ARROWS, AROUND A.D. 400.

The Hopewell may have used more exotic materials, but Indians across the country also made high-quality ornaments, tools and weapons. Men and women were placing a greater emphasis on personal appearance and status, and it shows in the pendants that were made. Earlier pendants were small- to medium-sized, thin and fairly crude. In Woodland times, people wore larger, well-defined ornaments which they made from high grades of slate. Though bell designs and keyhole shapes were made by the Adena, polished anchor and shovel pendants are also from this period. Etched pendants with a weeping eye motif and fringed types would have been made in Mississippian times. You can identify a fringed pendant by its triangular shape, small size and deeply notched base. Pebble pendants, made at various times, have been found in all parts of North America. Slightly modified before drilling, these pretty stones might have edge decorations, two flat surfaces or contouring of natural lines.

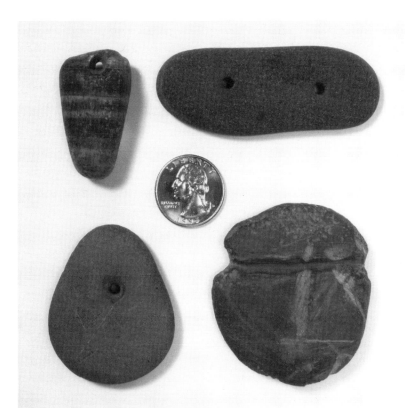

Figure 9-8. Though Indians did not always fasten their ornaments in the same way, you can usually tell the difference between pendants and gorgets by the number and position of holes. Pendants hang straight with one hole at the center of gravity (upper and lower left). A strap through two equidistant holes would secure a gorget (upper right) to an atlatl or arm. Since cords could stretch, drilled ornaments were safer than those with notches or a groove. The grooved pendant just may have slipped off a cord.

Gorgets, like other atlatl weights from earlier times, were also common in the Woodland period. Though most are drilled in two equidistant places from the ends, there are varieties that have anywhere from one to five holes. Some gorgets, however, are not drilled at all. Others are notched, grooved or both. Whether they were placed on atlatls or used as ornaments, plain types with double drilling are usually identified as artifacts from the Archaic or Woodland periods.

For flavor and aroma, people mixed leaves and stems with the tobacco they grew and used the blends in **pipes**. The Adena made tubular pipes, sometimes blocking the mouthpiece with a pebble to prevent the mixture from entering the tube. Hopewell Indians made effigies of birds and animals or used a platform style with ornate designs. Shaping bowls and hollow stems from clay was much easier than chipping pipes from soapstone, sandstone or limestone. A clay pipe of any shape or design would be from Woodland, Mississippian or later times.

Figure 9-9. Sometimes prehistoric graves are discovered in fields when grave goods are plowed to the surface. An extraordinary artifact lying on a field, such as an elaborately designed and detailed effigy pipe, is an indication that a tomb was disturbed. If you find an artifact that could have been plowed from a grave, speak with the landowner immediately and notify your state historic preservation agency.

Stone tools, weapons and artifact fragments can be dated more accurately when pieces of pottery are near. Archaeologists like sherds because they can date them by examining the decorations and materials. Indians from the Southwest drilled decorative pieces of broken pottery and wore the sherds as pendants. Clay pendants and other fragments with special features, such as tallied rims, etched weeping eyes, rolled clay coils or painted designs, can link pottery to a particular culture. When sherds are identified this way, the age of other artifacts in the immediate vicinity can also be estimated.

It would be extremely rare to discover an unbroken vessel of pottery on a plowed field. Fired clay decays in acidic soils and acid rain, and breaks up even further during plowing. If you find a shell-tempered cup, a small bowl, a miniature grit-tempered pot or prehistoric sherd—especially a rim, handle or decorated piece—it should be professionally studied.

MISSISSIPPIAN PERIOD

Around A.D. 800, life became centered around village and town life. In the **Mississippian period**, many people settled in river valleys and flood plains, cultivating crops near towns on a much bigger scale than before. Farming the surrounding land not only provided food for the day, it also allowed larger quantities to be stored. Since full-time residency was required for farming, and storing food permitted a settled life, permanent villages grew and flourished.

To raise maize, beans, squash, native sunflowers, tobacco or other crops, Indian farmers raked soil with hoes of stone, bone or shell, and shoveled earth with percussion-flaked spades. While the crops supplied domesticated food, people continued to hunt and gather. Using bows and arrows to hunt wild game such as deer, squirrel, rabbit, turkey and partridge, they also caught fish and collected river mussels—favorite foods of the time. People filled their baskets with hickory nuts, ground protein-rich seeds, and made flours that were new to the diet.

THE FARMERS

Like the earlier Mound Builders, Mississippians honored their dead with great ceremony and laid them to rest in burial mounds. During Mississippian times, Indians built massive temple mounds that compare with the Mayan and Egyptian pyramids. Temple mounds are enormous sites where farmers, arrowhead makers, potters, jewelers, leather workers and weavers attended grand ceremonies and rituals. Terraced structures with level summits, they were also places where aristocrats and rulers lived. The higher the house was on a terrace, the more lofty the personal status.

You can visit the most famous temple mound in Cahokia, Illinois. **Cahokia** was a major Mississippian center that existed for about six hundred years. With an estimated population of forty thousand and an area of nearly six square miles, it was the largest city in prehistoric America. The temple mound there was built in fourteen stages and despite the hard work of many laborers, it took almost three years to complete. Monk's Mound is about one hundred feet high, has two major terraced levels, and a base that covers fourteen square acres. A building the size of three tennis courts once stood on the flat, elevated summit. The structure, made from wood and thatch, could have been a temple or the home of a ruler. The large plaza below the summit would have served as a marketplace and gathering spot for city residents.

INDIANS MAY HAVE BUILT TEMPLE MOUNDS IN DEVOTION TO THEIR GODS.

Farmers and common folk didn't wear the antlered headdresses, fancy robes or the feathers of the nobles. But whether aristocrat, priest, soldier, artisan or laborer, people still used tools and weapons or wore ornaments that were made from natural resources. Spades and hoes for digging and smoothing earth during Woodland times were further developed in the Mississippian period. Skilled at grinding and polishing, Mississippians also improved the quality of other tools and weapons and made beautiful ceremonial objects.

Spuds and spatulates are not difficult to date because both originated in the Mississippian period. Unfortunately, the artifacts are even more scarce than photos and you'll have to look hard to find either one. Because they're high-quality polished tools that everyone can appreciate, it's much more common to see them at museums or artifact shows.

It's helpful to know the general locations where broken spatulates and large, whole spuds have been found. Though archaeologists have excavated some from ceremonial centers like

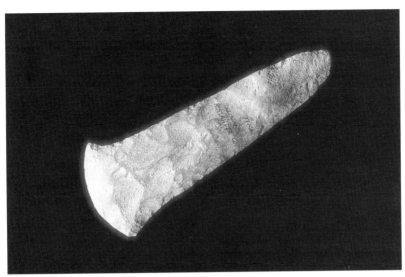

Figure 9-10. A spud is usually classified as a ceremonial ornament or woodcutting tool. This one happens to be a weapon. Although it compares more with war hatchets and iron tomahawks made in later times, it's also correctly identified as a flare-bitted celt. Discovered in Alexander County, Illinois, and made from chert, the material was heat-treated before being chipped down to a length of eight inches. Iron Horse collection. Photo by R.M. Gramly.

Cahokia, they appear throughout the Midwest, in the Mississippi Valley region and also in the South. Spuds and spatulates are rare in the North, but you might find a fluted spud in the upper Midwest. Mississippians who once lived in Wisconsin fluted their spuds on both sides of the shaft. Since these tools were ceremonial, the design was probably for ornament.

Bows and arrows were used for about four hundred years prior to the Mississippian period. Experts at making projectile points, Mississippians kept theirs small and simple. The most common type of arrowhead of this time has the basic shape of a triangle. Many triangular arrowheads have smooth or serrated edges, but most were made without notches. Though Cahokia points are triangular, the features are an exception to the rule. Refined and distinctive, Cahokia points have a notch on each side and one in the center of the base.

Points of Interest

Cultures by Region

While prehistoric periods are divisions in time that have been classified by lifeways, archaeologists have also divided North America into culture areas according to culture traits. Cultures with similar life-styles are grouped into regions, such as the Northwest Coast, Northeast and Great Lakes, Southeast or Plateau. To become proficient at identifying artifacts, learn about the cultures in your region long ago. If you live in the Southwest or the Great Basin, study the Anasazi, the Hohokam, Mogollon or the Cochise. Evidence shows that Desert culture hunters arrived there in the cool, moist climate of Paleo-Indian times. Later, Archaic gatherers foraged for plant food, processing it with ground tools. Throughout the Southwest, Woodland period Basket Makers wove yucca fibers into mats, baskets and sandals. A people who were also skilled potters, they began living in pueblos during Mississippian times. Are you from the Great Plains, or do you live in Alaska? Become familiar with herdsmen and horsemen, or Arctic fishermen who inhabited your area. Use resources to learn more about the prehistory of your region, because Indian cultures varied from place to place.

War points are Mississippian arrowheads that are less than one inch long. Sharp, dainty and lethal, these multipurpose points were suitable for both hunting and warfare. Since flaking is delicate and edges may be smooth, be sure to inspect the features of small stone triangles you see. Because the sizes are petite, war points are often found in one whole lovely piece! The discovery of a small war point is a big clue that you've found a Mississippian site.

ORIGINAL LOCATIONS OF MAJOR TRIBES

Figure 9-11. Use this map to find the geographic locations of major tribal families. Which trade-era tribe once lived in your area? To identify a ground tool, a flaked weapon or an ornament as historic, refer to the region and compare the artifact to others made by the tribe.

177

As Europeans arrived and wrote about their experiences across the land, the Mississippian period gradually shifted into the **trade-era**. While the new immigrants described strange and wondrous things in parchment letters, diaries and manuscripts, Indian lifeways and customs began to change once again. They still made stone tools and weapons for at least another two hundred years, but during this time they also worked a fair amount of metal. From the exchange of materials and finished goods with the early settlers, historic Indians met even more of their needs through trade.

FANCY PIPE-TOMAHAWKS WITH ORNATE HANDLES ARE CONSIDERED TRADE-ERA PIPES, NOT WEAPONS.

Most of the artifacts from this period that are identified with Native Americans were actually made by Europeans in the American colonies, Canada and Europe. Some, such as hand-forged iron axes, Dutch trader pipes and copper kettles, were used by the settlers, but more were created specifically for trade. In the eighteenth and nineteenth centuries, hatchets, tomahawks, steel-edged axes, steel projectile points and other sharp objects were in demand. When fur trading was in full swing, ornaments were also popular, especially glass beads. Glass trade beads were colorful, attractive and made of a material that was new to Indians. By 1870, glass telegraph insulators became another source of raw material for some of the arrowheads made during late historic years.

Because archaeological names, such as Paleo-Indian, Archaic, Woodland and Mississippian, are current classifications, prehistoric people did not identify themselves as we do now. No matter what the prehistoric culture happens to be, remember that the people are the ancestors of the present Native American Indians. The American Indian tribes you are familiar with, such as Apache, Cherokee, Iroquois and Sioux, were first recorded to have inhabited areas shown on the map in Figure 9-11. Since the style of a prehistoric point you find may resemble a type made by historic Indians, refer to the map for the name of the trade-era tribe. To estimate the age of your find, use resources to trace the history of the tribe back to earlier, prehistoric times.

Although much can be said about artifacts and the remarkable people who worked stone, there is much more to be learned. Why did Indians polish stones for recreation? What is the meaning of tally marks? Were cup stones used for starting fires or processing food? Did the Poverty Point culture manufacture clay biscuits in molds? Why were eyes significant on birdstones? How were ceremonial artifacts used in rituals? Why did flourishing cultures fade and disappear? What types of tools, weapons and ornaments have not survived the ravages of time?

By sharing information from discoveries, people help each other learn about prehistory. Assorted points and stone tools stored in a closet or artifacts without written back-up provide no more information than those which are being lost to looting. To save information and provide clues to the puzzles of the past, you'll want to keep an artifact journal.

Figure 10-1. You saw the worked sides of these unifacial scrapers in Chapter 8, Figure 8-5. We've turned the tools over to show how they can be labeled. While people do not label artifacts in the same way, the information should link the finds to the details written in artifact journals.

Keeping a Journal

Indians tended fires to heat rocks, hurled spears from throwing sticks, made massive axes for ceremonies, and arrow-heads smaller than a fingernail. They used sharp woodcutting tools, designed pretty ornaments of bone, shaped rocks into game stones, cultivated large crops, and built ten thousand mounds in the Ohio Valley alone. Did you ever imagine that Native American prehistory could be so diverse? Artifacts are the remnants of this colorful past. When you discover an artifact on the surface and decide to bring it home, you'll need to give it a meaningful future.

As you learn about prehistory from the artifacts you find, remember that it's the information from your discoveries that is of utmost importance. Whatever your age, your career, or your level of experience, you'll want to share the information from your finds with others who are interested in researching the past. People will appreciate the details you can supply and scientists may learn even more from your contributions. Though some feel strongly that surface hunting hampers the study of archaeology, their opinion may change as more arrowhead hunters record and report artifacts. To help preserve archaeological information and improve relations with the professional community, keep an artifact journal.

An artifact journal is a written archaeological record that provides information about artifacts, sites and prehistory. Whether your find is a knife fragment, a splintered bone with a drilled hole, a whole arrowhead, or a sharp flake that you believe to be a flake tool, the discovery should be recorded in your journal. Small pieces of broken, worked stone can be good sources of information, and "keepers" may be as well. Though you may be unable to determine why your find is damaged or identify exactly what it might be, you can supply facts, write about features, and furnish other information that could be helpful in a future study.

Your journal is also an arrowhead hunting diary that you can appreciate in years to come. It preserves the memory of the day you discovered an artifact, and it's a personal account that you'll want to share with family and friends.

You'll be labeling the finds you bring home as you record information. Labeling is important because it connects the artifacts to the journal entries. Labeling and recording are easy and fun to do, especially if you've taken good notes, mapped the site, and snapped a few photos. It's always best to record as soon as possible, while your hunting experience is still fresh in your mind. If you've put surface finds in containers for temporary storage, try to make time for inspection within the week. When you label and journalize promptly, you eliminate the chance of a crude artifact getting mixed up and tossed out with non-cultural stones.

LABELING

Artifacts can be labeled in more than one way. The adzes and the boatstone shown in Chapter 9 have been marked with indelible India ink. Because the ink cannot be erased or washed off, the artifacts are permanently linked to written records. While many people use this method to mark their discoveries, it might be better for those who are new to the hobby to use self-adhesive labels. Since you'll be recording "keepers" as well as artifacts, you may want to update the information at a later time. A self-adhesive label can be replaced with a new one without marring an artifact.

Self-adhesive labels are available at stores that carry school or office supplies. Choose the type you like, because they come in a variety of sizes and colors. Use dots on war points and small fragments since they'll cover only a bit of surface. Clear labels or translucent tints are even better for artifacts with delicate bifacial flaking. To include more information, such as the date found or type of material, consider small rectangles. If other members of your family surface hunt, use different shapes or colors for a quick way to associate artifacts with the right journals.

After you've inspected your finds and made a decision about which ones need to be recorded, you may begin labeling. Get your notes, maps and photos out, because you'll be referring to them as you record. The information you enter on a label is an important clue for locating the rest of the data. Archaeologists use a trinomial system—numbers for states, letters for counties, and numbers for sites. To learn the codes for using this nation-wide system, contact your SHPO. Another way to label is to use consecutive numbers. For whole artifacts, worked fragments and "keepers," assign a number to each. Use a pen, writing on labels before pressing them on your finds.

People who label numerically sometimes like to include other information, such as the county of the site or the name of the landowner. Others label by date, and note the name of the town. Whatever method you choose, be consistent. Whether you record with state codes, numbers, dates, letters, towns or surnames, using the same system is key to easily locating the expanded information you'll be logging in your journal.

RECORDING

You don't need to purchase anything expensive to keep an artifact journal. Most amateur archaeologists record information in a notebook. If you have a home computer, you might want to consider using software instead. Computer-generated journal pages should be printed out for proofing at the time information is entered. File the sheets in a folder or three-ring binder, and be sure to save the document to a disk. Either way you choose to record, label the hard copy with your full name.

Let's suppose you've decided to number your finds and write in a notebook. Place the artifact you've just labeled in front of you, check the number, and copy it to the first page. Then, transfer the information from the notes you took next to the number in the journal. Refer to your map for paces, landmarks or other details that may not be in the notes, and examine photos for features of the artifact and hunting site.

If your notes are sketchy, having the artifact in front of you may jog your memory. Do the best you can to be accurate. Record the name of the artifact, where you found it, the date and a description of the hunting site. Include the features of your find, such as dimensions, type of stone or the type of flaking. It's also helpful to write your opinions about why the artifact was at the site or how it surfaced.

Always skip a few lines between entries. Later, you might determine the prehistoric period, the culture, or other important details that you'll want to include in the record. Leave some space for information you learn in the future, and you'll also keep a neat journal.

If you've filled out a report form for a surface find, you've already recorded it properly. You've documented information to the best of your ability, and shared it with professionals as well. Though you may also want to keep a personal notebook, your record of a registered find is almost complete. To connect your labeled artifact to the completed form, simply write the label number at the top of your copy.

When using notes to record in a journal, it's not necessary to reword phrases into complete sentences. As long as your descriptions are clear, the short phrases you've jotted down are perfectly acceptable. You examined a sample sketch map and two completed forms in Chapter 6, but suppose it was *you* who discovered the celt in Scott Mills. Your first journal entry might look something like this:

1.	CELT found 11/9/96.	
	Gray granite	
	5⅛" long. 2½" wide.	
	Property owner: David R. Thomas	
	RD2	
	Scott Mills, WI	
	Site: Southwest corner of potato field, near fence. From corner of house closest to field, go 17 paces east and 103 paces south. Field was recently plowed. Heavy rain on 11/8/96. Location is a good place for a campsite.	
	Report filed 11/11/96.	
	Back-up: original notes, map and negatives.	

Original notes, maps and photo negatives are the back-up to journal entries. When you've finished recording, write the number of your label with the date of the find on all back-up documents. Store them in a safe place, such as a fireproof box or safe deposit box. Should your journal be destroyed by fire or water, the information will not be lost.

In the process of learning about artifacts, you may discover an error in identification. What should you do if months later you realize that the celt you recorded is actually an adze? If you've filed a report form, send a corrected copy with a note of explanation to the preservation agency, and update your journal entry as shown:

	ADZE (correction sent to ~~SHPO~~ on 1/14/97)
	1. ~~CELT~~ found 11/9/96. Gray granite 5⅛" long. 2½" wide.
	Property owner: David R. Thomas RD2 Scott Mills, WI
	Site: Southwest corner of potato field, near fence. From corner of house closest to field, go 17 paces east and 103 paces south. Field was recently plowed. Heavy rain on 11/8/96. Location is a good place for a campsite.
	Report filed 11/11/96. Back-up: original notes, map and negatives.

Use the extra space at the top to make a legible revision and add notations. For journalizing with a computer, try to using the strikeout code rather than deleting any of the original information.

PHOTO DISPLAYS AND
ARTIFACT STORAGE

Whether you leave an artifact at the site or bring it home, you might like to make a collage of arrowhead hunting photos. Did you take any pictures of scenery or wildlife? Arrange them around a color photograph of your find on its site. If you have a favorite print, consider enlarging it to poster-size. Or, keep all of your hunting snapshots in a special album. Show it to others and tell them the stories behind your discoveries. Point out the features of a site, and explain why you decided to hunt it. Describe the details of the artifacts, and you may teach others in the process. Remember that when you share your hunting experiences and the information you've learned, everyone can benefit.

If you've brought artifacts home for study, you'll need to think about where they should be kept. Museums are the most appropriate places for public display and preservation of artifacts, but it's not practical for every Native American artifact found to be shown or curated. There are limits to the amount of display space available, and storage space in back rooms is often inadequate. While you may want to loan an artifact to a large museum so that more people can see it, you might have to wait your turn. Try smaller, local or private museums whenever this occurs.

The care that you take in recording information should also be extended to storage. Finds should not be placed into a shoe box or put in an empty coffee can where they can rattle around and break. To prevent chipping, scratching or other damage, wrap each piece of worked stone in cotton or soft tissue, and gently lay the fragments in a box or drawer. For a whole, flaked artifact, such as a projectile point, secure it in a box by nestling it into a matching pattern cut in foam. Keep a pecked and ground artifact, such as a grinding stone, in a curio cabinet or bookcase with glass doors. Always store an artifact so you can examine it for study and find the condition to be the same.

<u>*Points of Interest*</u>

Saving Information

Label your finds

Keep a journal

File a report

Store a copy of records

Store artifacts safely

A trophy is precious to a champion because it's an award for achievement and excellence. A wedding ring is cherished not for the gold, but for the love it symbolizes. Photographs that capture moments in time are priceless because they remind us of special people, events or places. Meaningful objects are treasured and ultimately passed on to others who appreciate them. The artifacts you find are scientific treasures. Treat them with the respect they deserve and pass along the information they provide.

Arrowhead hunting is much more than just hunting for arrowheads. Things change when you have a personal experience with artifacts. You see rocks in a new way, geography in a new light, and think about history and people altogether differently. When you reach out to pick up an artifact, you make a connection between the past and the present. You become the first person to hold the stone tool that was last held by an Indian hundreds, or perhaps thousands of years ago. Discovering an artifact opens up a whole new world, and is an experience that you never forget.

Glossary

abrading stone (ə-brād′ing) - A sandstone or limestone rock that was used to smooth or sharpen antler, bone, wood and other stone.

A.D. - Represents years in the Christian era.

Adena (ə-dēn′ə) - The first major people of the Woodland period. Had cultural influences in Indiana, Kentucky, Maryland, New York, Ohio, Pennsylvania and West Virginia.

adze (adz) - A tool that was used like a chisel to work wood.

amateur archaeologist - An individual who has an active interest in archaeology, but does not make a living as an archaeologist.

anvil (an′vəl) - A rock slab that was used as a level base for chipping other stone into tools or weapons. See *chipping stone*.

archaeologist (ärkēol′ə-jist) - One who recovers and studies evidence of human life and culture from past ages.

Archaic period (är-kā′ik) - From 8000 B.C. to 1000 B.C., the seven-thousand-year span after Paleo-Indian and before Woodland times.

arrowhead hunting - An archaeological hobby that includes searching the surface of the ground for arrowheads and other artifacts, and recording information. See *surface hunting*.

artifact (är′tə-fakt) - An object made or used by people that has archaeological significance.

atlatl (at-la′təl) - A wooden stick with a hooked end that was used to fling spears.

atlatl weight - A drilled or grooved stone that was used to weight atlatls.

KEY	ä: car	i: sit	ō: note	o͞o: tool	û: urge
a: cat	e: pet	ī: mice	ô: paw	ou: pout	ǔ: cut
ā: page	ē: keep	o: cot	oi: coil	u: put	ə: about

authentic - True or genuine. Artifacts made in prehistoric times.

axe - A large chopping tool with a groove for hafting.

bannerstone - An atlatl weight with a centered hole, or a ceremonial ornament.

barb - A sharp, protruding shoulder on a point.

base - The bottom part of a point or knife.

B.C. - Before Christ.

bevel (bev′əl) - A sloped edge.

bifacial (bī-fā′shəl) - Worked on both sides.

bifurcate (bi′fər-kāt) - A type of stem that describes points and knives with a central notch separating the ears.

billet (bil′ət) - An antler flaking tool used in flintknapping to chip preforms into weapons and tools.

birdstone - An atlatl weight shaped like a bird, or a ceremonial ornament.

blade - The cutting portion of a knife or point. Also, a cutting tool that is at least twice as long as it is wide.

blowout - A patch of land in plains states where soil is blown away by wind.

boatstone - An atlatl weight shaped like watercraft, or a ceremonial ornament.

boiling stone - A stone that was used as a heat source during cooking. Woodland or Mississipian boiling "stones" may be made of clay. See *cooking stone*.

buffalo jump - A site at bluffs and cliffs where buffalo were killed and slaughtered.

buffalo wallow - A wet or moist area where buffalo gathered.

cache (kash) - A group of similar implements, usually knives or points, that have been stored in one place for safekeeping. Also, a hiding place for supplies.

Cahokia (kə-hō′kē-ä) - A major Mississippian center that began as early as A.D. 800 and lasted until approximately A.D. 1400.

celt (selt) - A thin, ungrooved axe with a sharp edge for cutting or chopping.

ceremonial stone - An oversized, finely crafted or elaborately decorated artifact that shows no sign of use.

chert (chûrt) - An impure form of flint that appears in limestone.

chipping stone - A flat cobble that was used as a level base for chipping other stone into tools or weapons. See *anvil*.

chunkey stone (chŭng'kē) - A small, disc-shaped stone that was used with wooden poles in a game. See *discoidal*.

Clovis (klō'vis) - A Paleo-Indian culture named after Clovis, New Mexico, near where the first fluted point of its type was found and documented.

conchoidal fracture (kän-koid'l) - A break in rock resulting in a circular, shell-like pattern. This typically occurs in rock such as flint, chert or obsidian.

cooking stone - A stone that was used as heat source during cooking. Woodland or Mississipian cooking "stones" may be made of clay. See *boiling stone*.

core - A stone from which flakes were produced.

cultural - Worked or used by people.

cup stone - An artifact with one or more depressions, thought to have been used in the fire-starting process. See *nut stone*.

discoidal (dis-koid'l) - A disc-shaped, polished stone that was used for recreation or ceremonial purposes. See *chunkey stone*.

drill - A slim tool with three or four flaked sides that was used to bore holes.

ears - Rounded or pointed extensions at the bottom of stems.

effigy (ef'ə-jē) - An image or representation of an animal, bird or human.

end scraper - A scraper with pressure flaking along an end edge.

excavation (ek-skə-vā'shən) - A cavity or hole in the earth formed by digging. Also, the unearthing of buried artifacts or other materials by digging.

fire-cracked - Altered color and texture in stone that results from repeated exposure to fire.

fired clay biscuit - A problem artifact, such as those found in Kentucky, Missouri and Illinois, that appears to have been made in a mold.

KEY	ä: car	i: sit	ō: note	o͞o: tool	û: urge
a: cat	e: pet	ī: mice	ô: paw	ou: pout	ŭ: cut
ā: page	ē: keep	o: cot	oi: coil	u: put	ə: about

flake - A piece of stone that has been removed from a core. Also, to chip pieces of stone from a rock.

flake tool - A naturally sharp scraping tool that resulted from chipping flakes off a core during flintknapping.

flaking - The chipping seen on flaked artifacts. Also, the process of chipping pieces of stone from a rock. See *flintknapping*.

flaking tool - An antler, bone, or wood and copper flintknapping tool used to chip preforms into weapons and tools.

flint - A hard quartz that produces sparks when struck with rock high in iron content.

flintknapping (flint′nap-ing) - A means of working stone into flaked weapons or tools. See *flaking*.

flute - A long, thin channel on a tool. Also, a vertical groove on the body of a point struck from the base. See *impact fracture*.

Folsom (fōl′səm) - A Paleo-Indian culture named after Folsom, New Mexico, near where the first fluted point of its type was found and documented.

game stone - A ground and polished circular stone that was used for amusement or ceremonial purposes.

geode (jē′ōd) - A hollow rock with quartz crystals lining the inside wall.

gorget (gôr′jət) - A thin, rectangular atlatl weight with two drilled holes, or an ornament.

graver - A small tool with a sharp tip that was used to engrave bone, stone and other materials.

grinding - A stone-working method used to smooth stone.

grinding stone - An artifact that was used to grind food or abrade antler, bone, wood and other stone.

haft (haft) - A means of attaching a tool or weapon to a shaft, handle or holder.

hammerstone - A rock, usually a cobble, that was used in the hand to strike or pound other objects.

handaxe - A large, randomly flaked woodcutting tool with heavy wear on edges.

hard-hammer percussion - A flintknapping technique used to break down large rock by striking one stone against another.

hearth stone - A stone that was used to line fire hearths.

heat-treating - A heating process used on stone to make flaking easier. Stone to be treated was first buried and then heated by tending a hot fire above it for several days.

Hopewell - Major Mound Builders of the Woodland period. Established trade ties across approximately two-thirds of the U.S. and into Canada.

impact fracture - A result of impact, a vertical groove that begins at the tip of a point. See *flute*.

invertebrate (in-vûr′tə-brit) - Soft- or hard-bodied animals, such as clams, crabs, snails and insects, that do not have a backbone. See *trilobite*.

knife - A bifacial tool with blade edges.

lanceolate (lan′tsē-ə-lāt) - A narrow, tapered projectile point or knife.

lobate (lō′bāt) - A type of stem that describes points and knives with curved or rounded ears.

lookout site - A high location where Indians would keep watch and sharpen weapons.

mano (mä′nō) - A stone with a flat side that was used to grind edible substances.

maul (môl) - A pounding tool that was pecked, ground, grooved and hafted.

Mississippian period - The span after Woodland times and before the trade-era, beginning at approximately A.D. 800.

mortar (môr′tər) - A grinding slab on which food and other substances were crushed.

multipurpose tool - A tool that was used for several purposes.

net weight - A crude drilled or notched tool that was used to weight nets.

nodule (nä′jo̅o̅l) - A cobble of flint, chert, granite or other rounded mass of mineral matter.

non-cultural - Natural. Not worked or used by people.

KEY	ä: car	i: sit	ō: note	o̅o̅: tool	û: urge
a: cat	e: pet	ī: mice	ô: paw	ou: pout	ŭ: cut
ā: page	ē: keep	o: cot	oi: coil	u: put	ə: about

notches - Indentations for hafting. On points and knives, notches are beneath the shoulders or in the base.

NRHP - National Register of Historic Places. Roster of historic property, archaeological sites and other protected places.

nut stone - An artifact with one or more depressions, thought to have been used in food preparation. See *cup stone*.

oblique flaking (ō-blēk') - A diagonal chipping pattern seen on points and knives.

obsidian (ob-sid'ē-ən) - A dark volcanic glass formed when lava cools quickly.

opaque (ō-pāk') - A characteristic that does not permit light to pass through.

ornament - An artifact that was worn for adornment or used for ceremonial purposes.

outcropping - A rock formation that protrudes above the ground.

Paleo-Indian period (pālē-o-in'dē-ən) - From 13,000 B.C. to 8000 B.C., the five-thousand-year span before Archaic times.

parallel flaking - A horizontal chipping pattern seen on points and knives.

patina (pat'ə-nə) - A lustrous coating caused by oxidation over long periods of time.

pecking - Battering with a hammerstone.

pendant - A stone or bone ornament, usually with one drilled hole in the center of gravity.

percussion - The removal of flakes by blows with a hammerstone or strikes with a billet.

perforator - A sharp, spiked tool that was used for puncturing and making holes in softer materials.

pestle (pes'əl) - A club-shaped tool that was used to mash or crush food and other substances.

pipe - A hollow instrument for smoking consisting of a bowl and tube.

polishing - A stone-working method used to buff ceremonial stones and ornaments after grinding.

polishing stone - A pebble with one or more flattened surfaces, thought to have been used for smoothing or shaping pottery.

pothunter - One who ignores the rules of surface hunting to collect or sell artifacts.

pottery - Earthenware made from moist clay and hardened with heat.

preform (prē′fôrm) - A piece of stone that has been worked into the basic shape of a point or tool.

prehistoric periods - Increments of time before written records, determined by how people lived.

pressure flaking - A flintknapping technique used to remove tiny flakes by pressing a sharp flaking tool against stone.

private property - Land that is owned by citizens and not by the government.

projectile point - An arrowhead or a spear point.

provenance (prä′və-nənts) - The spatial relationship of an artifact to its site.

public land - Federal, state and county lands where artifacts, plants, animals, rocks, shells and all other historic and natural features are protected by law, and all land owned by the U.S. government that is not reserved for other purposes.

radiocarbon dating - A lab test used to estimate the age of organic materials.

random flaking - Irregular chipping in no particular pattern.

reproductions - Modern representations of ancient artifacts made with no intent to deceive.

scraper - A sharp-edged tool that was used to scrape animal hides and soft materials.

serrations (se-rā′shəns) - Saw-toothed cutting edges.

sherd (shûrd) - A fragment of pottery.

shoulders - The flared areas on points and knives that are above the stem and below the body.

SHPO - State Historic Preservation Officer. An individual who supervises historic preservation efforts for a particular state.

side scraper - A scraper with pressure flaking along a side edge.

KEY	ä: car	i: sit	ō: note	ōō: tool	û: urge
a: cat	e: pet	ī: mice	ô: paw	ou: pout	ŭ: cut
ā: page	ē: keep	o: cot	oi: coil	u: put	ə: about

site - An area of land.

site protection regulations - Laws that protect public and private lands having archaeological resources.

sketch map - A drawing that marks the location where an artifact was found.

soft-hammer percussion - A flintknapping technique used with antler billets to chip stone into preforms.

spatulate (spach'ə-lit) - A long and narrow, highly polished ceremonial artifact with a flat, broad end.

spokeshave (spōk'shāv) - A small scraping tool with cutouts that was used to smooth and straighten sticks.

spud (spŭd) - A long, narrow tool with a sharp, flared blade, usually used for ceremonial purposes or chopping wood.

spur - A spike or projection.

steep-edge scraper - A conical scraper with steep, sloping sides. Also called a humpback or turtleback scraper.

stem - The area of a point or knife at the base and beneath the shoulders that is used for hafting.

surface find - An object found on the surface of the ground that has archaeological interest.

surface hunting - An archaeological hobby that includes searching the surface of the ground for arrowheads and other artifacts, and recording information. See *arrowhead hunting*.

tally marks - Narrow lines that are etched in stone.

tangs - Rounded or pointed extensions at the bottom of stems.

thumb scraper - A scraper about the size of a thumb. Also called a thumbnail scraper.

thumbnail scraper - A scraper about the size of a thumbnail. Also called a thumb scraper.

topographic map (täp-ə-graf'ik) - An accurate and detailed map of the physical features of a region.

trade-era - Historic times of trade with Europeans after the Mississippian period.

translucent (trants-loo'sənt) - A characteristic that permits some light to pass through. Translucence in artifacts indicates high-quality stone.

trilobite (trī′lə-bīt) - An extinct marine invertebrate that was probably a bottom-feeding predator.

unifacial (yo͞on-ə-fā′shəl) - Worked on one side.

USGS - U.S. Geological Survey. A government agency that produces and provides maps.

war point - A very small Mississippian arrowhead that has a triangular shape.

washout - A groove or furrow in the earth created by heavy rain.

Woodland period - From 1000 B.C. to A.D. 800, the span of nearly three thousand years after Archaic and before Mississippian times.

worked - Modified by flaking, pecking, grinding, polishing, drilling or etching.

KEY	ä: car	i: sit	ō: note	o͞o: tool	û: urge
a: cat	e: pet	ī: mice	ô: paw	ou: pout	ŭ: cut
ā: page	ē: keep	o: cot	oi: coil	u: put	ə: about

Artifacts and Features

You know how to identify the features of worked stone and you have a basic understanding of functions. You're also aware that different types of artifacts often have similar characteristics. To determine which kind of artifact your find could be, use this identification section as a supplemental guide. While the questions provide specific information about the most common materials and features, you'll want to consider the clues about style variations, provenance and other artifact classes. Be sure to cross-check your finds with other artifact types whenever more than one possibility is indicated.

Abrading stones
Is the material sandstone or limestone?
Is the stone small enough to fit in your hand?
Does it have slender, shallow grooves?
Are the grooves nearly parallel?
Do they run along the length of the stone?
Have you found a large, stationary abrading stone?

Adzes
Is the material hematite or other hard stone?
Is the stone pecked and ground?
Does one end taper into a sharp blade edge?
Does it have a flat surface on one side?
Was it made without a groove?
Or does it have notches, grooves or knobs?
Do you think it might be a celt?
Or have you found a chipped, heat-treated adze?

Anvils

Is the material a type of hard stone?
Does your broad, thick rock have one level surface, or two?
Is there pitting in the center of one or both level sides?
Did you find it at a flintknapping site?
Could your flat cobble be a chipping stone?

Atlatl weights

Is the material slate, quartzite or hard stone?
Is it pecked, ground and polished?
Does it have a distinct shape, such as a butterfly, boat or bird?
Or does it have a geometric design, such as a rectangle or tube?
Are there any drilled holes, narrow grooves or notches?
Is it perhaps a gorget?
Or have you found an effigy of an animal?
Could it be a ceremonial stone or an ornament?

Axes

Is the material granite, quartzite or hematite?
Is the stone pecked and ground?
Does it have a groove?
Does one end taper into a sharp blade edge?
Have you found one with barbs or flutes?
Or is it a different kind of chopping tool, such as a handaxe?

Bannerstones

Is the material slate, quartzite or hard stone?
Is it pecked, ground and polished?
Is the shape like a butterfly, hourglass, crescent or bow tie?
Or is it rectangular, triangular, round, tubular or ridged?
Does it have a round or an oblong hole in the center?
Is it notched instead?
Is it a smaller atlatl weight or a larger ceremonial stone?

Birdstones

Is the material slate, quartzite or hard stone?
Is it pecked, ground and polished?
Does the stone have the shape of a sitting bird at rest?
Are the eyes a prominent feature?
Are there drilled holes at each end of the base?
Is it a smaller atlatl weight or a larger ceremonial stone?

Boatstones

Is the material slate, quartzite or hard stone?
Is it pecked, ground and polished?
Does the stone have the shape of simple watercraft?
Is one side flat, scooped or hollow?
Are the ends pointed, curved or squared?
Does it have drilled holes near the ends, or a central groove?
Is it a smaller atlatl weight or a larger ceremonial stone?

Boiling stones

Is the material sandstone, hard stone or fired clay?
Is the stone basically round?
Is it about the size of a small tangerine?
Are there any crusty black particles adhering to surfaces?
Is your stone fire-cracked?
Or is the "stone" a chunk of compressed clay?

Celts

Is the material granite, hematite, basalt or slate?
Is the stone pecked and ground?
Is the shape triangular, rectangular or cylindrical?
Does one end taper into a sharp blade edge?
Is the other end rectangular, pointed or rounded?
Was it made without a groove?
Do you think it might be an adze?
Or have you found a chipped, heat-treated celt?

Ceremonial stones

Is the material a type of hard stone?
Is it pecked, ground and polished?
Is the stone decorated, finely crafted or oversized?
Does it have a geometric or an ornamental design?
Has it been drilled, grooved or notched?
Have you found a tool, a weapon or an atlatl weight?
Is it a birdstone, boatstone or bannerstone?
Or a gorget, discoidal, spud or spatulate?

Chipping stones

Is the material a type of hard stone?
Does your cobble have one level surface, or two?
Is there pitting in the center of one or both level sides?
Have you found one that was also used as a hammerstone?
Could your broad, flat rock be a stationary anvil?

Chunkey stones
Is the material a type of hard stone?
Is it pecked, ground and polished?
Is the stone in the shape of a disc?
Are the faces concave or convex?
Have you found one with an indented center or a drilled hole?
Are there any tally marks?
Is there damage from use, or is it flawless?
Wouldn't your flawless disc be a ceremonial stone?
Could your "stone" discoidal be a fired clay biscuit?

Cooking stones
Is the material sandstone, hard stone or fired clay?
Is the stone basically round?
Is it about the size of a small tangerine?
Are there any crusty black particles adhering to surfaces?
Is your stone fire-cracked?
Or is the "stone" a chunk of compressed clay?

Cores
Is the material flint or chert?
Is the stone in the shape of a cone?
Are there flaking scars on all surfaces?
Do you see any evidence of heat-treating?

Cup stones
Is the material sandstone?
Does the stone have one or more hollows?
Is the size of the hollows between a quarter and a silver dollar?
Are the hollows no more than one inch deep?
Do you think it was used as a nut stone?

Discoidals
Is the material a type of hard stone?
Is it pecked, ground and polished?
Is the stone in the shape of a disc?
Are the faces concave or convex?
Have you found one with an indented center or a drilled hole?
Are there any tally marks?
Have you found a flawless disc, or is there damage from use?
Is it a ceremonial stone or a game stone?
Could your "stone" disc be a fired clay biscuit?

Drills

Is the material flint or chert?
Does the stone have a long, narrow shaft?
Does the shaft have three or four flaked sides?
Does the base resemble a type on a point or knife?
Do you see any evidence of heat-treating?

Effigies

Is the material a type of hard stone?
Is it pecked, ground and polished?
Does it resemble a reptile, fish, bird, animal or human?
Does it have grooves or drilled holes?
Wouldn't that make it an atlatl weight or a ceremonial stone?

Fire-cracked rock fragments: cooking stones, boiling stones and hearth stones

Is the material sandstone?
Does the rock seem to be blackened or fire-reddened?
Is the fragment chunky rather than jagged?

Fired clay biscuits

Is the material fired clay?
Is the object in the shape of a disc?
Does the disc have two flat sides?
Is there a ring on the edge that may have come from a mold?
Are there any crusty black particles adhering to surfaces?
Could it be a chunkey stone?

Flake tools

Is the material flint, chert or obsidian?
Have you found a thin, sharp flake?
Is there perhaps a bit of chipping on part of an edge?
Does your flake have a "handle" opposite the sharp edge?
Do you see any evidence of heat-treating?

Game stones

Is the material a type of hard stone?
Is it pecked, ground and polished?
Is the shape perfectly round?
Or is it in the shape of a disc?
Have you found a chunkey stone?
Could it be a ceremonial stone?

Gorgets

Is the material slate?
Is it pecked, ground and polished?
Is the stone flat and thin?
Does it have a rectangular shape?
Are there two evenly spaced holes?
Or have you found one with three, four or maybe more?
Does it have any tally marks along edges?
Is it an atlatl weight, an ornament or a ceremonial stone?

Gravers

Is the material flint or chert?
Is the stone percussion-shaped and pressure-flaked?
Does it have one or more short, sturdy tips?
Or is the spur flaked on a corner of an end scraper?
Do you see any evidence of heat-treating?

Grinding stones

Is the material sandstone, river rock or granite?
Is the stone small or large?
Does it have a defined shape?
Or is it just easy to hold?
Is there at least one flat, smooth surface?
Does the smooth surface have one-way grinding scars?
Does your rough stone have grinding scars or parallel grooves?
Is it a mano or a pestle?
Have you found a polishing stone or an abrading stone?

Hammerstones

Is the material a type of hard stone?
Does the rock fit comfortably in your hand?
Is your cobble nicked and chipped at one end?
Did you find residue flakes or other artifacts in the area?
Was your hammerstone also used as a chipping stone?

Handaxes

Is the material flint or chert?
Is the stone flaked over all surfaces?
Is the size at least as large as your hand?
Is there extensive damage on edges?
Could it be a large scraper or a preform?
Do you see any evidence of heat-treating?

Heat-treated stone: points, knives, scrapers and other tools
Is the material flint or chert?
Does the stone have a gloss or waxy luster?
Are there tinges of yellow, orange, pink or rose?
Are there surface areas that are rough and red, or dark?
Do surfaces have any small, concave craters?
Is your stone flaked, or was it spoiled by "pot-lid" fractures?

Knife fragments
Is the material flint or chert?
Is the stone flaked over all surfaces?
Does it have deep, uneven notches and unequal shoulders?
Does it have a wide, sturdy base?
Does it have a blunt tip, or is it sharp?
Are the edges beveled or serrated?
Does the flaking have a pattern, or is it random?
Do you see any evidence of heat-treating?
Have you found a rare fluted fragment?
Could your fragment be part of a projectile point?

Manos
Is the material river rock, basalt or granite?
Is the shape oval or round?
Does it have a convex side that fits comfortably in your hand?
Is there a flat side?
Does the flat side have one-way grinding scars?
Have you found one with two flat sides?
Did you find any flakes or other artifacts in the area?

Mauls
Is the material a type of hard stone?
Is the stone pecked and ground?
Does it have a groove?
Is it a cross between a hammerstone and an axe?
Is it nicked and chipped at one end?

Mortar fragments
Is the material a type of hard stone or limestone?
Have you found part of a flat or scooped surface?
Does the fragment have one-way grinding scars?
Did you find a mano in the area?

Multipurpose tools
Is the material flint or chert?
Are there features that serve two or more purposes?
Such as scraping, slitting, puncturing or etching?
Does the stone have unifacial or bifacial flaking?
Do you see any evidence of heat-treating?

Net weights
Is your stone a pebble or a core?
Are rough notches chipped on two opposite sides?
Or is a hole drilled through it instead?

Nut stones
Is the material sandstone?
Does the stone have one or more hollows?
Is the size of the hollows between a quarter and a silver dollar?
Are the hollows no more than one inch deep?
Do you think it was used as a cup stone?

Ornaments
Is the material stone, bone or shell?
Has the stone been polished?
Does it have drilled holes, grooves or notches?
Is it decorated with tally marks or etched with designs?
Is it a pendant, gorget or reworked spatulate?

Pendants
Is the material slate, hard stone or bone?
Has the stone been polished?
Does it have a geometric shape, or is it in another design?
Is it small—between one and five inches long?
Does it have a drilled hole at one end?
Have you found one with two holes, a groove or notches?
Are there any tally marks or decorative lines?

Perforators
Is the material flint or chert?
Is the stone percussion-flaked?
Does it have a sharp spike?
Is there any pressure flaking?
Do you see any evidence of heat-treating?

Pestles

Is the material granite?
Is the stone pecked and ground?
Does it have the shape of a rolling pin, bell, hoof or tube?

Pipe fragments

Is the material fired clay, soapstone or hard stone?

Bowls: Are the surfaces smooth?
Is the fragment thin and rounded?
Have you found part of a rim?
Or does the base curve into part of the stem?
Are there any decorative etched lines?
Or does the bowl have the shape of an animal or human?
Did you see any black smudges on the concave surface?

Stems: Is the shape cylindrical or square?
Is the fragment also hollow?

Polishing stones

Is the material a type of hard stone?
Is the stone small enough to hold with your fingers?
Does it have one or more flat surfaces?
Do the flat surfaces have one-way grinding scars?
Did you find any pottery sherds in the area?

Pottery sherds

Is the material fired clay?
Do you see tiny bits of shell or stone mixed in it?
Are the surfaces dull instead of glossy?
Have you found one with blackened interior surfaces?
Does the fragment have any etched lines or other designs?
Could it be part of a rim or handle?
Did you remember to record any "keepers" from the area?

Preforms

Is the material flint or chert?
Is the stone flaked over all surfaces?
Does it seem to have the basic shape of a point or knife?
Or is it in the rough form of a tool, such as a chipped adze or celt?
Did you find any flakes or other artifacts in the area?
Do you see any evidence of heat-treating?

Projectile point fragments

Is the material flint or chert?
Is the stone flaked over all surfaces?
Does it have a notch, stem, tang, tip, flute or barb?
Is there an impact fracture?
Are there smooth edges on your base or stem?
Are other edges serrated, beveled or ground?
Does the flaking have a pattern, or is it random?
Do you see any evidence of heat-treating?
Could your fragment be part of a knife?

Scrapers

Is the material flint or chert?
Are edges percussion-flaked, pressure-flaked or both?
Is there chipping on surfaces or only at edges?
Does the stone have unifacial or bifacial flaking?
Does the tool have a rock "handle," or is it chipped for hafting?
Is deep flaking in a good spot for a handhold?
Are there other features that would make it a multipurpose tool?
Do you see any evidence of heat-treating?

Spatulates

Is the material a type of hard stone?
Is it pecked, ground and polished?
Does the shape remind you of a spatula?
Is the shaft long and narrow?
Is one end flat and broad?
Do you think it might be a spud?
Is it a large ceremonial stone?
Or have you found a smaller shovel-shaped pendant?

Spokeshaves

Is the material flint or chert?
Does an edge have one or two small cutouts?
Is the stone flaked on only one side?

Spuds

Is the material flint or chert?
Is the tool well made?
Is the shaft long and narrow?
Does one end flare into a sharp blade?
Does it remind you of a celt or a spatulate?
Could it be a ceremonial stone, a chopping tool or a weapon?

State Historic Preservation Agencies

Since 1966, when the National Historic Preservation Act was passed, states have had the responsibility of protecting historic resources. Under the act, the governor of each state is required to appoint a person to supervise preservation efforts. That person is your SHPO.

The agency your SHPO works for strives to preserve, protect and interpret history. It provides information, literature, special services, and programs to inform and assist the public. Individuals interested in preserving and protecting historic resources should contact their agency to explore the services it offers.

The people working for historic preservation agencies appreciate individuals like yourself who surface hunt and participate in preservation efforts. You can nominate a place for designation in the National Register of Historic Places by working with your state agency. Get approval to make a nomination from the property owner first, because the owner will have the responsibility of looking after the site.

Listing on the NRHP is an honor. Sites qualify landowners for certain tax breaks, and sometimes sites could receive special public funds as well. To be considered for the roster, any site nominated must first be determined eligible. State agencies are responsible for identifying sites and administering nomination applications, so contact your SHPO. Final designation would be made by the National Park Service.

The prehistoric people may be long since gone, but their history remains in the artifacts and sites you find. Reporting artifacts and sites is not a requirement, but a matter of choice and conscience. Help keep historic preservation alive and well by working with the SHPO of your state.

ALABAMA

Alabama Historical Commission
468 S Perry St
Montgomery, AL 36130-0900
(334) 242-3184
(334) 240-3477 FAX

ALASKA

Division of Parks
Office of History and
Archeology
PO Box 107001
Anchorage, AK 99510-7001
(907) 762-2622
(907) 762-2535 FAX

ARIZONA

Arizona State Parks
1300 W Washington
Phoenix, AZ 85007
(602) 542-4174
(602) 542-4180 FAX

ARKANSAS

Arkansas Historic Preservation Program
323 Center St Ste 1500
Little Rock, AR 72201
(501) 324-9880
(501) 324-9184 FAX

CALIFORNIA

Dept of Parks and Recreation
Office of Historic Preservation
PO Box 942896
Sacramento, CA 94296-0001
(916) 653-6624
(916) 653-8924 FAX

COLORADO

Colorado Historical Society
1300 Broadway
Denver, CO 80203
(303) 866-3355
(303) 866-5507 FAX

CONNECTICUT

Connecticut Historical Commission
59 S Prospect St
Hartford, CT 06106
(860) 566-3005
(860) 566-5078 FAX

DELAWARE

Division of History and Cultural Affairs
Historic Preservation Office
15 The Green
Dover, DE 19901-3611
(302) 739-5685
(302) 739-5660 FAX

DISTRICT OF COLUMBIA

Dept Consumer and Regulatory Affairs
614 H St NW Rm 305
Washington, DC 20001
(202) 727-6053
(202) 727-5445 FAX

FLORIDA

Division of Historical Resources
Bureau of Archaeological Research
500 S Bronough St
Tallahassee, FL 32399-0250
(904) 487-2299

GEORGIA

Office of Historic Preservation
205 Butler St SE Ste 1462
Atlanta, GA 30334
(404) 656-2840
(404) 651-5871 FAX

HAWAII

Dept of Land and Natural Resources
PO Box 621
Honolulu, HI 96809
(808) 548-6550

IDAHO

Idaho Historical Society
210 Main St
Boise, ID 83702
(208) 334-2682
(208) 334-2775 FAX

ILLINOIS

Illinois Historic Preservation Agency
One Old State Capitol Plaza
Springfield, IL 62701-1512
(217) 785-1153
(217) 524-7525 FAX

INDIANA

Dept of Natural Resources
Indiana Government Center S
402 W Washington St Rm W256
Indianapolis, IN 46204
(317) 232-4020
(317) 232-8036 FAX

IOWA

State Historical Society of Iowa
600 E Locust
Des Moines, IA 50319
(515) 281-8837
(515) 242-0560 FAX

KANSAS

Kansas State Historical Society
Memorial Bldg
120 SW 10th Ave
Topeka, KS 66612-1291
(913) 296-3251
(913) 296-1005 FAX

KENTUCKY

Kentucky Heritage Council
300 Washington St
Frankfort, KY 40601
(502) 564-7005
(502) 564-5820 FAX

LOUISIANA

Dept of Culture, Recreation and Tourism
PO Box 44247
Baton Rouge, LA 70804
(504) 342-8200
(504) 342-8173 FAX

MAINE

Maine Historical Preservation Commission
55 Capitol St Station 65
Augusta, ME 04333
(207) 287-2132
(207) 287-5335 FAX

MARYLAND

Division of Historical and Cultural Programs
Dept of Housing and
Community Development
100 Community Pl 3rd Fl
Crownsville, MD 21032-2023
(410) 514-7661
(410) 514-7678 FAX

MASSACHUSETTS

Massachusetts Historical Commission
80 Boylston St Ste 310
Boston, MA 02116
(617) 727-8470
(617) 727-5128 FAX

MICHIGAN

Office of the State Archaeologist
Michigan Historical Center
717 W Allegan St
Lansing, MI 48918-1847
(517) 373-0511
(517) 373-0851 FAX

MINNESOTA

Minnesota Historical Society
345 Kellogg Blvd W
St Paul, MN 55102-1906
(612) 296-2747
(612) 296-1004 FAX

MISSISSIPPI

Mississippi Dept of Archives and History
PO Box 571
Jackson, MS 39205-0571
(601) 359-6850

MISSOURI

State Dept of Natural Resources
205 Jefferson St
PO Box 176
Jefferson City, MO 65102
(573) 751-4422
(573) 526-2852 FAX

MONTANA

State Historic Preservation Office
1410 8th Ave
PO Box 201202
Helena, MT 59620-1202
(406) 444-7715
(406) 444-6575 FAX

NEBRASKA

Nebraska State Historical Society
1500 R St
PO Box 82554
Lincoln, NE 68501-2554
(800) 833-6747
(402) 471-3270

NEVADA

Historic Preservation Office
Capitol Complex
101 S Steward St
Carson City, NV 89710
(702) 687-6360

NEW HAMPSHIRE

State Historic Preservation Office
19 Pillsbury St
PO Box 2043
Concord, NH 03302-2043
(603) 271-3483
(800) 735-2964 TDD

NEW JERSEY

New Jersey Dept of Environmental Protection and Energy
CN402, 401 E State St
Trenton, NJ 08625-0404
(609) 292-2885
(609) 292-7695 FAX

NEW MEXICO

Historic Preservation Division
Office of Cultural Affairs
Villa Rivera Bldg
228 E Palace Ave
Santa Fe, NM 87503
(505) 827-6320
(505) 827-6338 FAX

NEW YORK

Parks, Recreation and Historic Preservation
Agency Bldg 1
Empire State Plaza
Albany, NY 12223
(518) 474-0443

NORTH CAROLINA

Division of Archives and History
109 E Jones St
Raleigh, NC 27601-2807
(919) 733-7305
(919) 733-8807 FAX

NORTH DAKOTA

State Historical Society of North Dakota
612 E Blvd Ave
Bismarck, ND 58505-0830
(701) 328-2666
(701) 328-3710 FAX

OHIO

Ohio Historic Preservation Office
1982 Velma Ave
Columbus, OH 43211-2497
(614) 297-2470
(614) 297-2546 FAX

OKLAHOMA

Oklahoma Historical Society
Capitol Complex
2100 N Lincoln Blvd
Oklahoma City, OK 73105
(405) 521-2491
(405) 521-2492 FAX

OREGON

State Parks and Recreation Dept
1115 Commercial St NE
Salem, OR 97310-1001
(503) 378-5019
(503) 378-6447 FAX

PENNSYLVANIA

Pennsylvania Historical and Museum Commission
PO Box 1026
Harrisburg, PA 17108
(717) 787-2891

RHODE ISLAND

Rhode Island Historical Preservation Commission
Old State House
150 Benefit St
Providence, RI 02903
(401) 277-2678
(401) 277-2968 FAX

SOUTH CAROLINA

Dept of Archives and History
PO Box 11669
Columbia, SC 29211
(803) 734-8609
(803) 734-8820 FAX

SOUTH DAKOTA

South Dakota State Historical Society
Cultural Heritage Center
900 Governors Dr
Pierre, SD 57501-2217
(605) 773-3458
(605) 773-6041 FAX

TENNESSEE

Tennessee Division of Archaeology
5103 Edmondson Pike
Nashville, TN 37211
(615) 741-1588

TEXAS

Texas Historical Commission
Capitol Station
PO Box 12276
Austin, TX 78711-2276
(512) 463-6100
(512) 475-4872 FAX

UTAH

Utah State Historical Society
300 Rio Grande
Salt Lake City, UT 84101
(801) 533-3500
(801) 533-3503 FAX

VERMONT

Agency of Development and Community Affairs
135 State St 4th Fl
Montpelier, VT 05633-1201
(802) 828-3211

VIRGINIA

Dept of Historic Resources
Commonwealth of Virginia
221 Governor St
Richmond, VA 23219
(804) 786-3143
(804) 225-4261 FAX

WASHINGTON

Office of Archaeology and Historic Preservation
111 W 21st Ave SW
PO Box 48343
Olympia, WA 98504-8343
(360) 753-4011
(360) 586-0250 FAX

WEST VIRGINIA

West Virginia Dept of Culture and History
1900 Kanawha Blvd E
Charleston, WV 25305-0300
(304) 558-0220

WISCONSIN

Office of the State Archaeologist
State Historical Society of Wisconsin
816 State St
Madison, WI 53706
(608) 264-6500
(608) 264-6404 FAX

WYOMING

Wyoming State Historic Preservation Office
6101 Yellowstone Rd 2nd Fl
Cheyenne, WY 82002
(307) 777-7697
(307) 777-6421 FAX

Historic Preservation Project Opportunities

Would you like to work with an archaeologist on a professionally supervised dig? Or help a forest ranger track prehistory on a trail adventure? Would you rather assist preservation specialists restore a prehistoric ruin, repair a historic log cabin, or be a guardian to an archaeological site? If you want to take part in an archaeological excavation, a back country expedition, be a site steward, or preserve cultural resources in some other way, volunteer to participate in a historic preservation project.

To become part of a preservation project team, all you really need is interest. Sometimes specialists need volunteers who can sketch, take photos, write clearly, or interview. Other times, they look for volunteers who know about carpentry, masonry, drafting or lab techniques. Often, they want people who like hiking or camping. You'll be a good candidate because of your surface hunting experience. You can choose to map sites, identify or catalog artifacts, research historical records, or volunteer for other activities that require some archaeological knowledge. No matter how you participate, you'll make a valued contribution to the team and also learn new skills under the guidance of professionals.

The organizations listed offer preservation project opportunities to people of all ages and educational backgrounds, but there are many others that have excellent programs, too. You can get more information from archaeological societies, museums and universities. Since these types of organizations conduct their own projects, be sure to check the listings in other sections of the *Resources*.

American Anthropological Association *Field School Guide*
1703 New Hampshire Ave NW
Washington, DC 20009
(202) 232-8800

Excavations in the U.S. and Canada. Opportunities are described in the *Field School Guide.*

Arkansas Archeological Survey
PO Box 1249
Fayetteville, AR 72702
(501) 575-3556
(501) 575-5453 FAX

Excavations in Arkansas.

Center for American Archeology
Kampsville Archeological Canter
PO Box 366
Kampsville, IL 62053
(618) 653-4316
(618) 653-4232 FAX

Educational and field school programs for middle and high school students, and adults. Excavations, tours, research and conservation of sites.

Earthwatch
680 Mt Auburn St
PO Box 9104
Watertown, MA 02172-9104
(800) 776-0188
(617) 926-8200

Excavations in the U.S. and around the world.

Foundation for Field Research
PO Box 2010
Alpine, CA 92001
(619) 450-3460

Private organization. Professionally supervised investigations.

Ontario Archaeological Society
126 Willowdale Ave
Ontario M2N 4Y2 Canada

Summer digs in Ontario.

Partners in Preservation Program
Heritage Resources Management
Los Padres National Forest
6144 Calle Real
Goleta, CA 93117
(800) 281-9176
(805) 681-2723
(805) 681-2729 FAX

Modeled after the Arizona Site Steward Program. Main objective is to prevent destruction of prehistoric and historic sites in Los Padres National Forest through site monitoring. Site stewards are trained by Forest Service archaeologists and law enforcement personnel. Stewards document archaeological sites in danger of artifact theft, destruction or deterioration. Calendar of events is published in a quarterly bulletin, the *Site Monitor.*

Passport in Time

Passport in Time Clearinghouse
PO Box 31315
Tucson, AZ 85751-1315
(800) 281-9176
(520) 722-2716
(520) 298-7044 FAX

Work with professional archaeologists and historians. Excavations, ruins stabilization, historic structure restoration, oral history, research projects and more. Opportunities across the U.S. are described in the *Pit Traveler*, a free biannual newsletter. A program of the U.S. Department of Agriculture Forest Service, all PIT projects are conducted under the direct supervision of the Forest Service Heritage staff.

Smithsonian Associates

Research Expeditions
490 L'Enfant Plaza SW Ste 4210
Washington, DC 20560
(202) 287-3210

Private organization. Professionally supervised investigations.

University Research Expeditions Program

University of California
Berkeley, CA 94720-7050
(510) 642-6586

Private organization. Professionally supervised investigations.

Archaeological Societies and Other Memberships

The best way to meet other people who are interested in Native American prehistory is through an archaeological society or organization. Being a member of a society is like belonging to an archaeology club. Societies provide opportunities to exchange information and ideas, and make contacts in the field of archaeology. Each organization has its own individual benefits and services. You can enjoy shows, meetings, special events, workshops, fieldwork opportunities and publications. Some societies offer programs that include public education, certification, and awards. Others would welcome your support on a committee or task force.

All of the organizations included in this section do not have the same objectives. In making a decision about which one to join, consider the society's goals. Regardless of whether the headquarters is located in your state, you'll get much more out of your membership if you choose one that reflects your views on the study of archaeology. Nationwide societies holding annual meetings in different regions often include excavations, lectures, special activities and shows—and may last for up to a week. Join one of these and plan to attend for a few days. You'll get to know others while learning about archaeology in a hands-on way.

Incidentally, addresses of some of these non-profit organizations may change annually, when new individuals begin service as officers. Should you need more current information, contact another society, a local museum or your SHPO. You may also want to inquire about other associations that are not listed on the following pages.

American Society for Amateur Archaeology

PO Box 1264
Buffalo, NY 14205-1264
(716) 849-0149
(800) 279-ASAA (members)

North American membership. All ages. Dedicated to the advancement of amateur archaeology and science for the general public. Advocates free exchange of knowledge about America's past. Clearinghouse for information about the latest discoveries, archaeological activities, laws and publications. Supervised excavations, lectures and an artifact show at annual meetings in different regions. Telephone line connects members with the organizer. Journal, *The Amateur Archaeologist*, at least twice a year.

Archaeological Conservancy

5301 Central Ave NE Ste 1218
Albuquerque, NM 87108
(505) 266-1540

Most members are not professional archaeologists. Works to preserve prehistoric and historic sites for research. Operates with government agencies, universities and museums. Quarterly publication, the *Archaeological Conservancy Newsletter.*

Archaeological Institute of America

675 Commonwealth Ave
Boston, MA 02215-2010
(617) 353-9361
(617) 353-6550 FAX

Educational and scientific society for those interested in study and research. Sponsors programs for middle school children. Annual publication, *Archaeological Fieldwork Opportunities Bulletin,* lists excavation sites and field schools for volunteers. Quarterly journal, *American Journal of Archaeology,* and quarterly newsletters. Publishes the magazine, *Archaeology* (see *Subscriptions*).

Archaeological Society of New Jersey

PO Box 23
Rahway, NJ 07065

Amateur-friendly society for those interested in intelligent conservation of sites and artifacts. Fieldwork, lab procedures, report preparation, exhibitions and quarterly meetings. Two publications, the *Bulletin* and the *Newsletter*. New Jersey and adjacent states.

Archaeological Society of Ohio

2505 Logan-Thornville Rd
Rushville, OH 43150
(800) 736-7815

Nationwide membership of amateurs and professionals. Excavations, artifact shows, chapter and annual meetings. Quarterly magazine, the *Ohio Archaeologist.* Robert N. Converse, editor (see *Additional Reading*).

Archeological Society of Virginia

562 Rossmore Rd
Richmond, VA 23225

Arizona Archaeological and Historical Society

3255 Camino Campestre
Tucson, AZ 85716
(520) 795-4581

On the Council of Affiliated Societies of the Society for American Archaeology.

Arizona Archaeological Society
725 W Brown #18
Tempe, AZ 85281
(602) 968-1683

On the Council of Affiliated Societies of the Society for American Archaeology.

Badger State Archaeological Society of Wisconsin
240 N High St
Randolph, WI 53956

Amateur-friendly member of the Central States Archaeological Societies, Inc. See *Subscriptions* for quarterly publication, the *Central States Archaeological Journal*.

Central States Archaeological Societies, Inc.
11552 Patty Ann
St. Louis, MO 63146

Amateur-friendly society. Endeavors to develop a better understanding among students, collectors, professionals, museums and schools by publishing articles and photos. Member states: Alabama, Arkansas, Georgia, Illinois, Indiana, Iowa, Kentucky, Michigan, Missouri, North Carolina, South Carolina, Tennessee and Wisconsin. See Badger State Archaeological Society of Wisconsin, Greater St. Louis Archaeological Society, Green River Archaeological Society of Kentucky, Hawkeye State Archaeological Society of Iowa, Illinois State Archaeological Society, Indiana Archaeological Society, Northwest Arkansas Archaeological Society, Peach State Archaeological Society of Georgia, Piedmont Archaeological Society of North and South Carolina, Rebel State Archaeological Society of Alabama, Volunteer State Archaeological Society of Tennessee, or Wolverine State Archaeological Society of Michigan. See *Subscriptions* for the *Central States Archaeological Journal*.

Colorado Archaeological Society
1300 Broadway
Denver, CO 80203
(303) 440-8572

On the Council of Affiliated Societies of the Society for American Archaeology.

Early Sites Research Society
c/o James Whittall
Long Hill
Rowley, MA 01969
(508) 948-2410

For those interested in the study of unidentified stone artifacts or other unexplained antiquities in the U.S. Operates a field school for children. Annual bulletin and periodic newsletters.

Eastern States Archaeological Federation
RD 2 Box 166
Dover, DE 19901

Amateur-friendly archaeological society. Nationwide membership.

Greater St. Louis Archaeological Society
PO Box 665
Bridgeton, MO 63044

Amateur-friendly member of the Central States Archaeological Societies, Inc. See *Subscriptions* for quarterly publication, the *Central States Archaeological Journal*.

Green River Archaeological Society of Kentucky
Box 923
Benton, KY 42025

Amateur-friendly member of the Central States Archaeological Societies, Inc. See *Subscriptions* for quarterly publication, the *Central States Archaeological Journal*.

Hawkeye State Archaeological Society of Iowa

407 Kindler Ave
Muscatine, IA 52761

Amateur-friendly member of the Central States Archaeological Societies, Inc. See *Subscriptions* for quarterly publication, the *Central States Archaeological Journal.*

Houston Archaeological Society

PO Box 6751
Houston, TX 77265-6751

On the Council of Affiliated Societies of the Society for American Archaeology.

Illinois Association for Advancement of Archaeology

RR 1 Box 63
Huntsville, IL 62344

Offers certificates to members sixteen years and older who participate in supervised excavations or workshops. Annual statewide meetings. Quarterly bulletin, *Illinois Antiquity,* and *Rediscovery,* an occasional journal. Separate dues required for membership in local chapters. On the Council of Affiliated Societies of the Society for American Archaeology.

Illinois State Archaeological Society

2910 Vigal Rd
Springfield, IL 62707

Amateur-friendly member of the Central States Archaeological Societies, Inc. Artifact shows and competitions. Annual show in Collinsville, Illinois, is one of the largest in the country. Quarterly publication, the *Central States Archaeological Journal,* and *Field Notes,* a quarterly newsletter.

Indiana Archaeological Society

107 Vantassel Dr
Monticello, IN 47960

Amateur-friendly member of the Central States Archaeological Societies, Inc. Artifact shows, junior shows, competitions, awards and more. Quarterly publication, the *Central States Archaeological Journal,* and newsletters.

Institute for American Indian Studies

38 Curtis Rd
PO Box 12601
Washington, CT 06793-0260
(860) 868-0518
(860) 868-1649 FAX

Family and individual memberships. Sponsors summer youth programs, craft workshops, film festivals and archaeological training sessions. Native American Art and Literary Competition for 1st through 8th graders. Indoor and outdoor exhibits. Archaeological excavations. Quarterly journal, *Artifacts,* and newsletters.

Iowa Archeological Society

c/o Office of the State Archaeologist
Eastlawn
University of Iowa
Iowa City, IA 52242-1411

Amateur-friendly society for those interested in Iowa archaeology. Has a good working relationship with professionals. Promotes the study, investigation and interpretation of prehistoric and historic remains. Field excavations, presentations and exhibits. Biannual meetings in different regions. Annual publication, *The Journal of the Iowa Archeological Society,* and quarterly newsletters.

Kansas City Archaeological Society
Museum of Anthropology
University of Kansas
Lawrence, KS 66045
(913) 864-4245

On the Council of Affiliated Societies of the Society for American Archaeology.

Louisiana Archeological Society
7628 N Coventry Circle
Baton Rouge, LA 70808
(504) 766-7142

On the Council of Affiliated Societies of the Society for American Archaeology.

Maine Archaeological Society
PO Box 9715-253
Portland, ME 04140
(207) 657-4574

On the Council of Affiliated Societies of the Society for American Archaeology.

Massachusetts Archaeological Society
12 Long Ave
Greenfield, MA 01301
(413) 773-7870

On the Council of Affiliated Societies of the Society for American Archaeology.

Mississippi Archaeological Association
PO Box 571
Jackson, MS 39205-0571
(601) 359-6863

On the Council of Affiliated Societies of the Society for American Archaeology.

Missouri Archaeological Society
PO Box 958
Columbia, MO 65205
(573) 882-3544

For those interested in archaeology but who choose not to collect artifacts. On the Council of
Affiliated Societies of the Society for American Archaeology.

New York State Archaeological Association
84 Lockrow Ave
Albany, NY 12205
(518) 459-4209

Amateur-friendly organization. Membership across the U.S., Canada and Europe. Founded in 1916
and chartered in 1927 by the Board of Regents of the State of New York. Long Island Chapter built
the Southhold Indian Museum (see *Places to Go and Things to See*). Non-profit.

Northern Illinois Archeological Society
c/o Mix's Trading Post
602 Clark St
Utica, IL 61373
(815) 667-4120

For those who choose to collect artifacts and are interested in sharing information at artifact shows.
NIAS has been conducting shows for approximately forty years. Biannual.

Northwest Arkansas Archaeological Society
20 Evesham Ln
Bella Vista, AR 72714

Amateur-friendly member of the Central States Archaeological Societies, Inc. See *Subscriptions* for quarterly publication, the *Central States Archaeological Journal.*

Oklahoma Anthropological Society
RT 1 Box 62 B
Cheyenne, OK 73628

Amateur-friendly society. Nationwide membership. Certification programs in archaeological photography, archaeological research design, lithic technology and analysis, and organic remains analysis. Excavations, artifact shows, meetings, newsletters and more.

Oregon Archaeological Society
PO Box 13293
Portland, OR 97213

For those interested in archaeology but who choose not to collect artifacts. Nationwide membership.

Peach State Archaeological Society of Georgia
3327 Woodview Dr
Smyrna, GA 30082

Amateur-friendly member of the Central States Archaeological Societies, Inc. See *Subscriptions* for quarterly publication, the *Central States Archaeological Journal.*

Piedmont Archaeological Society of North and South Carolina
159 Marshdale Ave SW
Concord, NC 25025-5647
(704) 786-6294

Amateur-friendly member of the Central States Archaeological Societies, Inc. The Piedmont Archaeological Society of North and South Carolina is a non-profit organization organized to discover and conserve archaeological sites and materials within the States of North and South Carolina, to seek and promote a better understanding among students and collectors, professionals and non-professionals of archaeological material, and to promote archaeological knowledge through publications and meetings. See *Subscriptions* for quarterly publication, the *Central States Archaeological Journal.*

Rebel State Archaeological Society of Alabama
PO Box 635
Rogersville, AL 35652

Amateur-friendly member of the Central States Archaeological Societies, Inc. See *Subscriptions* for quarterly publication, the *Central States Archaeological Journal.*

Sacramento Archaeological Society
2601 Sierra Blvd
Sacramento, CA 95864
(916) 485-5976

On the Council of Affiliated Societies of the Society for American Archaeology.

Society for the Documentation of Prehistoric America
3416 Lucas-Hunt Rd
St Louis, MO 63121

Amateur-friendly archaeological society. Nationwide membership. Artifact shows and meetings. Quarterly journal, the *Prehistoric American.*

Texas Archaeological Society
14804 Great Willow Dr
Austin, TX 78728
(512) 251-2639

For those interested in archaeology but who choose not to collect artifacts. On the Council of Affiliated Societies of the Society for American Archaeology.

Texas Cache Amateur Archeological Association
8901 Hwy 67 #10
San Angelo, TX 76904
(800) 7-CLOVIS
(915) 947-7616

Nationwide membership. Members may document artifact finds in the TCAAA archaeological database. Journal of submissions printed annually. Unlimited access to the TCAAA library. Representatives will come to your town to hold a membership drive, promote amateur archaeology, document point types, and photograph artifacts from your area. Artifact and flintknapping shows, competitions, excavations and more. See *Subscriptions* for magazine, *The Texas Cache*.

Utah Statewide Archaeological Society
441 S 400 W
Vernal, UT 84078

On the Council of Affiliated Societies of the Society for American Archaeology.

Volunteer State Archaeological Society of Tennessee
510 N Russell St
Portland, TN 37148

Amateur-friendly member of the Central States Archaeological Societies, Inc. See *Subscriptions* for quarterly publication, the *Central States Archaeological Journal*.

West Virginia Archeology Society
PO Box 5323
Charleston, WV 25361-0323

Amateur-friendly society. Biannual publication, the *West Virginia Archeologist*, and *Field Notes*, a bimonthly newsletter.

Wisconsin Archaeological Society
4600 N Morris Blvd
Milwaukee, WI 53211
(414) 963-1072

On the Council of Affiliated Societies of the Society for American Archaeology.

Wolverine State Archaeological Society of Michigan
2611 Niles Rd
St. Joseph, MI 49085

Amateur-friendly member of the Central States Archaeological Societies, Inc. See *Subscriptions* for quarterly publication, the *Central States Archaeological Journal*.

World Archaeological Society
120 Lakewood Dr
Hollister, MO 65672
(417) 334-2377

Members are amateur and professional archaeologists, anthropologists and art historians from over thirty countries. Promotes the study of archaeology, anthropology and art history. Periodic *WAS Newsletter*, *WAS Fact Sheet* and special publications.

Subscriptions

Artifact magazines, antiquity newspapers and other periodicals will help keep you abreast of archaeological news, artifact shows, books, films and more. Before ordering a subscription, request a sample copy to see how you like it. While an issue is sometimes provided free of charge, you might have to pay the individual, nominal cost. To receive a publication from an archaeological society, membership may be required. Typically, membership dues are comparable with prices of subscriptions. Consider joining a society not only for its publications, but for all other benefits as well. Though issues of some subscriptions included in this section can be found at bookstores or libraries, consult a librarian or contact an archaeological society for information about other periodicals that are available.

Amateur Archaeologist, The
PO Box 1264
Buffalo, NY 14205-1264
(716) 849-0149
(800) 279-ASAA (members)

Biannual journal. Features the archaeology of individual states. Reliable information about laws, prehistory, laws, laboratory tests and more. Photographs of artifacts from all over the country. Special issues. American Society for Amateur Archaeology membership required.

American Indian Art
7314 E Osborn Dr
Scottsdale, AZ 85251

Magazine. Native American, Old West and Southwest art, collectibles and antiques.

Ancient American, The
PO Box 370
Colfax, WI 54730

Bimonthly magazine. Mysteries of prehistory in a four-color format.

Archaeology
Subscription Service
PO Box 420425
Palm Coast, FL 32142-9808
(800) 829-5122

Bimonthly magazine. Archaeology around the world. Information on tours, excavations, surveys and lab work. Articles on archaeological topics, book and film reviews and exhibition news. Archaeological Institute of America lecture schedule for the U.S. and Canada.

Central States Archaeological Journal
11552 Patty Ann
St Louis, MO 63146

Archaeological society quarterly. A combined publication of member societies from thirteen states. Articles and photos of interest to both professional and amateur archaeologists. Calender of events. Subscription by membership only.

Chips Magazine
PO Box 702
Branson, MO 65615

Quarterly. Learn how tools and weapons were made. All articles are reader contributions. Nationwide calender for knap-ins, primitive technology, workshops and field trips. D.C. and Valerie Waldorf, editors *(see Additional Reading)*.

Enchanted Rock Magazine
209 E Main
Llano, TX 78643
(800) 865-6163

Monthly. A guide to the Texas Hill Country. Tales of cowboys and Indians, legends of conquistadors, family histories, and the way it was. Everything from hunters and gatherers to adventure maps for today. Named after Enchanted Rock, a place that Indians held sacred.

Flint Knapper's Exchange, The
278 W 8th St
Peru, IN 46970

Bimonthly newsletter. Information on stone-working techniques and materials.

Indian-Artifact Magazine
RD 1 Box 240
Turbotville, PA 17772
(717) 437-3698
(717) 437-3411 FAX

Quarterly. For American Indian and artifact enthusiasts. Educational information, perspectives on amateur archaeology, and human interest stories. Shows, meetings, humor, current laws and much more. Easy to read and understand. Photographs of artifacts from all parts of the country.

Indian Relic Trader
PO Box 88
Sunbury, OH 43074

Antiquity newspaper. Photographs of artifacts and up-to-date news.

Indian Trader, The
PO Box 1421
Gallup, NM 87305
(505) 722-6694

Antiquity newspaper. Information on the arts, crafts and cultures of the American Indian. Features Old West news.

223

National Geographic Magazine
National Geographic Society
1145 17th St NW
Washington, DC 20036-4688
(202) 857-7000
(202) 775-6141 FAX

Monthly. Scientific and educational information on explorations and research projects. Photographs, maps and special issues.

Prehistoric Antiquities and Archaeological News Quarterly
7045 E State RT 245
PO Box 296
North Lewisburg, OH 43060
(937) 747-2225

Antiquity magazine. Approximately one hundred pages. Articles about prehistory, information on books, calendar of events, and plenty of photographs.

Southwest Art
PO Box 53186
Boulder, CO 80321-3186

Monthly magazine. Covers arts of the American West. Events calendar for intertribal ceremonials, art festivals, antique Indian art exhibitions, Old West shows and galleries across the country.

Texas Cache, The
8901 S Hwy 67 #10
San Angelo, TX 76904
(800) 7-CLOVIS
(915) 947-7616
TXCACHE@AOL.COM

Quarterly amateur archaeological society magazine. Features artifacts from Texas and the Southwest. Column, "Ask An Archeologist," by Dr. Michael Gramly *(see Additional Reading)*. Calender of events.

Maps

When it comes to arrowhead hunting, some types of natural features are just more promising than others. As you scout for sites, think of the necessities of life in the way people did long ago. Keep in mind that while fresh water was a prime requisite, there was also a need for workable stone, wood for campfires, and protection from the elements. Whether big-game hunters, coastal fishermen, cave dwellers, Desert gatherers, Mound Builders, Basket Makers or Pueblo farmers, the culture of a given group of people had a considerable effect on the choice of a village site. To be successful in your search for surface artifacts, take into account the requirements of prehistoric daily life and the geography of your area.

You can find information about local natural resources by checking maps. It's possible to discover tributaries, small lakes, large creeks, and other sources of fresh water just by looking at ordinary road maps. When you use standard maps to find bodies of water, think about the size of the supply. A Mississippian village would have required a large, permanent source. A smaller body of water, such as a spring, would have been sufficient for a small family camp or a temporary stay.

Consider both past and present as you assess the supply, because water tables can drop or rise over the years. A creek that you see on a map today might not have existed in prehistory and a plentiful water supply may have entirely disappeared. In the Southwest, for example, large interglacial lakes are now deserts. The only indications of these lakes are terraces which mark the positions of ancient shorelines. It is at the terraces—places that are now waterless—where Anasazi cliff dwellings and apartment houses are being studied.

When evidence of the former presence of water is found in the topography, you'll scout more effectively if you examine a topographic map. If you're not familiar with the area you plan to hunt, you might want to bring along a quadrangle map. A quadrangle map is a topographic map which shows just the kinds of geographic features that you like to hunt. Use a topographic map to locate streams, springs, ponds, drainage areas, and quarries. Study variations in elevation to discover rises, knolls, and hills near water. Refer to the map and your compass to find a trail or dirt road in the woods, and it will keep you from getting lost.

For topographic, geologic, land use, county or state maps, and more, stop in at a map store or large bookstore and ask for assistance. The types of maps you'll want are reasonably priced and map specialists will help you choose the right one. Refer to your *Yellow Pages Directory* for the nearest map dealer, or use the information below to order USGS maps by mail. Before placing an order, request an index of map coverage and its companion catalog for your state. Published by the USGS under the National Mapping Program and provided at no charge, the index and catalog provide useful information about how to select and purchase maps.

Map Express
PO Box 280445
Lakewood, CO 80228-0445
(800) MAP-00EX
(303) 969-8195 FAX

**U.S. Department
of the Interior
Headquarters**
Bureau of Land Management
18th and C St NW
Washington, DC 20240
(202) 343-5717

U.S. Geological Survey
Bldg 810
Denver Federal Center
Denver, CO 80225
(303) 202-4700

**U.S.G.S. Earth Science
Information Centers**
(800) USA-MAPS

U.S.G.S. Information Service
Box 25286
Denver, CO 80225
(800) HELP-MAP

Places to Go and Things to See

Though arrowhead hunting may be one of your favorite activities, include other kinds of field trips in your schedule. There's a variety of interesting, inexpensive places to explore where you can also learn about archaeology. Gather your family or call a friend, and have fun discovering them together. Go to a city museum, see rock writing at a state historic site, study an exhibit in your hometown, or visit an effigy mound. For locations of cultural parks, university museums, radiocarbon labs, and much more, use this section to find out where they are. To learn about other excellent resources that we could not include, contact any of the organizations listed for your state.

ALABAMA

Alabama Dept of Archives and History
624 Washington Ave
Montgomery, AL 36130
(334) 242-4363

Indian Mound
Court St
Florence, AL 35630
(205) 760-6427

Russell Cave National Monument
Bridgeport, AL 35740
(205) 495-2672

ALASKA

Alaska State Museum
395 Whittier St
Juneau, AK 99801-1718
(907) 465-2901

Anchorage Museum of History and Art
121 W 7th Ave
Anchorage, AK 99501
(907) 343-6173

Kodiak Alutiiq Culture Center
214 W Rezanoff
Kodiak, AK 99615
(907) 486-1992

Pratt Museum
3779 Bartlett St
Homer, AK 99603
(907) 235-8635

University of Alaska Museum
University of Alaska
Fairbanks, AK 99701
(907) 474-7505

ARIZONA

Arizona State Museum
University of Arizona
Tucson, AZ 85721
(520) 621-6281

Besh Ba Gowah Archaeology Park
150 N Pine St
Globe, AZ 85501
(520) 425-0320

Grand Canyon National Park
Box 129
Grand Canyon, AZ 86023
(520) 638-2305

Heard Museum
22 E Monte Vista Rd
Phoenix, AZ 85004
(602) 252-8840

Hopi Tribe
Cultural Preservation Office
PO Box 123
Kykotsmovi, AZ 86039
(520) 734-6636

Museum of Northern Arizona
Fort Valley Rd
Flagstaff, AZ 86001
(520) 774-5211
(520) 779-1527 FAX

Radiocarbon Lab
University of Arizona
Dept of Geosciences
Tucson, AZ 85721
(520) 621-1638

Tempe Historical Museum
809 E Southern Ave
Tempe, AZ 85282
(602) 350-5105

ARKANSAS

Arkansas Museum of Science and History
503 E 9th St
Little Rock, AR 72202
(800) 880-6475
(501) 396-7054 FAX

Arkansas State University Museum
Box 490 State University
Jonesboro, AR 72467-0490
(501) 972-2074
(501) 972-2793 FAX

Hampson Museum State Park
2 Lake Dr
PO Box 156
Wilson, AR 72395-0156
(501) 655-8622

Henderson State University Museum
HSU Box H-7657
Arkadelphia, AR 71923
(501) 246-7311

Hot Springs National Park Museum
Central and Reserve Ave
Hot Springs National Park, AR 71902

University Museum
University of Arkansas
Fayetteville, AR 72701
(501) 575-3555

CALIFORNIA

Adan E. Treganza Anthropology Museum
San Francisco State University
160 Holloway Ave
San Francisco, CA 94132
(415) 338-1642

American Rock Art Research Association
PO Box 65
San Miguel, CA 93451
(805) 467-3704

Museum of Anthropology
California State University
9001 Stockdale Hwy
Bakersfield, CA 93311-1099
(805) 664-2305

Natural History Museum of Los Angeles County
900 Exposition Blvd
Los Angeles, CA 90007
(213) 774-3382

Santa Barbara Museum of Natural History
2559 Puesta del Sol Rd
Santa Barbara, CA 93105
(805) 682-4711

Southwest Museum
PO Box 41558
Los Angeles, CA 90041-0558
(213) 221-2164

UCLA Fowler Museum of Cultural History
Box 951549
Los Angeles, CA 90024-1549
(310) 825-4361

University of California
Phoebe A. Hearst Museum of Anthropology
103 Kroeber Hall
Berkeley, CA 94720-3712
(510) 642-3681

COLORADO

Colorado History Museum
1300 Broadway
Denver, CO 80203
(303) 866-3682

Denver Museum of Natural History
2001 Colorado Blvd
Denver, CO 80205-5798
(303) 370-6388

Koshare Indian Museum, Inc.
PO Box 580
115 W 18th St
LaJunta, CO 81050
(719) 384-4411

Louden-Henritze Archaeology Museum
Freudenthal Memorial Library
Trinidad State Junior College
Trinidad, CO 81082
(719) 846-5508

Museum of Western Colorado
248 S 4th St
PO Box 20000
Grand Junction, CO 81502-5020
(970) 242-0971

Rangely Museum
434 S Main St
PO Box 131
Rangely, CO 81648
(970) 675-2612

University of Colorado Museum
Henderson Bldg
Boulder, CO 80309
(303) 492-6892

Wray Museum
205 E 3rd St
Wray, CO 80758
(970) 332-5063

CONNECTICUT

Bruce Museum
One Museum Dr
Greenwich, CT 06830
(203) 869-0376

Connecticut State Museum of Natural History
University of Connecticut
U-23
Storrs, CT 06279-3023
(860) 486-4460

Day-Lewis Museum of Indian Artifacts
158 Main St
Farmington, CT 06032
(860) 677-2140

Institute for American Indian Studies
PO Box 1260
38 Curtis Rd
Washington, CT 06793-0260
(860) 868-0518

Museum of Connecticut History
231 Capitol Ave
Hartford, CT 06106
(860) 566-3056

New Britain Youth Museum
30 High St
New Britain, CT 06051
(860) 225-3020

Peabody Museum of Natural History
Yale University
170 Whitney Ave
PO Box 6666
New Haven, CT 06511-8161
(203) 432-3770

Stamford Museum and Nature Center
39 Scofieldtown Rd
Stamford, CT 06903
(203) 322-1646

Tantaquidgeon Indian Museum
RT 32
Norwich-New London Rd
Uncasville, CT 06382
(860) 848-9145

DELAWARE

Hagley Museum
Barley Mill Rd
Greenville, DE 19807

Iron Hill Museum
1355 Old Baltimore Pike
Newark, DE 19702
(302) 368-5703

DISTRICT OF COLUMBIA

Indian Craft Shop
1050 Wisconsin Ave NE
Washington, DC 20007
(202) 342-3918

National Conference of State Historic Preservation Officers
444 N Capitol St NW Ste 342
Hall of the States
Washington, DC 20001-1512
(202) 624-5465
(202) 624-5419 FAX

National Gallery of Art
4th St and Constitution Ave NW
Washington, DC 20565
(202) 737-4215

National Museum of American History
Smithsonian Institution
NMAH 1040 MRC 605
Social and Cultural History
Washington, DC 20560
(202) 357-2216

National Museum of the American Indian
Smithsonian Institution
470 L'Enfant Plaza Ste 7102
Washington, DC 20560

National Park Service
Archeological Assistance Division
PO Box 37127
Washington, DC 20013-7127

U.S. Dept of the Interior
Indian Arts and Crafts Board
1849 C St NW USDI Rm 4004
Washington, DC 20240-0001
(202) 208-3773

FLORIDA

Canaveral National Seashore
308 Julia St
Titusville, FL 32796
(407) 267-1110

Florida Museum of Natural History
Florida State University
Dept of Anthropology
Gainesville, FL 32611
(352) 392-1721

Historical Museum of Southern Florida
101 W Flagler St
Miami, FL 33130
(305) 375-1492

Indian Temple Mound Museum
139 Miracle Strip Pkwy
Fort Walton Beach, FL 32548
(904) 243-6521

Museum of Archaeology
203 SW 1st Ave
Ft Lauderdale, FL 33301
(954) 525-8778

South Florida Museum and Planetarium
201 10th St W
Bradenton, FL 34205
(813) 746-4131

St. Petersburg Historical Museum
335 2nd Ave NE
St Petersburg, FL 33701
(813) 894-1052

GEORGIA

Columbus Museum
1251 Wynnton Rd
Columbus, GA 31906
(706) 649-0713

Etowah Mounds State Historic Site
RT 2
Cartersville, GA 30120
(770) 382-2704

Kolomoki Mounds State Historic Park
RT 1 Box 114
Blakeley, GA 31723
(912) 723-5296

Ocmulgee National Monument
1207 Emery Hwy
Macon, GA 31201
(912) 752-8257

Rock Eagle Effigy Mound
350 Rock Eagle Rd NW
Eatonton, GA 31024
(706) 485-2831

Thronateeska Heritage Foundation Museum
100 Roosevelt Ave
Albany, GA 31701
(912) 432-6955

Track Rock Archaeological Area
Chattahoochee National Forest
Georgia Dept of Natural Resources
205 Butler St SE
Atlanta, GA 30334
(404) 536-0541

HAWAII

Bernice Pauahi Bishop Museum
Anthropology Dept
1525 Bernice St Box 19000-A
Honolulu, HI 96817-0916
(808) 848-4110

IDAHO

Alfred W. Bowers Lab of Anthropology
University of Idaho
Moscow, ID 83844-1111
(208) 885-6123

Herrett Museum
College of Southern Idaho
315 Falls Ave
PO Box 1238
Twin Falls, ID 83303-1238
(208) 733-9554

Idaho Historical Museum
Julia Davis Park
610 N Julia Davis Dr
Boise, ID 83702
(208) 334-3847

Idaho State University
Idaho Museum of Natural History
PO Box 8096
Pocatello, ID 83209
(208) 236-3366

Intermountain Cultural Center and Museum
PO Box 307
Weiser, ID 83672
(208) 549-0205

Nez Perce National Historical Park
PO Box 93
Spalding, ID 83551
(208) 843-2261

Redfish Rock Shelter Site
Headquarters Office Star RT
Ketchum, ID 83340
(208) 726-7672

ILLINOIS

Burpee Museum of Natural History
737 N Main
Rockford, IL 61103
(815) 965-3433

Cahokia Mounds State Historic Site
30 Ramey Dr
PO Box 681
Collinsville, IL 62234
(618) 346-5160
(618) 346-5162 FAX

Center for American Archeology
Kampsville Archeological Center
PO Box 366
Kampsville, IL 62053
(618) 653-4316
(618) 653-4232 FAX

Dickson Mounds Museum
10956 N Dickson Mounds Rd
Lewistown, IL 61542
(309) 547-3721

Douglas County Museum
700 S Main
Tuscola, IL 61953
(217) 253-2535

Fermi National Accelerator Lab
Kirk Rd and Pine
Batavia, IL 60510
(630) 840-3000

Field Museum of Natural History
Roosevelt Rd at Lake Shore Dr
Chicago, IL 60605
(312) 922-9410

Ford County Historical Society
Court House, Heritage Rm
PO Box 213
Paxton, IL 60957

Illinois State Museum
State Museum Bldg
Springfield, IL 62706
(217) 782-7386

Lakeview Museum of Arts and Sciences
1125 W Lake Ave
Peoria, IL 61614
(309) 686-7000

Lithic Casting Lab
577 Troy-O'Fallon Rd
Troy, IL 62294
(618) 667-2447

Madison County Historical Museum
715 N Main St
Edwardsville, IL 62025
(618) 656-7562

Midwestern Archaeological Research Center
Illinois State University
Dept 4641
Normal, IL 61761
(309) 438-2271

Natural History Museum
Northern Illinois University
DeKalb, IL 60115
(815) 753-0230

Old Barn Museum
7127B Oak Brook Rd
Newark, IL 60541
(815) 553-5997

Quincy Museum
1601 Main St
Quincy, IL 62301
(217) 224-7669

Southern Illinois University
University Museum and
Center for Archeological
Investigations
Carbondale, IL 62901

University of Illinois
Museum of Natural History
438 Natural History Bldg
1301 W Green St
Urbana, IL 61801
(217) 333-2517

INDIANA

Angel Mounds State Historic Site
8215 Pollack Ave
Evansville, IN 47715
(812) 853-3956

Children's Museum of Indianapolis
3000 N Meridian St
PO Box 3000
Indianapolis, IN 46206
(317) 924-5431

Eiteljorg Museum of American Indian and Western Art
500 W Washington St
Indianapolis, IN 46204-2707
(317) 636-WEST

Fulton County Museum
37 E 375 N
RR 3 Box 89
Rochester, IN 46975
(219) 223-4436

Glenn A. Black Laboratory of Archaeology
Indiana University
9th and Fess St
Bloomington, IN 47405
(812) 855-9544

Indiana State Museum
202 N Alabama St
Indianapolis, IN 46204
(317) 232-1637

Mathers Museum
Indiana University
416 N Indiana Ave
Bloomington, IN 47405
(812) 855-MUSE

Miami County Museum
51 N Broadway
Peru, IN 46970
(317) 473-9183

Minnetrista Cultural Center
PO Box 1427
Muncie, IN 47308

Mounds State Park
4306 Mounds Rd
Anderson, IN 46017
(317) 642-6627

Wyandotte Cave
Leavenworth, IN 47137
(812) 738-2782

IOWA

Blood Run National Historic Landmark
Lyon County Conservation
Board
311 1st Ave E
Rock Rapids, IA 51246
(712) 472-2217

Grout Museum of History and Science
Park Ave at South St
Waterloo, IA 50701

Mills County Historical Museum
PO Box 255
Glenwood, IA 51534
(712) 527-5038

Sanford Museum and Planetarium
117 E Willow
Cherokee, IA 51012
(712) 225-3922

Sioux City Public Museum
2901 Jackson St
Sioux City, IA 51104
(712) 279-6174

State Historical Society of Iowa Museum
600 E Locust
Des Moines, IA 50319
(515) 281-5111

University of Iowa
Museum of Natural History
Macbride Hall
Iowa City, IA 52242
(319) 355-0481

KANSAS

Barton County Historical Museum
85 S Hwy 281
PO Box 1091
Great Bend, KS 67530
(316) 793-5125

Coronado-Quivira Museum
105 W Lyon St
Lyons, KS 67554
(316) 257-3941

Ellsworth County Historical Society
Hodgden House Museum
Main St
Ellsworth, KS 67439
(913) 472-3059

Kansas Museum of History
6425 SW 6th St
Topeka, KS 66615-1099
(913) 272-8681

Kansas State Historical Society
Memorial Bldg
120 SW 10th Ave
Topeka, KS 66612-1291
(913) 296-3251

Museum of Anthropology
University of Kansas
Spooner Hall
Lawrence, KS 66045
(913) 864-4245

Pawnee Indian Village Museum
RT 1 Box 475
Republic, KS 66964
(913) 361-2255

Roniger Memorial Museum
Union and Oak St
PO Box 70
Cottonwood Falls, KS 66845
(316) 273-6310

KENTUCKY

Big Bone Lick State Park
3380 Beaver Rd
Union, KY 41091
(606) 384-3522

Blue Licks Pioneer Museum
PO Box 66
Mt Olivet, KY 41064
(606) 289-5507

J.B. Speed Art Museum
2035 S 3rd St
Louisville, KY 40208
(502) 636-2893

Mammoth Cave National Park
Mammoth Cave, KY 42259
(502) 758-2251

William S. Webb Museum of Anthropology
University of Kentucky
Lafferty Hall
Lexington, KY 40506-0024
(606) 275-7112

LOUISIANA

Louisiana State Exhibit Museum
3015 Greenwood Rd
PO Box 9067
Shreveport, LA 71139
(318) 226-7123

Marksville State Commemorative Area
700 Martin Luther King Dr
Marksville, LA 71351
(318) 253-8954

Tunica-Biloxi Regional Indian Center and Museum
Tunica-Biloxi Reservation
Louisiana Hwy 1
PO Box 231
Marksville, LA 71351
(318) 253-8174

Williamson Museum
Northwestern State University
210 Kyser Hall
Natchitoches, LA 71497
(318) 357-4364

MAINE

Abbe Museum
Acadia National Park
PO Box 177
Bar Harbor, ME 04609

Aroostook Historical and Art Museum
109 Main St
Houlton, ME 04730
(207) 532-4216

Hudson Museum
University of Maine
5746 Maine Center for the Arts
Orono, ME 04469-5746
(207) 581-1901

Maine State Museum
State Capitol Complex
State House Station 83
Augusta, ME 04333-0083
(207) 289-2301

MARYLAND

Andover Foundation for Archaeological Research
Box 83
Andover, MA 01810
(508) 470-0840

Dorchester Heritage Museum
1904 Horn Point Rd
Cambridge, MD 21613
(301) 228-5530

Historic St. Mary's City
Box 39
St Mary's City, MD 20686
(301) 862-0090

Jefferson Patterson Park and Museum
10515 Mackall Rd
St Leonard, MD 20685
(410) 586-8500

MASSACHUSETTS

Center for Materials Research in Archaeology
Massachusetts Institute of Technology
Rm 8-138
Cambridge, MA 02139
(617) 253-1375

Children's Museum, Inc.
Russells Mills Rd
Dartmouth, MA 02714

Cohasset Historical Society
14 Summer St
Cohasset, MA 02025
(617) 383-1434

Concord Museum
200 Lexington Rd
Concord, MA 01742
(508) 369-9609

Fruitlands Museums
102 Prospect Hill Rd
Harvard, MA 01451
(508) 456-3924

Memorial Hall Museum
8 Memorial St
Deerfield, MA 01342
(413) 774-7476

Peabody Essex Museum
Archaeology Dept
E India Square
Salem, MA 01970
(508) 745-1876

Peabody Museum of Archaeology
Harvard University
11 Divinity Ave
Cambridge, MA 02138
(617) 495-2248

Robert S. Peabody Museum of Archaeology
Phillips Academy
Main St
Andover, MA 01810
(508) 749-4490

MICHIGAN

Chippewa Nature Center
400 S Badour Rd
Midland, MI 48640
(517) 631-0830

Great Lakes Indian Museum
6325 W Jefferson Ave
Detroit, MI 48209
(313) 833-7900

Historical Museum of Bay County
321 Washington Ave
Bay City, MI 48708
(517) 893-5733

Jesse Besser Museum
491 Johnson St
Alpena, MI 49707
(517) 356-2202

Kalamazoo Public Museum
315 S Rose St
Kalamazoo, MI 49007
(616) 345-7092

Michigan State University Museum
W Circle Dr
East Lansing, MI 48823
(517) 355-2370

Museum of Anthropology
University of Michigan
1109 Geddes Ave
Ann Arbor, MI 48109-1079
(313) 764-0485

Public Museum of Grand Rapids
54 Jefferson St SE
Grand Rapids, MI 49503
(616) 456-3977

MINNESOTA

Archaeometry Laboratory
University of Minnesota
10 University Dr
Duluth, MN 55812-2496
(218) 726-7957

Grand Mound Center
6749 Hwy 11
International Falls,
MN 56649-9019
(218) 285-3332

Helmer Myre State Park
RT 3, Box 33
Albert Lea, MN 56007
(507) 373-5084

Itasca State Park
Lake Itasca, MN 56460
(218) 266-3634

Jeffers Petroglyphs Site
RR 1 Box 118
Bingham Lake, MN 56118
(507) 877-3647

Pipestone National Monument
PO Box 727
Pipestone, MN 56164
(507) 825-5464

Science Museum of Minnesota
Dept of Anthropology
30 E 10th St
St Paul, MN 55101
(612) 221-9424

MISSISSIPPI

Grand Village of the Natchez Indians
400 Jefferson Davis Blvd
Natchez, MS 39120
(601) 446-6502

Mississippi State Historical Museum
Capitol and North State St
PO Box 571
Jackson, MS 39205
(601) 359-6920

Mississippi State University
Cobb Institute of Archaeology
PO Drawer AR
Mississippi State, MS 39762
(601) 325-3826

Natchez Trace Parkway
RR 1 NT-143
Tupelo, MS 38801
(601) 842-1572

MISSOURI

Clay County Historical Museum
14 N Main St
Liberty, MO 64068
(816) 781-8062

Kimmswick Museum
Kimmswick, MO 63052
(314) 464-2976

Line Creek Archaeological Museum
5940 NW Waukomis
Kansas City, MO 64151
(816) 587-8822

Missouri Historical Society
Jefferson Memorial Bldg
Forest Park
St Louis, MO 63112
(314) 361-1424

Southeast Missouri State University Museum
One University Plaza
Cape Girardeau, MO 63701
(573) 651-2260

St. Joseph Museum
11th and Charles St
St Joseph, MO 64501-2874
(816) 232-8471

University of Missouri-Columbia
Museum of Anthropology
104 Swallow Hall
Columbia, MO 65211
(573) 882-3573
(573) 884-5450 FAX

MONTANA

Annual Crow Fair and Powwow
Crow Tribal Administration
Crow Agency, MT 59022
(406) 638-2601

Mt. Ulm Pishkun Park
Dept of Fish, Wildlife and Parks
PO Box 6610
Great Falls, MT 59406
(406) 454-5840

Museum of the Plains Indian
PO Box 400
Browning, MT 59417

Museum of the Rockies
Montana State University
Archaeology and Anthropology
Dept
Bozeman, MT 59717
(406) 994-2251

Park County Museum
118 W Chinook
Livingston, MT 59047
(406) 222-3506

NEBRASKA

Hastings Museum
1330 N Burlington Ave
Hastings, NE 68901
(402) 461-2399

Museum of Nebraska History
Nebraska State Historical
Society
1500 R St
Lincoln, NE 68501-2554
(402) 471-4754

National Park Service
Midwest Archaeological Center
Federal Bldg Rm 474
100 Centennial Mall N
Lincoln, NE 68508-3873

Scottsbluff National Monument
PO Box 427
Gering, NE 69341
(308) 436-4340

University of Nebraska State Museum
307 Morrill Hall
14th and U St
Lincoln, NE 68508-0338
(402) 472-6032

NEVADA

Churchill County Museum
1050 S Main St
Fallon, NV 89406
(702) 423-3677

Lost City Museum of Archeology
PO Box 807
Overton, NV 89040
(702) 397-2193

Nevada Historical Society
1650 N Virginia St
Reno, NV 89503
(702) 688-1190

Nevada State Museum
600 N Carson St
Carson City, NV 89710
(702) 687-4810

Nevada State Museum and Historical Society
700 Twin Lakes Dr
Las Vegas, NV 89107
(702) 486-5205

NEW HAMPSHIRE

American Institute for Archaeological Research
24 Cross Rd
Mt Vernon, NH 03057
(603) 673-3005

Laconia Public Library
695 Main St
Laconia, NH 03246
(603) 524-4775

Libby Museum
PO Box 629
Wolfeboro, NH 03894
(603) 569-1035

Manchester Historic Association
129 Amherst St
Manchester, NH 03101
(603) 622-7531

Phillips Exeter Academy
P. Phillips Foundation Museum
20 Main St MSC #81337
Exeter, NH 03833-2460
(603) 772-4311 ext 3452

University of New Hampshire
Anthropology Laboratory
Parsons Hall, College Rd
Durham, NH 03824
(603) 862-1547

Woodman Institute Museum
182-192 Central Ave
Dover, NH 03820
(603) 742-1038

NEW JERSEY

Morris Museum
6 Normandy Heights Rd
Morristown, NJ 07960
(201) 538-0454

New Jersey State Museum
205 W State St
Trenton, NJ 08625-0404
(609) 292-2023
(609) 984-0578 FAX

Newark Museum
49 Washington St
Newark, NJ 07102
(201) 596-6550

Seton Hall University
Archaeological Research
Center and Museum
Fahy Hall
S Orange Ave
South Orange, NJ 07079
(201) 761-9543

Space Farms Zoological Park and Museum
218 RT 519
Sussex, NJ 07461
(201) 875-5800

NEW MEXICO

Bandelier National Monument
HCR1 Box 1
Los Alamos, NM 87544
(505) 672-3861

Chaco Culture National Historical Park
Star RT 4 Box 6500
Bloomfield, NM 87413
(505) 988-6727

El Morro National Monument
Ramah, NM 87321
(505) 783-4226

Geronimo Springs Museum
211 Main St
Truth or Consequences, NM 87901
(505) 894-6600

Gila Cliff Dwellings National Monument
RT 11 Box 100
Silver City, NM 88061
(505) 536-9461

Gran Quivera
PO Box 498
Mountainair, NM 87036
(505) 847-2770

Indian Arts and Crafts Association
122 LaVeta NE
Albuquerque, NM 87108
(505) 265-9149

Institute of American Indian Arts
Traveling Exhibit
108 Cathedral Pl
Sante Fe, NM 87501
(505) 988-6281

Inter-tribal Indian Ceremonial Association
PO Box 1
Church Rock, NM 87311
(800) 233-4528

Museum of Indian Arts and Culture
Laboratory of Anthropology
PO Box 2087
Sante Fe, NM 87504-2087
(505) 827-6344
(505) 827-6497 FAX

Wheelwrite Museum of the American Indian
704 Camino Lejo
Santa Fe, NM 87505
(800) 607-4636
(505) 982-4636

NEW YORK

American Museum of Natural History
Central Park W at 79th St
New York, NY 10024
(212) 769-5100

Brooklyn Museum
200 Eastern Pkwy
Brooklyn, NY 11238
(718) 638-5000

Buffalo Museum of Science
Anthropology Division
1020 Humbolt Pkwy
Buffalo, NY 14211-1293
(716) 896-5200

Chenango County Historical Society Museum
45 Rexford St
Norwich, NY 13815
(607) 334-9227

Fred L. Waterman Conservation Center
403 Hilton Rd
PO Box 377
Apalachin, NY 13732-0377
(607) 625-2221

Hartwick College
Yager Museum
Oneonta, NY 13820
(607) 431-4480

Iroquois Indian Museum
PO Box 7
Howes Cave, NY 12092
(518) 296-8949

Old Stone Fort Museum & William W. Badgley Historical Museum
RR 2 Box 30 A
Schoharie, NY 12157
(518) 295-7192

National Museum of the American Indian
Smithsonian Institution
One Bowling Green
New York, NY 10004-1415
(212) 825-6700
(212) 825-8180 FAX

New York State Museum
Empire State Plaza
Albany, NY 12223
(518) 474-5877

Owasco Teyetasta
Cayuga Museum
203 Genesee St
Auburn, NY 13021
(315) 253-8051

Rochester Museum and Science Center
657 E Ave
PO Box 1480
Rochester, NY 14603-1480
(716) 271-4552 ext 440

Seneca-Iroquois National Museum
Allegany Indian Reservation
PO Box 442
Broad St Ext
Salamanca, NY 14779
(716) 945-1738

Six Nations Indian Museum
HCR1 Box 10
Onchiota, NY 12968
(518) 891-2299

Southold Indian Museum
Bayview Rd
PO Box 268
Southold, NY 11971
(516) 765-5577

NORTH CAROLINA

Catawba College
Museum of Anthropology
South Campus
Salisbury, NC 28144
(704) 637-4111

Greenboro Historical Museum
130 Summit Ave
Greenboro, NC 27401
(919) 373-2043

Morrow Mountain State Park Natural History Museum
49104 Morrow Mountain Rd
Albemarle, NC 28001
(704) 982-4402

Museum of the Cherokee
U.S. 441 at Drama Rd
Cherokee, NC 28719
(704) 497-3481

Oconaluftee Indian Village
PO Box 398
Cherokee, NC 28719
(704) 497-2315
(704) 497-2111

Research Laboratories of Anthropology
University of North Carolina
CB3120 Alumni Bldg
Chapel Hill, NC 27599-3120
(919) 962-6574

Schiele Museum of Natural History
1500 E Garrison Blvd
Gastonia, NC 28053
(704) 866-6900

Wake Forest University
Museum of Anthropology
PO Box 7267
Winston-Salem, NC 27109
(919) 759-5282

NORTH DAKOTA

Knife River Indian Villages National Historic Site
RR 1 Box 168
Stanton, ND 58571

Three Affiliated Tribes Museum
PO Box 147
New Town, ND 58763
(701) 627-4477

Ward Earth Lodge Village Historic Site
Bismarck Parks and Recreation District
215 N 6th St
Bismarck, ND 58501

Writing Rock State Historic Site
State Historical Society of North Dakota
612 E Blvd Ave
Bismarck, ND 58505-0830
(701) 328-2666

OHIO

Allen County Museum
620 W Market St
Lima, OH 45801
(419) 222-9426

Cleveland Museum of Art
11150 E Blvd at University Circle
Cleveland, OH 44106
(216) 421-7340

Cleveland Museum of Natural History
Wade Oval University Circle
Cleveland, OH 44106
(216) 231-4600

Clinton County Historical Society and Museum
149 E Locust St
PO Box 529
Wilmington, OH 45177
(937) 382-4684

Dayton Museum of Natural History
2600 Deweese Pkwy
Dayton, OH 45414
(937) 275-7431
(937) 275-5811 FAX

Firelands Museum
4 Case Ave
PO Box 572
Norwalk, OH 44857
(419) 668-6038

Indian Ridge Museum
8714 W Ridge Rd
Elyria, OH 44035
(216) 323-2167

Miami County Archaeological Museum
8212 W Lauver Rd
Pleasant Hill, OH 45359
(937) 676-5103

SunWatch 12th Century Indian Village
2301 W River Rd
Dayton, OH 45418-2815
(937) 268-8199

Warren County Historical Society
105 S Broadway
PO Box 223
Lebanon, OH 45036-0223
(513) 932-1817

Western Reserve Historical Society
10825 E Blvd
Cleveland, OH 44106
(216) 721-5722

Wyandot County Historical Society
130 S 7th St
Upper Sandusky, OH 43351
(419) 294-3857

OKLAHOMA

A.D. Buck Museum of Science and History
Willis Rd
PO Box 515
Tahlequah, OK 74465
(918) 456-6007

American Indian Heritage Center
Harwelan Bldg
2210 S Main
Tulsa, OK 74114

Indian City, U.S.A.
PO Box 695
Anadarko, OK 73005
(405) 247-5661

Museum of the Great Plains
PO Box 68
Lawton, OK 73502
(405) 581-3460

No Man's Land Historical Museum
207 W Sewell St
PO Box 278
Goodwell, OK 73939
(405) 349-2670

Southern Plains Indian Museum
Hwy 62 E
PO Box 749
Anadarko, OK 73005

University of Oklahoma
Oklahoma Museum of Natural History
1335 Asp Ave
Norman, OK 73019-0606
(405) 325-4711

Woolaroc Museum
RT 3
Bartlesville, OK 74003
(918) 336-0307

OREGON

Cape Perpetua Visitor Center
U.S. 101
PO Box 274
Yachats, OR 97498
(541) 547-3289

Confederated Tribes of Warm Springs Museum
PO Box C
Warm Springs, OR 97761
(541) 553-3331

Deschutes County Historical Society
129 NW Idaho St
PO Box 5252
Bend, OR 97708
(541) 389-1813

Favell Museum of Western Art and Indian Artifacts
125 W Main St
Klamath Falls, OR 97601
(541) 882-9996

Hells Canyon National Recreation Area
PO Box 490
Enterprise, OR 97828
(503) 426-4978

Schminck Memorial Museum
128 South E St
Lakeview, OR 97630
(503) 947-3134

Tahkenitch Landing Archaeological Site
Siuslaw National Forest
545 SW 2nd Ave
Corvallis, OR 97333
(541) 757-4480

Tillamook County Pioneer Museum
2106 2nd St
Tillamook, OR 97141
(503) 842-4553
(503) 842-4553 FAX

University of Oregon
Museum of Natural History
Eugene, OR 97403
(541) 686-3024

Wallawa County Museum
Main St
Joseph, OR 97846
(541) 432-1015

PENNSYLVANIA

Annual Artifact and Fossil Show
Saegertown American Legion Hall
Saegertown, PA 16433
(814) 398-4814

Carnegie Museum of Natural History
4400 Forbes Ave
Pittsburgh, PA 15213
(412) 662-3131

Franklin and Marshall College, North Museum
College and Buchanan Ave
PO Box 3003
Lancaster, PA 17604-3003
(717) 291-3941

Indian Steps Museum
205 Indian Steps Rd
Airville, PA 17302
(717) 862-3948

Matson Museum of Anthropology
Pennsylvania State University
409 Carpenter Bldg
University Park, PA 16802
(814) 865-3853

Mercer Museum
84 S Pine St
Doylestown, PA 18901
(215) 345-0210

Monroe County Historical Association
900 Main St
Stroudsburg, PA 18360
(717) 421-7703

Museum of Indian Culture
Lenni Lenape Historical Society
2825 Fish Hatchery Rd
Allentown, PA 18103-9801
(610) 797-2121

Pyramid Shop
Museum of Archaeology and Anthropology
University of Pennsylvania Museum, etc.
33rd and Spruce St
Philadelphia, PA 19104
(215) 898-4045

State Museum of Pennsylvania
3rd and North St
PO Box 1026
Harrisburg, PA 17108-1026
(717) 787-4978

Tioga Point Museum
724 S Main St
Athens, PA 18810
(717) 888-2005

Venango County Courthouse
Liberty and 12th St
Franklin, PA 16323

RHODE ISLAND

Brown University
Haffenreffer Museum of Anthropology
Mt Hope Grant
Bristol, RI 02809
(401) 253-8388

Museum of Natural History and Cormack Planetarium
Roger Williams Park
Providence, RI 02905
(401) 785-9451

Museum of Primitive Art and Culture
1058 Kingstown Rd
PO Drawer A
Peace Dale, RI 02883-0117
(401) 783-5711

Tomaquag Indian Memorial Museum
325 Summit Rd
Arcadia, RI 02826
(401) 539-7213

SOUTH CAROLINA

Charles Towne Landing 1670
1500 Old Towne Rd
Charleston, SC 29407-6099
(803) 852-4200

South Carolina Institute of Archaeology/Anthropoloy
University of South Carolina
1321 Pendleton St
Columbia, SC 29208
(803) 777-8170

SOUTH DAKOTA

Cultural Heritage Center
900 Governors Dr
Pierre, SD 57501-2217
(605) 773-3458
(605) 773-6041 FAX

Mitchell Prehistoric Indian Village Museum and Site
PO Box 621
Mitchell, SD 57301
(605) 996-5473

Sherman Park Indian Burial Mounds
W 22nd St and Kiwanis Ave
c/o Park Dept
600 E 7th St
Sioux Falls, SD 57103

Wind Cave National Park
Hot Springs, SD 57747
(605) 745-4600

TENNESSEE

Chattanooga Regional History Museum
400 Chestnut St
Chattanooga, TN 37402
(423) 265-3247

Chucalissa Indian Town and Museum
Memphis State University
1987 Indian Village Dr
Memphis, TN 38109
(901) 785-3160

Cumberland Science Museum
800 Ridley Blvd
Nashville, TN 37203
(615) 259-6099

Pinson Mounds State Archaeological Area
460 Ozier Rd
Pinson, TN 38366
(901) 988-5614

Sequoyah Birthplace Museum
PO Box 69
Vonore, TN 37885
(423) 884-6246

Shiloh Mounds
Shiloh National Military Park
Shiloh, TN 38376
(901) 689-5275

Tennessee State Museum
Polk Cultural Center
505 Deaderick St
Nashville, TN 37219
(615) 741-2692

University of Tennessee
McClung Museum
1327 Circle Park Dr
Knoxville, TN 37996
(423) 974-2144

TEXAS

Alabama-Coushatta Indian Museum
RT 3 Box 640
Livingston, TX 77351
(800) 444-3507

Baylor University
Strecker Museum
BU Box 7154
Baylor University
Waco, TX 76798-7154
(817) 755-1110
(819) 755-1173 FAX

Caddo Indian Museum
701 Hardy St
Longview, TX 75604
(903) 759-5739

Institute of Texan Cultures
801 S Bowie St
San Antonio, TX 78205-3296
(210) 558-2300
(210) 558-2228

Panhandle-Plains Historical Museum
2401 4th Ave
Canyon, TX 79016
(806) 656-2244
(806) 656-2250 FAX

Sul Ross State University
Museum of the Big Bend
Box C-210
Alpine, TX 79831
(915) 837-8143

Texarkana Historical Museum
219 State Line Ave
PO Box 2343
Texarkana, TX 75501
(214) 793-4831

Texas Tech University Museum
Indiana Ave and 4th St
Box 43191
Lubbock, TX 79409-3191
(806) 742-2442

University of Texas
El Paso Centennial Museum
University Ave and Wiggins Rd
El Paso, TX 79968
(915) 747-5565

University of Texas at Austin
Texas Memorial Museum
2400 Trinity St
Austin, TX 78705
(512) 471-1604

Wilderness Park Museum
2000 Transmountain Rd
El Paso, TX 79999
(915) 755-4332

Witte Memorial Museum
3801 Broadway
Brackenridge Park
San Antonio, TX 78209

UTAH

Anasazi Indian Village State Park
PO Box 1329
Boulder, UT 84716
(801) 335-7308

Brigham Young University
Museum of People and Culture
710 N 100 E
Provo, UT 84602
(801) 378-6112

Canyonlands National Park
National Park Service
Moab, UT 84532-2995
(801) 259-7164

College of Eastern Utah
Prehistoric Museum
155 E Main
Price, UT 84501
(801) 637-5060

Utah Field House of Natural History State Park
235 E Main St
Vernal, UT 84078
(801) 789-3799

VERMONT

Chimney Point State Historic Site
Museum of Native American Heritage
RD 1 Box 3546
Vergennes, VT 05491
(802) 759-2412

Plumsock Mesoamerican Studies
RT 106
PO Box 38
South Woodstock, VT 05071
(802) 457-1199

VIRGINIA

Alexandria Archaeology
105 Union St
Alexandria, VA 22314
(703) 838-4691

Center for Historic Preservation
Mary Washington College
1301 College Ave
Fredericksburg, VA 22401-5358
(540) 899-4037

Historic Crab Orchard Museum and Pioneer Park, Inc.
RT 19 and 460
RT 1 Box 194
Tazewell, VA 24651
(540) 988-6755
(540) 988-9400 FAX

Institute of Early American History and Culture
PO Box 220
Williamsburg, VA 23187
(757) 253-4175

Pamunkey Indian Museum
Pamunkey Indian Reservation
RT 1 Box 2050
King William, VA 23086
(804) 843-4792

Peaks of Otter Visitor Center
Blue Ridge Pkwy
RT 2 Box 163
Bedford, VA 24523
(540) 586-4357

Valentine Museum
1015 E Clay St
Richmond, VA 23219
(804) 649-0711

WASHINGTON

Chelan County Historical Society Museum and Pioneer Village
600 Cottage Ave
PO Box 22
Cashmere, WA 98815
(509) 782-3230

Dry Falls Interpretive Center
HCR1 Box 36
Coulee City, WA 99115
(509) 632-5583

Fort Simcoe Museum
RT 1 Box 39
White Swan, WA 98952
(509) 874-2372

Makah Cultural and Research Center
PO Box 95
Neah Bay, WA 98357
(360) 645-2711

Museum of Native American Culture
E 200 Cataldo
Spokane, WA 99202
(509) 326-4550

Sacajawea State Park and Interpretive Center
2503 Sacajawea Park Road
Pasco, WA 99301
(509) 545-2361

Seattle Art Museum
1st Ave and University
PO Box 22000
Seattle, WA 98122-9700
(206) 625-8913

Sequim-Dungenes Museum
175 W Cedar
Sequim, WA 98382
(360) 683-8110

University of Washington
Thomas Burke Memorial State Museum
Seattle, WA 98195
(206) 543-5590

Washington State University
Museum of Anthropology
College Hall
Dept of Anthropology
Pullman, WA 99164-4910
(509) 335-3441

Yakima Indian Nation Cultural Heritage Center
151 Fort Road
Toppenish, WA 98948
(509) 865-2800

Yakima Valley Museum
2105 Tieton Dr
Yakima, WA 98902
(509) 248-0747
(509) 453-4890 FAX

WEST VIRGINIA

Blennerhassett Island
Blennerhassett Historical Park
Commission
Parkersburg, WV 26102
(304) 428-3000

Delf Norona Museum and Cultural Centre
801 Jefferson Ave
Moundsville, WV 26041

West Virginia State Museum
Capitol Complex
Charleston, WV 25305-0300
(304) 558-0220

WISCONSIN

Aztalan Museum
N 6264 Hwy Q
Jefferson, WI 53549
(414) 648-8845

Beloit College
Logan Museum of
Anthropology
Prospect at Bushnell
Beloit, WI 53511
(608) 363-2677

Burnett County Historical Society Museum
PO Box 31
Siren, WI 54872
(715) 349-2219

Devil's Lake State Park
S 5975 Park Rd
Baraboo, WI 53913-9299
(608) 356-8301
(608) 356-4281 FAX

Hoard Historical Museum
407 Merchants Ave
Fort Atkinson, WI 53538
(414) 563-7769

Milwaukee Public Museum
800 W Wells St
Milwaukee, WI 53233
(414) 278-2700

Neville Public Museum
210 Museum Pl
Green Bay, WI 54303
(414) 448-4460

Oconto County Historical Society Museum
917 Park Ave
Oconto, WI 54153
(414) 834-6206

Oneida Tribal Museum
Oneida Nation of Wisconsin
PO Box 365
Oneida, WI 54155

Oshkosh Public Museum
1331 Algoma Blvd
Oshkosh, WI 54901
(414) 236-5150

Sheboygan County Museum
3110 Erie Ave
Sheboygan, WI 53081
(414) 458-6144

State Historical Museum
30 N Carroll St
Madison, WI 53706
(608) 262-7700

University of Wisconsin, Stevens Point
Learning Resources Bldg
Stevens Point, WI 54481
(715) 346-2858

WYOMING

Annual Wild West Fine Art Show
1167 Sheridan Ave
Cody, WY 82414
(800) 505-CODY

Buffalo Bill Historical Center
720 Sheridan Ave
PO Box 2630
Cody, WY 82414
(307) 587-4771
(307) 587-3243

Greybull Museum
325 Greybull Ave
Box 348
Greybull, WY 82426
(307) 765-2444

Johnson County, Jim Gatchell Memorial Museum
100 Fort St
PO Box 596
Buffalo, WY 82834
(304) 684-9331
(307) 684-5829 FAX

Mammoth Visitor Center
Yellowstone National Park
PO Box 168
Yellowstone National Park,
WY 82190
(307) 344-7381

Natural History Museum
Western Wyoming Community
College
PO Box 428
2500 College Dr
Rock Springs, WY 82902-0428
(307) 382-1666
(307) 382-7665 FAX

Rockpile Museum
W 2nd St
Box 922
Gillette, WY 82716
(307) 682-5723

University of Wyoming
Anthropology Museum
Anthropology Bldg
PO Box 3431
Laramie, WY 82071
(807) 766-5136

Wyoming State Museum
AMH Dept
Barrett Bldg
24th and Central Ave
Cheyenne, WY 82002
(307) 777-7024

Additional Reading

Since books are a valuable source of information, they might just be your best resource. Reading is an excellent way to learn much of what you want to know, so examine library books and study the ones you own. The books listed in this section are about artifacts, prehistory and archaeology, and can be enjoyed by young people and adults alike. With colorful pictures and interesting text, you'll find the material informative and educational regardless of your age.

The best choice for comparing surface finds with photos would be an identification guide. If you've never seen an artifact identification guidebook before, you'll be amazed at the abundance and variety of photos. Be sure to read the corresponding captions because specific information that's often educational is also included. Try the Hothem or Overstreet guides, choose titles that include the names of Indian cultures or culture regions, or examine books that feature particular types of artifacts. To find more books about Native American relics or the study of archaeology, speak with your librarian or local bookseller.

Adkins Site, The: A Paleo-Indian Habitation and Associated Stone Structure. Richard Michael Gramly, Persimmon Press, 1988.

Album of Prehistoric Man. Tom McGowen, Children's Press, 1988.

All About Arrowheads and Spear Points. Howard E. Smith, Jr., Henry Holt and Company, 1989.

Amateur Archaeologist's Handbook, The. Maurice Robbins with Mary B. Irving, Harper and Row, 1981.

America and Its Indians. Dr. Jerome E. Leavitt, Children's Press, 1962.

American Indian Axes and Related Stone Artifacts. Lar Hothem, Collector Books, 1994.

American Indian, The: From Colonial Times to the Present. Michael Gibson, Putnam, 1974.

America's Ancient Treasures: A Guide to Archeological Sites and Museums in the United States and Canada. Franklin Folsom and Mary Elting Folsom, University of New Mexico Press, 1993.

Ancient Art of Ohio. Lar Hothem, Hothem House, 1994.

Ancient Indian Pottery of the Mississippi River Valley. Roy Hathcock, Hurley Press, 1976.

Ancient North America: The Archaeology of a Continent. Brian M. Fagan, Thames and Hudson, 1995.

Ancient Ones, The. Gordon C. Baldwin, Norton, 1963.

Archeology. Francis Celoria, Price Stearn Sloan, 1973.

Arrowheads and Projectile Points. Lar Hothem, Collector Books, 1995.

Arrowheads and Stone Artifacts. C.G. Yeager, Pruett Publishing, 1986.

Bows and Arrows of the Native Americans. Jim Hamm, Lyons and Burford, 1991.

Cherokee Indians, The. Nicole Claro, Chelsea House, 1991.

Children's Atlas of Native Americans. Rand McNally and Company, 1992.

Collecting Indian Knives: Identification and Values. Lar Hothem, Books Americana, 1986.

Discover Archaeology: An Introduction to the Tools and Techniques of Archaeological Fieldwork. George Sullivan, Viking Press, 1981.

Earliest Cities, The. Jean-Michel Coblence, Silver Burdett Press, 1987.

Early Archaic Indian Points and Knives. Robert Elder, Collector Books, 1989.

Early Humans. Nick Merriman, Alfred A. Knopf, Inc., 1989.

Early Man: Young Readers Edition. F. Clark Howell, Silver Burdett Press, 1977.

Everyday Life in Prehistoric Times. Marjorie and C.H.B. Quennell, David and Charles, 1980.

Field Guide to Stone Artifacts of Texas Indians, A. Ellen Sue Turner and Thomas R. Hester, Gulf Publications, 1985.

First Americans, The. Robert Claiborne, Time-Life Books, 1992.

First Hunters: Ohio's Paleo-Indian Artifacts. Lar Hothem, Hothem House, 1990.

Flint Blades and Projectile Points of the North American Indian. Lawrence N. Tully, Collector Books, 1986.

Florida's Prehistoric Stone Technology. Barbara A. Purdy, University Presses of Florida, 1986.

From Abenaki to Zuni: A Dictionary of Native American Tribes. Evelyn Wolfson, Walker and Company, 1988.

Glacial Kame Indians, The. Robert N. Converse, Archaeological Society of Ohio, 1980.

Glass Trade Beads in the Northeast: Including Aboriginal Bead Industries. Gary L. Fogelman, Fogelman Publishing, 1991.

Going On A Dig. Velma Ford Morrison, Dodd, Mead and Company, 1981.

Great Lakes Indians: A Pictorial Guide. William J. Kubiak, Baker Book House, 1970.

Guide to the Paleo-Indian Artifacts of North America. Richard Michael Gramly, Persimmon Press, 1992.

Handbook of North American Indians. Smithsonian Institution, Superintendent of Documents, U.S. Government Printing Office, Washington, D.C. 20402.

Hart's Prehistoric Pipe Rack. Gordon Hart, Hart Publishers, 1978.

History of the World: Civilizations of the Americas. Raintree Steck-Vaughn Publishers, 1990.

How to Collect North American Indian Artifacts. Robert F. Brand, Nacci Printing, 1984.

In Search of the Wild Indian. Tom Driebe, Maurose Publishing, 1996.

Indian Artifacts of the East and South: An Identification Guide. Robert Swope, Jr., R. Swope, 1982.

Indian Artifacts of the Midwest. Lar Hothem, Collector Books, 1996.

Indian Artifacts of the Midwest, Book II. Lar Hothem, Collector Books, 1995.

Indian Axes and Related Stone Artifacts. Lar Hothem, Collector Books, 1996.

Indian Baskets. Sarah Peabody Turnbaugh and William A. Turnbaugh, Schiffer Publishing, 1986.

Indian Crafts and Lore. W. Ben Hunt, Golden Press, 1976.

Indian Flints of Ohio. Lar Hothem, Hothem House, 1986.

Indian Sign Language. Robert Hofsinde, William Morrow Books, 1959.

Indian Tribes of America. Marion E. Gridley, Checkerboard Press, 1973.

Indians. Claude Appell, Follet, 1965.

Indians and Artifacts in the Southeast. Bert W. Bierer, B. Bierer, 1980.

Indians of the Arctic and Subarctic. Paula Younkin, Facts on File, 1991.

Indians of the Northeast Woodlands. Beatrice Siegel, Walker and Company, 1992.

Indians of the Plains. Elaine Andrews, Facts on File, 1991.

Indians of the Plateau and Great Basin. Victoria Sherrow, Facts on File, 1991.

Indians of the Southeast. Richard E. Mancini, Facts on File, 1991.

Indians of Southern Illinois. Irvin M. Peithmann, Charles C. Thomas Publishing, 1964.

Indians of Yellowstone Park, The. Joel C. Janetski, University of Utah Press, 1987.

Introduction to Archaeology. Shirley Gorenstein, Basic Books, 1972.

Koster: Americans in Search of Their Prehistoric Past. Stuart Struever and Felicia Antonelli Holton, NAL-Dutton, 1985.

Living Like Indians: A Treasury of American Indian Crafts, Games and Activities. Allan A. Macfarlan, Association Press, 1961.

Making Silent Stones Speak. Kathy D. Schick and Nicholas Toth, Simon and Schuster Trade, 1993.

Marshall Cavendish Illustrated History of the North American Indian, The. Marshall Cavendish and Maggie McCormick, M. Cavendish, 1991.

Mound Builders and Cliff Dwellers. Dale Brown, ed., Time-Life Books, 1993.

Mounds, Towns and Totems: Indians of North America. Robert Myron, World Publishing, 1966.

Native American Traditions. Arthur Versluis, Element Books, 1994.

Native Americans Before 1492: The Moundbuilding Centers of the Eastern Woodlands. Lynda Norene Shaffer, M.E. Sharpe, 1992.

North American Indian Artifacts. Lar Hothem, Books Americana, 1996.

North American Indian Arts. Andrew Hunter Whiteford, Western, 1990.

North American Indian Ornamental and Ceremonial Artifacts. Lar Hothem, Books Americana, 1993.

North American Indians, The. Ernest Berke, Doubleday, 1963.

Ohio Flint Types. Robert N. Converse, Archaeological Society of Ohio, 1994.

Ohio Slate Types. Robert N. Converse, Archaeological Society of Ohio, 1978.

Overstreet Indian Arrowheads Identification and Price Guide, The. Robert M. Overstreet, Gemstone Publishing, 1995.

Pictorial History of the American Indian, A. Oliver LaFarge, Crown Publishing, 1984.

Points and Blades of the Coastal Plains. John Powell, American Systems of the Carolinas, 1990.

Prehistoric Lithic Industry at Dover, Tennessee. Richard Michael Gramly, Persimmon Press, 1993.

Projectile Point Typology for Pennsylvania and the Northeast, A. Gary L. Fogelman, Fogelman Publishing, 1988.

Quapaw and Their Pottery, The. Roy Hathcock, Hurley Press, 1983.

Reader's Digest America's Fascinating Indian Heritage. James A. Maxwell, ed., Reader's Digest Association, Inc., 1994.

Richey Clovis Cache, The: Earliest Americans Along the Columbia River. Richard Michael Gramly, Persimmon Press, 1993.

Search for Early Man, The. John E. Pfeiffer, Harper Collins, 1963.

Shoop: Pennsylvania's Famous Paleo Site, Popular Version. Gary L. Fogelman, Fogelman Publishing, 1986.

Stone Age in North America, The, vol. I and II. Warren K. Moorehead, The Depot, 1987.

Story in Stone. Valerie and D.C. Waldorf, Mound Builder Books, 1987.

Sun Circles and Human Hands. Emma Lila Fundaburk and Mary Douglas F. Foreman, 1957.

Treasures of the Mound Builders. Lar Hothem, Hothem House, 1989.

Wampanoag, The. Laurie Weinstein-Farson, Chelsea House, 1989.

Wampanoag Indian Federation of the Algonquin Nation, The. Milton A. Travers, Christopher Publishing House, 1961.

Who's Who in Indian Relics, vol. 1. H.C. Wachtel, ed., 1960.

Who's Who in Indian Relics, vol. 2. H.C. Wachtel, ed., 1968.

Who's Who in Indian Relics, vol. 3. Cameron Parks and Ben W. Thompson, ed., Parks and Thompson, 1972.

Who's Who in Indian Relics, vol. 4. Cameron Parks and Ben W. Thompson, ed., Messenger Printing, 1976.

Who's Who in Indian Relics, vol. 5. Ben W. Thompson, ed., Messenger Printing, 1980.

Who's Who in Indian Relics, vol. 6. Ben W. Thompson, ed., Messenger Printing, 1984.

Who's Who in Indian Relics, vol. 7. Ben W. Thompson, ed., Messenger Printing, 1988.

Who's Who in Indian Relics, vol. 8. Ben W. Thompson, ed., Weidner Publishing, 1992.

Bibliography

Addington, Lucile R. *Lithic Illustration: Drawing Flaked Stone Artifacts for Publication.* Chicago, Illinois: The University of Chicago Press, 1986.

Archaeologists of the Americas. Washington, D.C.: Society for American Archaeology, 1994.

Directory of Certified Professional Archaeologists. Oklahoma City, Oklahoma: Society of Professional Archaeologists, 1995.

Encyclopedia of Associations, 30th ed., vol. 1. New York, New York: Gale Research Inc., An International Thomson Publishing Company, 1996.

Folsom, Franklin and Folsom, Mary Elting. *America's Ancient Treasures: A Guide to Archeological Sites and Museums in the United States and Canada, 4th ed.* Albuquerque, New Mexico: University of New Mexico Press, 1993.

Gramly, Richard Michael. *Guide to the Paleo-Indian Artifacts of North America, 2nd ed.* Buffalo, New York: Persimmon Press, 1992.

Gramly, Richard Michael. "Scanning Electron Microscopy," *The Amateur Archaeologist* 2, no. 1 (1995): 19-27.

Gramly, Richard Michael. "The National Register of Historic Places," *The Amateur Archaeologist* 2, no. 1 (1995): 28-29.

Gramly, Richard Michael. "What is Looting?" *Indian-Artifact Magazine* 15, no. 1 (1996): 53.

Hester, Peter. "Thoughts on Collecting," *Indian-Artifact Magazine* 9, no. 1 (1990): 9, 48-49.

Hothem, Lar. *Arrowheads and Projectile Points.* Paducah, Kentucky: Collector Books, A Division of Shroeder Publishing Co., Inc., 1995.

Hothem, Lar. *Collecting Indian Knives: Identification and Values.* Florence, Alabama: Books Americana, Inc., 1986.

Hothem, Lar. *Indian Artifacts of the Midwest.* Paducah, Kentucky: Collector Books, A Division of Shroeder Publishing Co., Inc., 1992.

Hothem, Lar. *Indian Artifacts of the Midwest, Book II.* Paducah, Kentucky: Collector Books, A Division of Shroeder Publishing Co., Inc., 1995.

Hothem, Lar. *Indian Axes and Related Stone Artifacts.* Paducah, Kentucky: Collector Books, A Division of Shroeder Publishing Co., Inc., 1994.

Hothem, Lar. *North American Indian Artifacts, 5th ed.* Florence, Alabama: Books Americana, Inc., 1994.

Hothem, Lar. *North American Indian Ornamental and Ceremonial Artifacts.* Florence, Alabama: Books Americana, Inc., 1990.

Hunt, W. Ben. *Indian and Camp Handicraft.* Milwaukee, Wisconsin: The Bruce Publishing Company, 1945.

Janetski, Joel C. *The Indians of Yellowstone Park.* Salt Lake City, Utah: Bonneville Books, University of Utah Press, 1987.

Lang, Gordon. *Miller's Antiques Checklist: Pottery.* London, England: Reed International Books Limited, 1995.

Maxwell, James A., ed. *America's Fascinating Indian Heritage.* Pleasantville, New York: The Reader's Digest Association, Inc., 1994.

Moore, Bill. "Ask An Archeologist," *Indian-Artifact Magazine* 9, no. 1 (1990): 24.

Morrison, Velma Ford. *Going On a Dig.* New York: Dodd, Mead and Company, 1981.

Ortega, Bob. "Nifty Spear Flinger Aztecs Called 'Atlatl' Makes a Comeback," *The Wall Street Journal*, 24 October 1995, Section A.

Overstreet, Robert M. and Peake, Howard. *The Official Overstreet Identification and Price Guide to Indian Arrowheads, 2nd ed.* New York, New York: The House of Collectibles, 1991.

Rhodes, Frank H.T., Zim, Herbert S. and Shaffer, Paul R. *Fossils: A Guide to Prehistoric Life.* New York, New York: Golden Press, 1962.

Robbins, Maurice with Irving, Mary B. *The Amateur Archaeologist's Handbook, 3rd ed.* New York, New York: Harper and Row, Publishers, Inc., 1981.

Shuttlesworth, Dorothy. *The Story of Rocks, rev. ed.* Garden City, New York: Doubleday and Company, Inc., 1966.

Smith, Howard E., Jr. *All About Arrowheads and Spear Points.* New York, New York: Henry Holt and Company, 1989.

Sofianides, Anna S. and Harlow, George E. *Gems and Crystals from the American Museum of Natural History.* New York, New York: Simon and Schuster, 1990.

Taylor, Jeb and Fogelman, Gary L. "Some Thoughts on Heat Treatment of Chert," *Indian-Artifact Magazine* 15, no. 2 (1996): 8, 65.

Walker, Laurence C. *Forests: A Naturalist's Guide to Trees and Forest Ecology.* New York, New York: John Wiley and Sons, 1990.

Yeager, C.G. *Arrowheads and Stone Artifacts.* Boulder, Colorado: Pruett Publishing Company, 1986.

Young, Phil. "Cultural Resource Protection Laws," *Indian-Artifact Magazine* 14, no. 3 (1995): 52-53.

Index

C

cache 53, 190

Cahokia 174, 175, 190

celt 47-48, 126, 133, 141, 165, 175, 190, 200

ceremonial stone 51-52, 139, 190, 200

chert 10, 12, 15-16, 19, 175, 191

chipping stone 18, 19, 21, 83, 134, 191, 200

chunkey stone 51-52, 191, 201

cleaning chart 115

Clovis 154, 160-161, 191

conchoidal fracture 12-13, 14, 15, 16, 191

cooking stone 51, 191, 201

core 17-18, 19, 20, 27, 191, 201

cultural 11, 27, 191

cup stone 72, 77, 78, 191, 201

D

discoidal 51-52, 120, 191, 201

drill 32, 127, 159, 191, 202

E

ears 37, 191

effigy 116, 138-139, 165-166, 172, 191, 202

end scraper 43, 158, 191

excavation 55, 98, 191, 212, 215

F

fire-cracked 51, 191, 202

fired clay biscuit 148-152, 191, 202

flake 12, 14-22, 26-27, 192

flake tool 18-23, 131, 192, 202

flaking tool 18, 21, 192

flint 10, 14-15, 27, 62, 132, 192

flintknapping 17-23, 192

flute 37, 39, 154, 160-161, 192

Folsom 160, 161

G

H

I

K

L

M

N

O

oblique flaking 22, 142, 194
obsidian 10, 16, 127, 194
ornament 51-53, 170-171, 194, 205
opaque 15, 194
outcropping 62, 65, 194

P

Paleo-Indian 154-162, 194
parallel flaking 22, 142, 194
patina 30, 114, 133, 194
pecking 25-27, 126, 194
pendant 116, 137, 170-172, 194, 205
percussion 19, 20-21, 26-27, 43, 123-125, 132, 194
perforator 14, 35, 194, 205
pestle 49-50, 110, 194, 206
pipe 116, 171-172, 194, 206
polishing 26, 134, 194
polishing stone 134-135, 194, 206
pothunter 93, 195
pot-lid 16
pottery 114, 116, 135, 167-168, 172, 195, 206
preform 20-21, 27, 132, 195, 206
prehistoric period 155-156
pressure flaking 21-23, 26-27, 43, 123-125, 195
private property 68, 92, 98, 195
projectile point 5, 20, 35-38, 40-41, 127, 195, 207
provenance 28, 195
public land 56, 97-98, 195

R

radiocarbon dating 117, 150, 195
random flaking 22, 124, 195
reproductions 23-24, 195

S

scraper 5-6, 36, 42-45, 128, 158-159, 180, 195, 207
serrations 22, 37, 124, 195
sherds 79, 113-116, 172, 195, 206
shoulders 37, 128, 195
SHPO 70, 98, 106-107, 183, 195, 208-209

side scraper 124, 195
site 105, 196
site protection regulations 98, 196
slate 165, 166, 167
sketch map 86, 90, 103, 196
soft-hammer percussion 20-21, 196
spatulate 140-141, 174-175, 196, 207
spear 35, 37, 137-138, 158
spear point 32, 38-39
spokeshave 45, 130, 196, 207
spud 140-141, 174-175, 196, 207
spur 45, 158, 196
steep-edge scraper 124, 129, 196
stem 26, 37-39, 196
surface find 6, 196
surface hunting 3, 93, 196

T

tally mark 52, 196
tang 37-38, 83, 196
thumb scraper 43, 129, 196
thumbnail scraper 124, 129, 196
topographic map 70, 86, 103, 196, 226
trade-era 177-179, 196
translucent 15, 196
trilobite 8, 197

U

unifacial 23-24, 42-43, 129-130, 180, 197
USGS 70, 86, 103, 197, 226

W

war point 39, 127, 177, 197
washout 58-59, 61, 197
Woodland 167-172, 197
worked 11, 23, 26-28, 122-123, 197

About the Authors

Sandy Livoti and Jon Kiesa are avocational archaeologists who believe constructive public attitudes and professional cooperation are fundamental for cultural resource preservation. *Adventures in Stone Artifacts* is the result of a mutual interest in surface hunting and is their first book. Residents of Woodridge, Illinois, they are members of the Illinois State Archeological Society, Central States Archaeological Societies, Inc., Texas Cache Amateur Archeological Association and American Society for Amateur Archaeology.